PARTIAL TRUTHS

A MEMOIR AND ESSAYS
ON READING, WRITING,
AND RESEARCHING

GLENDA L. BISSEX

HEINEMANN   Portsmouth, NH

Heinemann
A division of Reed Elsevier Inc.
361 Hanover Street
Portsmouth NH 03801-3912

Offices and agents throughout the world

The author and publisher thank those who have given permission to reprint borrowed material.

"Growing Writers in Classrooms" from *Language Arts*, October 1981. Copyright 1981 by the National Council of Teachers of English. Reprinted with permission.

"The Child as Teacher" from *Awakening to Literacy*, edited by Hillel Goelman, Antoinette Oberg, and Frank Smith (Heinemann, A division of Reed Elsevier Inc., Portsmouth, NH, 1984).

"Watching Young Writers" from *Observing the Language Learner*, edited by Angela Jaggar and M. Trike Smith-Burke. Published by IRA/NCTE. Copyright 1985 by the International Reading Association. Reprinted with permission.

"On Reading Nature's Writing" originally appeared in a slightly different version in *Vermont Natural History*, 1991. Adapted by permission of the Vermont Institute of Natural Science.

Acknowledgments for borrowed material continue on page 221, which constitutes an extension of the copyright page.

Library of Congress Cataloging-in-Publication Data
Bissex, Glenda L.
    Partial truths : a memoir and essays on reading, writing, and researching / Glenda L. Bissex.
        p.   cm.
    Includes bibliographical references.
    ISBN 0-435-07224-2
    1. Language arts—United States. 2. Reading—United States. 3. English language—Composition and exercises—Study and teaching—United States. 4. Children—Language. 5. Action research in education—United States. 6. Bissex, Glenda L. 7. English teachers—United States—Biography. 8. Bissex, Glenda L.
    I. Title.
    LB 1576.B494   1996
    372.6—dc20   96-26639
                                                                                                CIP

Editor: Carolyn Coman
Production: Melissa L. Inglis
Cover design: Judy Arisman/Arisman Design
Author photo: Carley Stevens-McLaughlin
Manufacturing: Louise Richardson

Cover photo of a hilltop field with apple trees in Plainfield, Vermont by Glenda L. Bissex.

Printed in the United States of America on acid-free paper
99 98 97 96   DA   1 2 3 4 5 6 7 8 9

Contents

iv

Acknowledgments

THE IDEA FOR THIS BOOK WAS PLANTED BY TIM GILLESPIE'S interview of me for the first issue of *Teacher Research*. I imagine that Ruth Hubbard, the journal's coeditor, put him up to it, so they're both a little bit responsible. When I discovered someone was interested in the life behind my work, I thought of putting together a chronological collection of my essays interspersed with commentaries about events that had led up to each one. As the commentaries grew, my writing group urged me not to interrupt the scenes of my life with the essays and to reveal more of myself in those scenes. So the commentaries became a memoir. For all their help in transforming my material and moving the memoir beyond a bed to bed story, I'm indebted to past and present members of my writing group: Joan Smith (my writing partner at the beginning of this project), Toby and Laura Fulwiler, Corrine Glesne, Charlie Rathbone, Michael Strauss, and Mary Jane Dickerson. I'm also grateful for their interest in my ducks.

Two groups of teacher-researchers who had at one time been in my Case Study course responded sensitively and graciously to my memoir manuscript. They, too, wanted to see more of my self, even as I felt I had stripped naked (for an academic). Thank you, Pat Fox, Rita Eastburg, Roseann Mason, Cheryl Timion, Kate Bradley, Ruth Heil, Shirley McPhillips, and Elsie Nigohosian.

Having my son, Paul, now twenty-seven years old and a writer himself, respond to drafts of some chapters was a special pleasure. So was his help, as a graphic designer, in selecting possible cover photos. My husband, Tom Kyle, has supported both my life and my work.

I'm grateful to Carolyn Coman, my editor at Heinemann, for her enthusiasm, her noninvasive and just criticisms, and her empathy for the sensitivities of a fellow writer.

I thank Melissa Inglis, my production editor, for all her work behind the scenes and for asking if I had any photos that might be used for the cover.

I'm indebted to everyone who helped locate former students of mine for permission to use their work of fifteen, twenty, and almost thirty years ago: Barbara Bohn, Sally Laughlin, Karen Luciano, and especially Debbie and Bill Halliday for their extraordinary efforts and ultimate success.

I cannot begin to acknowledge and thank all the people who influenced my life and learning, as represented in the essays as well as the memoir.

Introduction

ROBERT FROST DIDN'T LIKE TO TALK ABOUT HIS POEMS because they already said what he meant to say. The modern poets who were asked to choose a favorite poem and comment on it for a collection I used when I taught high school English, didn't *explain* their poems but offered some *context*—perhaps the occasion for writing the poem or a technical challenge they surmounted. Their comments gave me an inside view of poetry that made me feel included as a reader. The personal contexts shared by the poets in their ordinary voices served as a kind of bridge across which I could more easily walk into their poems. For me, people's work is never the same after I've been in their presence. I see the face, I hear the voice as I read; the writing is no longer disembodied. My memoir offers scenes from my life that are also a context for the scenes from my work—for the essays, some previously published and others new, that follow it. Memoir and essays, each is a partial truth about me.

Learning how to write the memoir took several years. Throughout my life I've written—journals, research papers, poems, speeches, editorial reviews, essays, books. Because I've always written and always saved things, I could look back on my life through cartons and files of artifacts. I studied them and tried to write this memoir like a researcher. But what I pieced together wasn't a story and wasn't alive. I had to relearn what my first writing group tried to teach me a good many years ago when I was, I thought, writing a personal introduction to a book of women's nature writings I was collecting. Only it wasn't very personal because I was writing as a researcher studying women's nature writings and only occasionally talking about my childhood and my mother and grandmother, who had helped connect me with nature. I felt naked without my academic robes, as I've felt naked now, telling my story without hiding behind the facts and artifacts that are my researcher's props. Readers of early drafts kept saying they wanted to see more of me while I felt I was spread out all over the page. How many students' voices I've coaxed out onto their pages, yet my own faltered. How often and earnestly I've taught what I needed to learn myself. After two writing blocks, I learned that the story wasn't in those boxes of artifacts: It was in me. Once I imaginatively re-entered and re-experienced those years, the writing spun itself out.

The themes of my life seem to have existed all along inwardly, though they've taken different forms through my outward roles. My roles as teacher, researcher, and writer are my professional identities: who I am known as, how my work is seen, and one way that I see myself. My characteristic processes—how I act and respond, such as by questioning, creating, seeking to see for myself, and distrusting categories—are closely related to themes. Themes—like my urge to look at individuals, my fascination with different points of view, my search to understand how learning occurs—provide inner continuity and run through my journals. My life has circled around certain themes. When I come back to these, I'm not coming back to the same places but, from another approach, rediscovering and reaffirming their importance for me. Sometimes I've been dismayed to find in old writings that something I'm thinking now I thought years ago—dismayed because it seems like forgetfulness, futility, reinventing the wheel. And yet, when I reread my earlier words, I understand them more fully.

I wonder why, given my distrust of categories, I've just proposed these categories of themes, processes, and roles as somehow structuring my life—a life, like others', that is full of contradictions and inconsistencies alongside the continuities. In spite of how I represent it through language, my life is shot through with these, keeping me aware, surprised, struggling, questioning and, out of it all, growing and learning. As a learner I keep finding that once the momentary fullness of an insight passes, I see how it might be questioned or qualified or be part of something else, which is why the phrase "partial truth" recurs in my journals and has given this book its title.

I sit here, in my study in my home, at what was my son's desk when he was younger, working on this book while watching the ducks and crows outside the window. Whether observing my son, my students, or life around my backyard pond, I'm intrigued with what is close at hand. My researching, writing, teaching, and personal lives commingle. Nature, always important in my personal life, entered my professional life as a researcher, and my research extended to include music, also personally important. New combinations open up new ways of seeing, just as new questions open the possibility of new juxtapositions. The territory of my life is out there in the world, but it's also inside me. I wander around both territories, moving not in a predetermined straight path to attain a particular external goal, but letting one experience lead to another and assessing each one largely in terms of my own learning and being.

The craft of words is hard, but the craft of living is harder.

Part I

Memoir

1

The Streets of Chicago

I GREW UP IN AN INSTITUTION. MY PARENTS WERE SOCIAL workers who lived as well as worked in a settlement house in Chicago. Like Jane Addams's Hull House, Chicago Commons was part of the neighborhood it served, a slum in the heart of the city, covered with an oily soot of coal dust from chimneys and freight trains—soot that peppered the white window sills in our apartment and smudged when you tried to wipe it off. From the window of my tiny bedroom I watched freight trains go by and waited eagerly before suppertime for the new, streamlined passenger trains to pass: The City of Denver and The City of San Francisco. Peddlers' carts rumbled in the alley below; the rag man and the knife and scissors sharpener sang out. Kids played ball or smashed bottles against the brick wall behind the row of trash cans. I watched and listened, learning to be an observer. The margins are a great place from which to observe, and I was a marginal character in the settlement house and its neighborhood.

Across the street in the public school playground was a wide wheel suspended on a metal centerpost, that I loved to spin around on. Farther back in the graveled playground on summer evenings men rolled bocce balls. Three blocks up the street the Italian grocery held strong-smelling olives in wooden barrels, sausages and cheeses hanging from hooks on the ceiling, pasta in shapes from tiny stars and alphabets to thick ziti arrayed in bins, and in the window my beloved, green-petaled artichokes. On the sidewalk in front of the meat market next to the grocery, chickens indignantly poked their heads out between the slats of their crates while crowded rabbits tried to hop inside their pens.

For a few days once a year a carnival enchanted the street a couple of blocks north of the settlement house. Festooned with booths, centipeded with people, and drenched in blaring music, Erie Street was transformed. The enormous Ferris wheel twinkled with lights while the air below was smoky and pungent with alien odors from food cooking in open pits. The dim grotto of St. Stephen's Church, only a short stone stairway down from the world of tenements and vacant lots and trucks and trolleys, was another magical yet alien world, aglow with candles burning in ruby glasses lit by women who crossed themselves before the statue of Mary and silently prayed. My family did not go to this church, they did not eat strange smelling food, they were not poor, and I did not go to the grim-looking public school or the parochial school with "Ad Maioram Gloriam Dei" carved above its pillars.

By grace of a scholarship, I went to a progressive school miles and worlds away in a borderland between middle-class homes and the swanky apartment buildings in which some of my school friends lived. When I went to their apartments after school or on weekends, I hardly knew how to behave in the presence of doormen, maids, and paper curls capping the ends of lamb chops. I was astonished at Claudette's private bathroom and Susan's canopied bed. For a couple of years Faith, another settlement house child, was in my class. She lived even farther from school, near the stockyards, whose odor, she said, you got used to. I did as we played cops and robbers with our water guns on the sidewalks of her neighborhood. Eating at the big table with her family and the rest of the Benton House staff and listening to their talk about social work felt familiar. Faith and I once gave a party for our classmates, at my settlement house, in the auditorium. How did my mother endure the pandemonium of a bunch of seventh graders let loose in a space where they could run, rearrange rows of folding chairs, open and close the stage curtains or wrap themselves up in them? They were envious, as though they thought I actually *lived* in this room, while I thought they'd be disgusted at the dingy neighborhood, so different from theirs.

The residents of Chicago Commons were a congregation of mostly middle-aged adults, mostly unmarried women, who had lived there as long as I could remember. We were the only family. Some residents, like my parents, were social workers. Others roomed there because it was inexpensive and companionable; they ate modestly at the long tables in the common dining room (olive drab spinach and rubber liver stand out, doubtless unfairly, in my memory) and volunteered time each week to operate the switchboard or do another chore. Younger staff members and residents (usually students) stayed more briefly and moved on. Among them was Ursel, who had fled World War II in Europe to wait years in uncertainty in this building for her fiancé to escape also. How could she wait and hope so long? In the end the serious-faced fiancé came and took her away with him. Until then, Ursel's visits to my bedside when I was sick cured my spirits. Her dark eyes sparkled with childlike mischief as we played "funny face," handing back and forth the sheet of paper, folded over, on which we'd drawn a segment of the person or fantastic creature we were constructing, ignorant of exactly what we added onto. When the feet were completed and a name given to the unseen creature, we unrolled the paper and laughingly beheld our creation. No other children lived in the settlement house. Thank you, Ursel, wherever you are— playing, I hope, with your grandchildren.

An only child, I lived in a world of adults, most of whom were not family. Few wanted to relate to children, perhaps especially to one as shy as I was. When I grew to crave the company of pets, I discovered they cared even less for animals. My family's apartment wasn't exactly sealed off from the rest of the building. Above the unlockable door—opening directly into our living room from the third floor landing—was a transom with its pane of glass missing. The rest of the third floor included the rooms of two of the older ladies: Hazel Macadam, who was at least jolly, and Millicent Callert, who was decidedly not. Why then did the cocoa colored litter of Mehitabel, my white mouse, and Archie, her brown mate, flee to Millie's room? And later, why did Uncle Zinnia, my cat (originally named Zinnia with Uncle added when "she" turned out to be "he"), choose Millie's room when he leapt from the top of the bookcase through the transom?

On the wooden stairway up to our third-floor apartment, I heard my mother's energetic, purposeful stride and my father's limping footsteps, sometimes dragging and sometimes almost skipping. His voice might burst out with a buoyant bit of "You Are My Sunshine" or "Jesus Wants Me for a Sunbeam," relics of his religious youth. I never knew if he was trying to lift his own spirits with those songs or if he was truly feeling exuberant.

Under the third-floor stairway was a long, steep stairway of old wood, painted brown, leading from the second-floor hallway down to a perpetually locked door to the street. The hallway was lit day and night by a feeble bulb overhead. Usually I hurried by this stairway and tried not to look down it as I passed. I never walked down it more than a few slow steps. I never saw anyone else on it, even to clean off the years of dust. I knew I'd feel trapped if I ever descended to its coffinlike bottom. I knew I'd feel inexplicably guilty if anyone ever saw me climbing it. Always it was there, this darkness I had to pass daily, dimly waiting, yawning, like a long, toothed crocodile jaw.

As a child, life was full of mysteries for me. There were mysterious places, like this dark stairway, St. Stephen's grotto, the cheap bars on Clark Street whose bright neon signs masked the human degradation within, and the Kansas of my father's youth where no trees grew. There were mysterious people like the grandfather whose black eyes stared out from a portrait over my grandmother's bed; like Hoodoo, someone in Kansas whom my father fleetingly referred to; like the drunk man Faith and I befriended on the Grand Avenue streetcar after we visited the dogs and cats at the Humane Society. There was so much I didn't know, didn't ask about, assumed I shouldn't know. And there were things adults wanted me to know that I didn't care about knowing then, like my mother's ancestry.

In adolescence, my life grew bright colored and passionate; the mysteries withdrew into irrelevance. I connected with the world. By myself I discovered some dialogues of Plato in the back of the school library stacks. I'd never read anything like them: The back and forth of arguments about truly important questions I'd just begun to ponder was a revelation, more delicious for being self-discovered. Through school plays I could become other people, like Electra, outraged at her father's murder, who freely expressed her emotions, as I could not. On Friday afternoons I sometimes climbed the long flights of stairs up to the gallery of Orchestra Hall to hear the Chicago Symphony for a couple of dollars. In the spring I might walk after school through Lincoln Park and down Michigan Avenue to take a streetcar the rest of the way home. Riding buses and elevated trains and street cars, and walking, I constructed my own mental map of the city. I joined a youth group at the settlement and finally made friends in the neighborhood, mostly boyfriends. I was no longer stumbling around in dim adult worlds I barely understood that receded into infinite pasts in places I had never seen and with people I would never meet. The treasure chest of the world opened to me: That was the gift of adolescence, and doubtless one reason why, when I became a teacher, I chose high school.

My neighborhood, once the territory of Cherry-Nose Gioia, supposedly a member of Al Capone's gang, was quieter as I was growing up until blacks moved in and a new kind of violence flared. Midnight of my sixteenth birthday, the sky was red. In the big tenement a block north, black Jessie Mae MacDonald, ten years old, burned. Her mother worked at night. Black Mrs. Griggs burned along with her three young children. Her sister, Mrs. Hector, and her three-year-old jumped from the third floor of the burning building. The stairway was in flames and there was no fire escape. They were killed. From a glow in the doorway, reported by a passing car, flames ran down the hallway (soaked with kerosene or benzene or naphtha or fuel oil, the detective's report said), up the stairway, through doors, shattering windows, as they reached for the sky.

"When I heard the screams I couldn't hate them any more. Everyone has a right to live," said one white neighbor. The screams of the burning and fallen and those who survived to witness this agony moved a white mother to offer to take in survivors. "Like hell you will," said her husband. "Not in my house." St. Stephen's church, less than a block away, did not open its doors.

Like me, Jessie Mae was her mother's one child. I was alive, she was dead. I was white, she was black: black as the faces crowded into the church for her funeral service, black as the faces of the children's choir singing "Going Home." When the coffin was opened at the end of the service, her mother screamed up at the blue ceiling painted with silent gold stars.

I left the settlement house and my small school and friends for a college I had never seen in a part of the country I had never visited. My parents took me and my suitcases in a taxi to the cavernous station, echoing with announcements of arriving and departing trains. I slept in my seat at night and wakened at dawn in the Berkshire hills of Massachusetts. The train disgorged lines of girls in Northampton and Wellesley, and ended its run in Boston. I had never been east of Indiana. I had never seen Harvard Square or the quadrangle of brick Radcliffe dorms where I learned that I had a midwest twang and tried to speak like the sophisticated New York girls. I thought I'd major in sociology—wasn't that natural, given where I'd come from?—but I graduated with a major in English Literature and an undergraduate thesis on Joseph Conrad. I had claimed my own territory. I would not be a social worker, but I had never dreamed of being one or of any other career. That puzzles me now, except that in the 50s neither the college nor my family was urging me to think about it. When I was a junior in college my father did ask me what I wanted to do and I said I'd thought of being a teacher. Saying it aloud confirmed it for me. So did his approval, for teaching, like social work, was a way of serving others, of trying to leave the world a better place than you had found it. My parents' lives made clear that that's what work and life were about, but my first years of teaching were about learning what kind of teacher I could be.

2

Who Am I to Stand Before You?

WHEN MY FIRST HIGH SCHOOL ENGLISH STUDENTS walked through the door of my classroom in Chicago, I knew they didn't see *me*. They saw a new teacher and they were curious. I recognized myself in them, for I had been a student most of my life. But I had never been a teacher. The rows of chairs on a polished wood floor and the oak desk with a blackboard on the wall behind it were a familiar scene, but not the faces all turned toward me. I felt the mantle of "teacher" fall on me as they clothed me with their expectations. I don't know if I grasped then that there are no generic teachers, only individual teachers—that I couldn't become *a* teacher but rather the particular teacher I could become, given who I was.

Because my first teaching positions were in independent schools, certification and hence student teaching weren't required: I simply catapulted from one side of the desk to the other. Without the support or criticism of an experienced teacher, I faced alone the daily revelations of my capabilities and liabilities in classrooms that were entirely my own. Were the lively classes that gathered momentum until shattered by the buzzer created by me or by the students? I was surer of my responsibility for the lifeless classes from which I awaited release by the buzzer, and the classes that slithered in and out of focus, in and out of control, fueling my inner critic and testing my will to endure. Who was I to stand before these students? Someone who had been to college and knew more than they about literature and about writing. But amazingly (as I see it now) I could not have answered, "Because I am a teacher." I wasn't a teacher yet—only someone hired to fill that space at the front of the room.

No wonder the beginning years of teaching are so grueling. I was expected to perform as a professional while I was only apprenticing without a master. There was no way I could practice alone, as one might practice painting or writing, afterwards trashing the bungled projects. Every mistake—every miscalculated teaching strategy, every unquelched rowdiness—was public. As I look back now, I'm grateful for the forgivingness of most of my first students and most of their parents instead of pained, as I was then, by the few who were unforgiving.

When a student who was upset about a grade tried to pressure me by threatening to tell the principal what was going on in my classroom, I imagined the lack of discipline must be worse than I had sensed. How could I judge it? I might have remembered beginning teachers I'd had as a student, like the young woman with plucked eyebrows over deep blue eyes whom my eighth-grade class drove from the room in tears. I don't remember what we did, but I remember the tears. I'd never seen a teacher cry. I might have remembered sitting with my best friend in history class, counting all the "uh"s interspersed among our new teacher's halting words to us. Instead, I probably had in mind all the orderly classes taught by experienced teachers, like those who surrounded me. Many had been *my* teachers when I was a student at the same school. They had been teaching so long and distinctively that they'd become institutions, while I struggled to define myself as a teacher.

Asking for help would have been, for me, admitting failure—my failure to be the teacher I thought I was expected to be. I saw my success as a teacher, as I saw almost everything else in my life, as a test of character. With little perspective beyond what my feelings told me, I took everything personally and bounced from despair at one student's quoting to me Shaw's "Those who can, do. Those who can't, teach" to joy when a group of juniors asked me to meet with them on weekends in their homes to discuss books they wanted to read. I sensed it wasn't just the reading but the contact they wanted. Since my own adolescence had been a great awakening, I loved the intellectual ferment in the adolescents around me. A streak of adolescent rebelliousness in me may have resisted enforcing discipline, as did doubts about my own authority—at least until I was able to hear that, despite their behavior, my students truly *wanted* the discipline I'd hesitated to assert. They were uncomfortable with the disruptions they created.

I believed that if I could teach good enough classes—ask interesting questions and keep discussions moving along—discipline would take care of itself. Almost any teaching method other than discussion would have offered easier control. But except for occasional lessons in grammar and literary terminology, I didn't consider teaching another way. Discussion, the medium of most of my high school classes as a student, I assumed would be the medium of my own teaching. I'd had no experience with worksheets or with small-group work and, as a person of few words, I couldn't hold forth in long lectures. Perhaps something essentially democratic in my upbringing by politically liberal parents made me believe in discussion. Or was it the same quality of mind to which Plato's dialogues appealed? Unfortunately, I'd never in my life led a discussion or had any training to do so. Sitting as a student in discussion classes years earlier, I hadn't thought about what my teachers were doing. Discussions just happened—except in the Humanities discussion section I'd eagerly chosen over lecture sections my freshman year in college. Led by a brilliant classicist and dominated by two or three outspoken students, it became a dialogue among them to which the rest of us merely listened. I asked to transfer to a lecture section. As a teacher, I learned what skilled creations discussions were—true discussions, in which everyone thought aloud together about questions that mattered to them. I had many qualities of a discussion leader: I was a good listener, a prolific questioner, and I cared about my students as individuals. But I was quiet and unconfident in interactions with people.

An experienced teacher, perhaps an emissary from a concerned administration, once visited my class and suggested to me afterward that I move my chair out from behind the desk. I understood her suggestion as both literal and metaphoric. Aware now of the desk as a barrier, I never again sat behind one while teaching. I even came to sit on the corner of the desk—a pose one boy mimicked so well that I instantly recognized myself as I walked into the room late for class one day. Moving my chair from behind the desk was the easy part. The hard part was putting my *self* out there; but the classroom offered me a context for taking that risk, and being a teacher committed to discussion gave me a motive. Teaching forced me to find ways to overcome my reticence. Perhaps teaching was the job I *needed* rather than the one I was at the moment best equipped for. The teacher I wanted to become was also the person I wanted to become, which is just as true today as it was forty years ago. I didn't envision then that this process of becoming would be endless.

My earliest teaching years don't replay themselves in stories and scenes but in single lines and snapshots of faces. I see again Barbara's round, earnest face as she walked into my classroom, Arthur Miller's *All My Sons* in hand, questioning me about something in the assigned reading even before she sat down. Another student stopped beside us and listened. They really wanted to know about the play and how I understood it! Such student questions sparked class discussions that felt more like conversations, moving along on their own energy. If I hadn't viewed such conversations as happy accidents,

I'd have learned more from them. I know now strategies I might have used to elicit more student questions. But then I didn't envision such strategies or didn't see cultivating students' questions as crucial to my role as teacher. Yet I was more alive thinking on my feet as I responded to students than I was teaching from my well-prepared questions, and more connected with the students.

Much of my energy as a young English teacher was spent on creating curriculum, which I felt more able to control than students. I taught in schools where I didn't have to teach a curriculum dictated by a textbook. My first meeting with literature textbooks had been in a college survey course. In the awkwardly large and weighty tan and maroon volumes, a page of Beowulf looked like a page of metaphysical poems: small print marshaled into double columns on thin paper—centuries of literature crammed in and visually homogenized, with no space to breathe or for me to comment in the margins. A textbook was not a curriculum. I loved literature and cared passionately about philosophical issues, spending years developing units on concepts of tragedy and on good and evil. Although I didn't engage in long discussions with colleagues about the nature of literature and consequent ways of teaching it, I did enter such discussions through books. One of these was Archibald MacLeish's *Poetry and Experience* which, I explained in a note I wrote at the time, "gave a decisive turn to my already changing views." I describe that turn in my curriculum report for the Junior English course I taught in 1960–61:

> Convinced that poetry speaks mainly to the emotions and imagination, not the intellect, I tried to teach it that way—a difficult undertaking since falling into the pit of intellectualization is so easy. Following MacLeish's lead, I started the three-week poetry unit with Oriental poems, only I used Haiku. Haiku cannot be understood—cannot seem more than trivial and childish observations—until the reader, through his participation, makes them poems. They are poetry stripped to its core. We spent two days on just a few of these tiny Haiku, but they yielded up a great deal of "meaning." One indignant student still exclaimed, "This is *poetry?*", whereupon his classmates leaped to its defense in an excited and exciting discussion.

A note to myself, "How to grade recent assignment?" no doubt refers to papers on the eighth-century Chinese poem "Jade Flower Palace." Grading presumes the teacher knows the right answers. Yet I had no information about "Jade Flower Palace" or its author or Chinese culture. Like my students, I had only the text of the poem in front of me. Behind me I had the encouragement of Archibald MacLeish—his authority as a poet—to risk such an assignment. I asked the class to respond with personal associations and images, not to explain what the poem "meant." (Did *I* know what it meant?) My assignment perhaps came as a relief to them, for although they'd been trained to track down messages, many felt that "digging for hidden meanings," as they put it, destroyed poetry. I was stunned and moved by their papers—by the personal engagement every one of them experienced and revealed in writing. How could I grade them? I celebrated by joyfully reading the responses aloud to the class. But after that poetry unit, I went back to teaching literature I "knew" and assigning grades, even though I agonized over them. For many years this incident haunted me. Finally I learned from it and wrote about it in "On Learning and Not Learning from Teaching."

"I can't stand teachers who act like they know the answer to everything. Why can't they sometimes say, 'I don't know,' like you did?" Molly's face burned with emotion as she talked to me after class one afternoon. (She later became a fine teacher at the same school years after I'd left.) She made me aware of how burdened I felt by what I thought were students' expectations of me as a knower, and she started my conscious liberation from that burden. As a person, I didn't feel entirely comfortable in the role of "authority." I did not seek power. Yet as a teacher it took me years to cast off the "authority" obligation and find another place to stand that wasn't merely in the midst of the adolescents around me. The issue had grown beyond personal authority in classroom management to pedagogical authority in curriculum: Who am I to say what this poem means? If only I could have envisioned myself then as a model *learner* rather than a model *knower*.

I'm freer now from that vision of teacher as knower and teller—an image that didn't fit me, yet one I couldn't shake without years of struggle, without the support of a few liberal educational institutions, and without students who valued the way I questioned and listened. But back in my early years of teaching, I was vulnerable not just because I lacked "authority," but because I lacked conviction about choosing not to use "authority." I first had to know I could teach and manage my classroom with authority before I could have that pedagogical and moral choice.

Sometimes I felt like a very slow learner as a teacher, so I was relieved when a seasoned supervisor of teachers commented that it took at least five years to develop into a teacher of the sort I was. Five years stretched from the day I first sat behind a teacher's desk past the "Jade Flower Palace" incident, and lasted much longer than five years do now. Perhaps I wasn't such a slow learner after all! I saw my efforts then as simply learning to become a better teacher, unqualified by who I was—my capacities and limits for growth—and the kind of teacher I was trying to become. Yet two years later I impressed interviewers from the Harvard Graduate School of Education by my response to a question about what kind of teachers I, as a possible master teacher of interns in English, would want to develop. I said I'd encourage teachers to develop their own styles. I was hired for the Harvard-Newton Summer Program, a position I wouldn't have sought out myself. Me, a "Master Teacher"? The interviewers had come to talk with another teacher at my school and asked him if they should consider anyone else there; he mentioned my name. And so I came into my adolescence as a teacher, moving out into the wider world of education.

The summers I spent working with interns—planning an English course that the group of us taught jointly, and observing and analyzing each other's teaching—opened my eyes. Interns with strong personalities already had distinctive teaching styles. Watching Norman sweat through a dynamic lecture and Janet go for the drama and Barry orchestrate a discussion made me more aware of my own teaching style by comparison. Observing and talking with beginning teachers made me see what I had learned about teaching that they hadn't yet. I also saw, in the comradeship and help they provided each other and in the mentoring I offered for their brave, initial trials, what I had missed as a new teacher.

The Newton High School teachers I met through the Harvard-Newton Program, especially my supervisor, Henry Bissex, whom I eventually married, moved me toward the next challenge I was ready to take on. I knew I was a teacher now, but could I stand up to teaching in a large public school?

3

"Like a Key to a Jail"

My first fall as a public school English teacher, I looked out the window of my screwed-down desk classroom at the throngs of students passing between the buildings that fortressed the campus, thinking that if they knew their power, they could take over the school. It was not the "model home, complete community, and embryonic democracy" that the Parker School, where I'd taught in Chicago, had aspired to be. Never again would I teach in a high school that I loved and fully believed in as an institution. Public school teaching stretched and toughened me; it disheartened me and it left me with a few treasures.

For the first time I confronted in my lowest track class an entire roomful of students who didn't want to be in school. They also didn't "discuss." What was a teacher who saw discussion as the essence of teaching and who'd focused on developing discussion-leading skills to do? One day I decided that dividing the class into small groups might enable them to talk and work together. The next day my department head reported to me that one of the girls in a group I'd sent to work in a nearby classroom had threatened to knife another girl after school. The message I heard was: Don't experiment, don't trust. In desperation I sometimes became with this class a kind of teacher I didn't want to be, sitting on them, asking factual questions, and doling out detentions. Once I caught these students really listening to me after one of them protested that I'd favored a member of the class. Unhesitatingly I explained that if everyone was exactly the same, then treating everyone identically would be "fair." But since everybody wasn't the same, like Lars who was just learning to speak English, treating him the same would be unfair. Their silence felt as though what I'd said hit home. This may have been another learning moment I missed—a chance to explore their ideas of fairness and their experiences of school.

14

I did experiment in and trust and learn from other classes, especially the last senior English class I taught there. I carried out with them my first teacher-research, though there wasn't a name for it then. This class showed me a great deal about discussion—and shows me still as I listen again to my old reel-to-reel tapes. Near the end of the senior year, the authority of the old power structure wanes in the face of the students' imminent release from it. There is a loosening up. Teachers may respond by becoming more despotic or more democratic—by tightening or loosening themselves. It became for me a time to try a different approach to discussion.

Student-led discussions grew as an idea between this class and myself. Not an outstanding group in terms of grades, they were more spirited and self-propelled than comparable public school senior classes I had taught. ("They" refers probably to the minority in any class which nevertheless gives the entire class a characteristic tone.) Even under more conventional procedures, they were good discussers; I don't know that I ever felt with them as though I were giving artificial respiration to a corpse. I assigned the reading, started off discussions of it, curbed and turned the discussions to other points as they went along, tried to keep tabs on the various interpretations argued by the students, but generally felt the discussions had some life of their own—dependent on the school setting, my assignments and my presence, but not dependent on me to keep pumping life into them. The students seemed comfortable with one another, spoke readily—often to each other rather than to the front of the room—and enjoyed arguing, sometimes beyond the point of productivity.

At the beginning of the fourth term, I asked the class for suggestions for what we might do the remainder of the year. Things to avoid, of course, came more easily than positive alternatives, but they suggested spending some class periods discussing topics they were concerned about. As I remember, Vietnam was specifically mentioned early in our talk. Then I asked in writing for other topics. A few slips of paper came in. I asked again and was finally able to compile an uninspiring looking list of topics. The list was narrowed down by asking students to check once topics they were interested in and twice topics on which they were willing to speak. Then students who had volunteered to take responsibility for discussion met in groups according to the topic of their interest. (This did not include all the students in the class.) After talking together for a while, some groups found that they didn't have a topic after all—for example, there was no difference of opinion about lowering the voting age, hence nothing to discuss. Exactly how these groups of usually four students were to conduct the class discussions I left up to them.

The issues they ended up discussing were the Vietnam War and the draft, mercy killing (which came to include abortion), religion, and teenage sexual morality. What mattered to them were current moral issues that affected their own lives. As I listen again to tapes of these discussions I'm distressed by the periodic noise and disorder and think how I could have managed things differently. I see it all once again from my point of view, but the students' evaluations of the discussions remind me that teachers can't see all of what happens in their classrooms. We know what's happening to ourselves, but that's not necessarily what's happening for the students. And since each student responds somewhat differently, what's going on is complex and eludes the grasp of summary. It goes on invisibly in the head of each student and also, invisibly to the teacher, outside of the classroom, as some student responses reminded me:

> "The class may have been disorganized and noisy, but there was a beneficial exchange of ideas in and out of the classroom."

> "Sure, they're shouting out their prejudices and opinions—but this is the whole stimulation. It antagonizes others to participate. They are thinking and discovering new ideas. This is the kind of experience that kids in a classroom need. They're bottled up from day-to-day in school, put through a system of questions and retorts, dictation, home lesson assignments. These discussions are like a key to a jail. It lets them out to express things they're silently carrying around inside of them. They are learning! I modified my opinions more than once and have had others approach me after a discussion with a new outlook."

Before students wrote their evaluations, I played back for them some of the taped discussions. They heard the noise, but one student observed the silences:

> "I think there was a lot of noise, but it was necessary because out of it came quite a bit of thought and reconsideration on the topics. You can hear many periods of silence when the class *was* listening to one person speak. I say it was *necessary* because if there had been any attempt to control it, we would have felt very restricted and we wouldn't have felt as free to express ourselves. It showed that many, or *most* of us do feel strongly about these subjects. The noise and yelling gave a chance for people to suddenly form new thoughts. The private discussions going on at the same time were good—and they were always about the topic."

I don't think I had many preconceptions about what the students would learn through these discussions. When I asked them what they'd learned, their responses included expected and unexpected things:

"Indirectly I learned that I know very little about various subjects i.e., Vietnam and birth control. I have also learned to keep my mouth closed when I can't say anything of great value (I used to shout my mouth off just for the sake of saying something). People in this class are pretty open-minded. I was glad to learn this. One last new bit of information was that some people, e.g. that lady without arms and legs, can still manage and be happy."

"Many small facts about the draft, about the ratings such as I-A."

"I guess what I learned about was people. Just how they react in arguments; either by gross overgeneralizations or stubbornness or like me—a big sister—just shout over the ruckus and say what you want to say. I learned too that very few people are reasonable in arguments (including me); they feel too threatened to give an inch. If they could really discuss and not end up arguing, the discussions would work out better. But what I learned was about people."

"I learned ways of holding my temper and expressing my feelings in ways other people could understand."

I wish I'd had the courage to invite as much student feedback on the discussions *I* led, but I'd at least stuck my toe in the waters of teacher-research. It enabled me to see a different side of my students and to relate to them more on their own ground.

The discussion that thrilled me the most that year was one I didn't initiate but only agreed to when Maureen, a student in the class I've been talking about, approached me in the final week or two of her senior year. She still owed me a paper. Instead of writing about *All the King's Men*, she asked, could she and her friend Debbie (also in this class) discuss at home some of the questions I'd proposed as paper topics, recording their conversation for me to listen to later? I couldn't think of a good reason to say no. Like me, Maureen in desperation had come up with a new idea. Freed by our approaching release from school, neither of us had stopped caring about learning but saw it more clearly as separable from certain institutional formalities.

Debbie and Maureen ended up talking about far more than the questions I'd posed. Their tape, like the responses to my "Jade Flower Palace" assignment, was an unexpected gift. Only as I listened to it recently did a comment by Maureen help me see how it grew out of my particular way of teaching and not just of out of the personalities and intellectual curiosities of the two girls. Near the end of the tape, when they've branched out into reflecting on what education might ideally be like, Maureen appreciates the discussion of "issues" in our class. Yes, I loved to discuss issues as much as

Debbie loved to talk about religion, as she says early in the tape, and as much as Maureen relished talking about good and evil. Since they knew I valued this kind of talk and had encouraged it in the student-led discussions, they could imagine me as an interested listener, silently supporting their discussion. While they are wonderfully engaged with one another, they occasionally speak directly to me in the tape, acknowledging my felt presence. What they learned about *All the King's Men*, Robert Penn Warren's novel of political corruption, was not a result of my "teaching," but it was no accident that this tape grew out of my class. I wasn't, in effect, standing before them but sitting with them—not as a peer but as a teacher. An authority that felt right.

Thankfully, I wasn't physically there to intervene, to steer the discussion back "on track" or to offer clues when they got stuck. And so they made their own discoveries in their own ways:

> Maureen poses a question Penn Warren and my assignment sheet did: Do you think that good can come from evil?
>
> *Debbie: Well. . .*
>
> [Maureen can't wait to give her answer.] Well, I do. Want me to explain why I do? OK, the hospital was involved in a lot of evil business, right? Getting the hospital built was all politics and everything and evil stuff, too, but the hospital was good, right?
>
> *Yeah, bad has to be involved to make good, but you can't just make good purely from bad, you know why?*
>
> No, you have to have some good in the beginning.
>
> *There has to be some good in the person who's doing the good.*
>
> That's right. I mean Willie [the powerful and corrupt political figure whose life affects all the major characters in the novel] was good because he wanted to build the hospital.
>
> *Right.*
>
> Which is the worst of two evils—which is the worse? of two evils—which is the worser?
>
> *[Debbie laughs.]*
>
> Which isn't the best, which is the not-so-good thing? To have a hospital built using evil means or not having the hospital and having everything good? But can everything be good without a hospital?

It depends on evil for who? If you're talking about which is better—which is worser, which is worse, which is the worst for the people, it's certainly good to have a hospital even though it was built with evil motives. But if you're talking about which was better for Willie Stark or for the pure independent thing of good, then—it's better to have no hospital even though if you have no hospital you can't do good, than have a hospital that came from pure bad. But—

It can't come from pure bad though.

Well, I know, but if you're going to talk ideally, it's better not to have a hospital than one that's all in corruption and everything. If you're going to talk practically, for the people's sake, you know, who're going to be using the hospital, it's better to have a hospital no matter how it was built.

That's right. I think he had a good motive. I think that was a good thing, but I think that good doesn't *always* have to come from bad. Of course if you look back—

It doesn't have to, but it can.

Yeah but look at how—what was supposed to start off this whole race? Wasn't it Adam and Eve? And they were certainly bad; they weren't good. Right? I mean they had some good characteristics but basically they were bad, right?

But no—Oh but listen! Adam and Eve were supposed to be—I'm not saying I believe in Adam and Eve because personally I don't—

Well, yeah, I know. Adam and Eve is just a story.

Right. But according to what we're supposed to believe about Adam and Eve, now they were supposed to be good until Eve went and had the apple, right?

Right—tempted Adam to eat the apple.

Yeah, but so did Eve.

I wonder if that has any relationship to Adam Stanton [the doctor in the novel who tries unsuccessfully to avoid any involvement with evil].

I doubt it.

It might though.

Anyway, Adam and Eve were supposed to be good until they ate that fruit, right? So if they were—

—innocent and all good and pure good, if they were supposed to be pure good and innocent and right, how could they *allow* themselves to—

—eat the apple?

I don't know because if they were supposed to be so brilliant and everything, they should have *known* that something would have happened like that. Why couldn't they have avoided the temptation? Well, I guess it's just a human thing that they couldn't avoid the temptation.

It was just a story made up.

I know. But, listen, I think there might be some connection between Adam Stanton and Adam and Eve because, you know, Adam—

Adam—he tried to be so good and everything.

Yeah! and as soon as he found out that he came from bad, he thought he was—

Oh, right! Until he found out his father—

Right! I told you that.

Right! He tried to be right and pure and everything until his sister—

Yeah?

—until—oh! and his sister would be like Eve, right?

Right!

And his father—he was created from his father who was bad, and he found out the flaw in his father's nature which was in his.

Right.

Which showed the flaw in his character, which showed that he couldn't always be completely separated from evil, right?!

That's right. That's very good—see it's all—did you hear that, Mrs. Bissex? That was me, Maureen O'Brien! [Both girls laugh.] See, that's a parallel because he thought he was all good, and as soon as he found out he wasn't all good—you know, in both cases, it really wasn't Adam's fault that he wasn't all good. I mean Adam Stanton and Adam and Eve, because it was Eve who—well, as the Biblical story goes—it was Eve who tempted him—

Right.

—into eating the apple, right?

They couldn't really call—

It was like an exterior force that caused them to be evil.

Right.

It wasn't really their own doing because—I think that's a definite parallel.

That is. Gee. When you first said that I thought, aw phooey.

I know you did, that's why you shut me up but I said it again anyway.

[Both girls laugh over this.]

More than twenty-five years later, I still love and learn from their discussion. I'm now more than ever fascinated by looking at how particular individuals learn and (as I did at length later on in *GNYS AT WRK*) looking at discrepancies between particular individuals' learning processes and what our teaching assumes about learning. Classrooms don't—can't—provide 45-minute blocks (the length of their tape) for the meandering, dialogic explorations of Maureens and Debbies. Is it distrust of meanderings and faith in efficiency and logic that would have led me, had I been standing in front of a class, to steer the discussion back on track—my track, that is? Would I have been in a position to appreciate the rich context of these students' intellectual discoveries—what they bring to bear from other parts of their lives and experiences; their ability to laugh together at their own actions and at their entanglements with English grammar; the ways they support each other's gropings ("Right?" "Right!") while also openly disagreeing? Meanwhile what of the twenty-five other learners who would be sitting in that classroom?

Maureen and Debbie themselves are interested in and articulate about their own ways of learning and about how these intersect with the realities of school. All three of us, in our own ways, are exploring the same questions.

Maureen: I don't know how much you've learned, but I've learned a lot from this discussion.

Debbie: Yeah, like about the Great Twitch and Adam.

Yeah, I think it's a much more valuable experience than writing a paper although both are equally important for education.

When you're talking you can—

When you're talking, you come up—I come up with ideas I had never thought of before. I would never have thought that thing about Adam unless we were talking about it, you know.

Remember when we were reading The Scarlet Letter *with Mr. Marshall?*

Yeah.

He gave us those questions, twenty-six questions or something like that. Well, Nancy and I decided to do the first ten or so together in study hall one day. She had tried it at home and she couldn't get it, and I had tried it at home and I couldn't get it. We pulled our chairs in the back of the room, we sat there and we talked and we came out with the most brilliant *stuff. We came out with the most detailed, brilliant stuff, the two of us together, just because we were sitting there talking about it.*

Right.

And, I'm not kidding, stuff that we couldn't have thought up in a million years, just because we were talking and our two ideas came together. And something about trying to explain what you believe to somebody else clarifies it in your own mind.

Oh, yeah. You have to have it so logical—

And you see the flaws in your own thinking.

Yeah, when you talk over things with someone, you do. My teachers lately have been bringing up so much about what is education. In French he said would you be here right now if you didn't need this course to get into college? And it really made me stop and think because I don't particularly enjoy French that much.

I don't enjoy French class but I would love to be able to speak French. All the stuff I'm learning in school, I think it's so interesting, but it's too bad I have to learn it in school.

That's right. If you could sit around in groups of maybe ten people and have the same classes with those ten or fifteen people, and you just sit in a circle and you just talk about anything. . . . I think we've done a lot toward that idea in English, although we haven't all the time. We've discussed issues that are always a part of education. It's not a normal English class—

[Debbie laughs and makes a reassuring aside to me] *She means that in a complimentary way.*

I think it's fantastic.

The only thing is you've got to realize that a class can't always be run that way.

That's right, you have to have lectures and you have to really work on some things.

In a school like this where the classes are so big, if you divide up in small groups, after a couple of days the kids will just start to talk. You have to have a teacher and you have to have somebody to supervise, and so in a class situation like ours it would be impossible to have these small groups.

That's true.

But if we had two teachers for every one that we have now or if we killed off half the kids in school, it would be very workable, it would be very, very good.

I think that's more like what education is.

For me, as for Maureen and Debbie, what the discussion comes essentially to be about is learning—the liveliness and unpredictability of learning as heard in their dialogue, and then in their reflections on the conditions enabling the dialogue of learning to occur. To capture persons in the *act* of learning is rare. School has most often been about presenting the *results* of learning, as teachers instruct and students answer teachers' questions, both teachers and students showing what they already know. One of the appeals and rewards of teaching adolescents was, for me, identifying with their excitement at intellectual discoveries, their fascination with moral issues, and their growing sense of the power of their own thinking and understanding. Maureen and Debbie's discussion reaffirms for me now my valuing of learning above teaching in the traditional sense. More and more I prize the learner in myself as part of who I am as a teacher, researcher, and person.

As I write this book, I learn more—or differently—from my high school teaching experiences than I did at the time, when I was abraded by the daily realities of my dissatisfaction with conventional education. Teaching in a public school, even a very good one, turned my focus outward from developing my own teaching style and competence to trying to make sense of how education could serve all kinds of students, especially those disaffected for varied reasons. I took their disaffection as a symptom of disease in the educational system. In the face of this, what had I to offer them? My discomfort was not just with myself as a teacher but with the context in which I taught. What was school learning about anyhow?

I was alienated by the sheer size of the school, by being part of something too large to know and to be known in. I had gone to a small school myself from first grade through high school, a school that had a fireplace in its front hall. Though rarely lit, it was a symbol as well as a gathering place. In college I sought refuge from a large dorm in a co-op house that had been an old home with a soapstone sink in the kitchen and a tin-plated copper bathtub on the second floor. But teaching in a 2,000-student high school on a faculty most of whom I didn't know, in a room that looked like every other room was not as uncomfortable as confronting every day a class that simply didn't want to be there. Their presence made me ask what I was doing there with them, and I didn't have a good enough answer.

I resigned that spring, not to leave teaching, but because I needed to find an answer and also because I was ready to start my own family. How could I give time to a child when teaching English was a 60-hour a week job with long hours spent reading and responding to papers and studying the literature I was to teach as well as planning how to teach it? This, alas! was before Writing Workshop, when I read every word I'd asked my students to write and commented extensively, revealing my fondness for one-on-one teaching. I was even feeling guilty as I trained interns into this consuming job of English teaching. My husband had at one time studied Reading and suggested I might want to teach that instead. I wasn't sure what "Reading" was but I was sure it would eliminate those piles of papers. I applied to the Harvard Graduate School of Education.

4

Why I Didn't "Go in with Some Specific Hypothesis"

AFTER TWELVE YEARS OF RESPONSIBILITY FOR EVERYTHING that happened in a classroom, twelve years of nonstop decision making on my feet, I relished the luxury of sitting down to read and study and reflect. My classes were often seminar-sized and taught by women professors. What a different world from the Harvard College lecture halls dominated by men that I'd experienced fourteen years earlier! And I was a different learner, pregnant to boot. Sitting in Courtney Cazden's Child Language course, I looked forward to observing my own child's language development. The baby growing inside me wouldn't have become the protagonist of GNYS AT WRK without the models of linguists who recorded and studied the language of individual children including their own. Not long after Paul was born, I had my tape recorder going. Several years later, when he started to write and read, I continued to observe, gathering material for what would become—though I had no idea of it then—my first book.

The Graduate School of Education was a different world from the English Departments that had earlier been my academic dwelling places. Reading "the literature" now meant reading the research on a particular topic, not reading Shakespeare or Yeats. I was steeped in humanities, from undergraduate and graduate study of (real) literature, from my love of music and other arts, from twelve years of teaching literature and writing. Most statistical research did not impress me: not its antiseptic methodology, nor the sterile, impersonal voice in which it was presented, and sometimes not even the too cleanly cut questions it asked.

Summarizing the research on language development, Cazden wrote that "On all the measures, in all the studies, children of upper socioeconomic status . . . are more advanced than those of lower socioeconomic status." Had those researchers lived among people of "lower socioeconomic status" as I had? Had they asked the right questions? What if, I speculated, one of the measures of language development was not differentiating meanings through extensive vocabulary (conjunctions, say) but distinguishing, through context, different meanings for a single conjunction (such as *and*, which lower class speakers "overuse")? Were their meanings necessarily as limited as their vocabulary? How sensitive to that possibility might researchers from a different socioeconomic class be? What if the tables were turned and the studies were conducted by researchers of lower status on speakers of higher status? In my first paper for Cazden's course, written in a deliberately pedantic and impersonal style, I spoofed the research and turned compensatory education upside down.

WHOSE SUBCULTURAL DEFICIENCIES?

One of the most reliable measures of linguistic development, it is clear from recent research, is the ability to differentiate multiple meanings of single terms. The study here reported investigated the ability of subjects to differentiate, through production and comprehension, the meanings of *and*. The subjects were eleven- and twelve-year-olds, ten from families of lower socioeconomic status and ten from families of higher socioeconomic status.

Their responses to informal questions on their experiences with policemen were taped and analyzed as the first measure in this study. The average frequency of *and* in the speech of lower SES subjects was 10.8 per hundred words; for higher SES subjects, 6.1 per hundred words. Data on differentiation among the meanings of *and* are summarized in Figure 1.

Figure 1

Meanings of "and"[1]	% of lower SES occurrences	% of higher SES occurrences
to signal co-ordination	36	68
to signal combination	14	32
to introduce	9	0
to signal consequence	13	0
to signal cause	10	0
to signal contrast	11	0
to signal a minor break in thought	7	0

[1]For a discussion of the correlation between number of available meanings of "and" and intelligence test results, see my article "Class Differences in Intellectual Endowment," *Scientific Studies*, 21, 190–237.

The second measure involved a listening comprehension test. Instances of *and* in all seven of its meanings were incorporated into sentences in stories. Questions were designed to elicit the listener's ability to distinguish the appropriate meanings of *and* for each occurrence. Results on this section correlated highly (.93) with those on the first section. While lower SES listeners differentiated all of the meanings of *and*, higher SES listeners were able to distinguish only two different meanings. It is not surprising, then, that higher SES subjects scored correctly on only 11%–48% of the appropriate meanings, and that lower SES subjects indicated the proper meaning in 76%–100% of the instances of *and*. The achievement of such scores is evidence that sufficient context clues were present in the sentences to differentiate the proper meanings of *and* provided the child had the fundamental knowledge of the range of meanings.

One implication of this research for language training to enrich the impoverished usage of *and* among higher SES children is clear: The existence of five additional meanings for the word must be brought to their awareness. Exposure of such children to speakers and writers who do utilize the full range of *and* meanings is, of course, essential. My colleague, Dr. Train M. Wright, has suggested in a recent article in *The Journal of Ortholinguistics* (1966, 460–75) that prohibiting higher SES children from using such "crutch" words as *then, therefore* and *because* would naturally induce them to attempt the more advanced task of differentiating among the meanings of the single term. And surely it is this matter of training which deserves our attention now, for the research evidence on subcultural differences in language ability is abundant and unequivocal: On all the measures, in all the studies, children of lower socioeconomic status are more advanced than those of upper socioeconomic status.

One of my first researches grew out of listening to interviews of a Harvard student William Perry was analyzing for his *Forms of Intellectual and Ethical Development in the College Years* (1970). Along with other graduate students in a discussion group with Perry, I had been distressed at what "Harvardization" appeared to have cost this young man in enthusiasm, optimism, humor, zest, directness of action, and speech. He had seemed to become paler, more formalized, more standardized. On the tape, his voice lost some of its vigor and dynamic over the four years, as well as the edge of its Dorchester accent. Since I was, before hearing this tape, already concerned about the devitalizing and de-individualizing effects of academic institutions, I was quite prepared to demonstrate these processes through my analysis of Michael's speech.

I searched for methods of language analysis in previous studies, but the methods I found were largely rooted in the purposes of those particular projects, which were not my purposes. So I simply immersed myself in the interviews themselves, hoping that salient features would rise to the surface, granting me some sense of where to begin. That's how I had learned to read English literature.

Certain words and phrases characteristic of, or even unique to Michael's language in a particular year began to stand out for me. As a freshman, he repeatedly referred to "learning the ropes." Also reflecting his concern with coping with his new situation were many, many instances of "how" (e.g. "How can I read that in just a week?"). The words "concrete" and "complex" stood out as peculiarly recurrent in his sophomore interview, as did the expressions "for instance" and "for example." As a junior, by contrast, he usually clarified statements not with concrete instances but with more abstract explanations, introduced by "I mean." This shift from concrete illustration and anecdote to restatement, generally on the same level of abstraction as his original statement, rendered his speech less colorful, more academic.

The words "decide" and "decision" were frequent in his last two years (21 instances in his junior interview, 22 in his senior). While the activities he described all four years involved decision making, it seemed that only as he confronted the longer range decisions of commitment to certain values and a career did his language explicitly reflect an awareness of decision making. His focus was now not so much on the externals of doing but on his inner judgmental processes: He was no longer so much in a world of *things* to be *done* as a world of *values* to be *chosen*. Thus I came to see that the changes were not all losses, and that the process was not one of constant grinding down but of transformation.

My approach to data was rather like my approach to my students: I wasn't eager to impose my authority and I enjoyed listening. I found my way through data by immersing myself in it, getting the feel of it and letting it lead me, rather than imposing a predetermined, standard analytical scheme. This immersion approach to research dismayed one faculty reader of another analysis I undertook. As an English teacher discovering what research on reading might have to say about interpreting literature, I plunged into a pile of essay test responses by high school English students to questions on a literary passage. My aim was "to see what they might reveal about the reading process. I was not so much concerned with answering questions as raising some that might be further investigated." My paper's critic responded: "In a study of this type it's much easier and more fruitful to go in with some specific hypothesis rather than try to make some sense out of a mass of data."

"Easier and more fruitful" for him, I suppose. Looking at those student responses to literature from a Reading teacher's perspective brought me new awarenesses and helped me build a bridge to my new area of teaching. My advisor, Jeanne Chall, was more encouraging. Although her approach to research was very different from mine, she was one of my strongest supporters during this year and my later doctoral research. "I found the paper extremely interesting and suggestive," she wrote. "While I agree that it is worthwhile to start with hypotheses, I think you ended up with at least two in your Final Thoughts section." In that section I reflected that:

> From my perspective as an English teacher, I have become aware of how many reading problems I once lumped together in my mind as "careless-ness," thus learning nothing more about them and providing little help for these students. I am aware, not for the first time, of how unenlightened and unenlightening is the emphasis on evaluation rather than understanding in most classrooms. I have found that students who are not answering *the* question are, when one takes the time to infer it from their responses, answering *a* question; and I wonder about the academic artificiality of answering someone *else's* questions all the time. I am also, as an English teacher, wondering what can be done to help students with "higher level'" reading problems. English teachers may go so far as to define "theme," for instance, but how many are even conscious enough themselves of the processes involved to explain to students how to find themes in a piece of literature? And what about training in question reading, especially for less academically successful students?
>
> Interpretation is not the mysterious or incomprehensible process students imply when they call it "digging for hidden meanings." The process of interpretation, of extracting meanings from events, seems, like language, to be inherent in the human mind.

As I tried to understand the nature of "reading comprehension" later that year, I saw that the area where the vast domain of human comprehension (meaning making, interpretation) and the smaller realm of reading overlap constitutes "reading comprehension." Twenty years later, my experiences of reading nature extend this awareness of the omnipresence of meaning making. I see that canoeists and fishermen read the water, farmers read the sky, hunters and loggers read the woods, each for their own purposes, geologists read rocks, and we all read faces. When I see how many texts I might read, I realize my illiteracies and know how narrow my notion of literacy has been. Reading, in one form or another, is what we all do to survive in and understand our worlds.

While my graduate work had most immediately turned me into a teacher of reading, it also turned me into a student of reading. This year changed my work, my thinking, and my life. In the summer we moved from inner-city Boston to a hill farm in Vermont. "We" included three-week-old Paul, who led me to rediscover childhood, expanding my interests as an educator and researcher. I couldn't have seen then how profoundly this move, this child, and my introduction to research would reshape my life.

One of my professors assumed I'd moved to Vermont because my husband had a job there but, in fact, he'd searched two years for the kind of job that would enable us to move into a new life in a small white farmhouse on a hill, looking thirty miles west to the Green Mountains and the peak of Camel's Hump. For me, living in this countryside was a new form of a treasured part of my youth, for my growing up wasn't entirely in the city.

Summers, my parents and I and our suitcases, including a partially zipped duffel bag inside which Uncle Zinnia meowed, boarded the orange electric train of the Chicago South Shore and South Bend Railroad. We rolled through South Chicago toward Indiana, the station stops chanted by the conductor: Calumet, Whiting (putrid with gas tanks), Hegewich, Hammond, East Chicago, Gary (clouded with steel mill smoke), Ogden Dunes, Mineral Springs, and on to Tremont, "gateway to the dunes" and home of "the old Indian medicine man" whose profile dignified a billboard. From the station we phoned for Mr. King to drive us in his black taxi the several miles to the bottom of the path up to our cottage. He spat tobacco juice out the window as he drove, but never hit me.

Our cottage was in the woods on a little hill. You didn't have to dig down very far to find out you were on a sand dune merely coated with topsoil—enough for blueberries and modest oaks and occasional dogwoods to grow. Although the cottage was only a few miles from Lake Michigan, I didn't get to the beach often until I was old enough to bike along Highway 12, then left onto a narrow ribbon of road through scrub, past the ditch where a few fiery cardinal lobelias bloomed and crayfish hid, past the Bob-O-Link Camp, up, up to the crest of the highest dune. Suddenly the lake spread out below all the way to the horizon—blue, or green, or gray; flat or dimpled or roiled with waves. Always a surprise. Always different.

I climbed the dunes on foot, too, scorching my feet on the sand, then running back down in leaps until my feet were blessed by the cool water. I charged into the waves and, at the right instant, turned and let them slide me, weightless, back to shore where I was solid flesh and bone again. Too solid, I felt, as I watched the beach grass bow and sweep. If only I could bend so with the wind, my hair and fingertips like grasses etching crescents in the sand. In my Chicago neighborhood everything was paved except a rubble-crusted vacant lot and two small triangles of grass in front of the settlement house, guarded by high, black iron fences with pointed pickets.

The places of my childhood will always be mine because I was born into them, as I was born into my family. The place I have chosen out of love, this Vermont hill farm, only slowly became familiar, like a spouse, as I lived with it over years. There was the land to know—the succession of wildflowers that kept repainting the fields in early summer from dandelion yellow to a tapestry of orange paint brush, purple vetch, and daisies; the woods with unfamiliar trees like iron wood and yellow birch and cedar; the little pools and waterfalls along our stream, and all of these transformed by fall and winter and spring.

And there were people to know. Bea Kellogg Johnson, once a school teacher and then proprietor of Kellogg's General Store, sold me ground cloves for the first batch of apple butter I ever made. "You won't want to use too much of these," she warned. They were so potent I never have used too much of them, and the partly empty jar still sits on my spice shelf more than twenty years later. When I first visited the three generations of neighbors sharing a farmhouse on the hill overlooking us, the only girl among the youngest generation was introduced to me as liking school and being a reader. The boys preferred an active, outdoor life. I was already identified as a teacher, and it was through teaching in the local school, more than through living on East Hill Road, that I entered the community.

5

"Sooner or Later I'm Going to Catch Up with All the Words"

THOUGH THE OPEN CLASSROOM MOVEMENT OF THE 60S had left the walls of the local high school intact, as their first, part-time reading teacher, I was free to create my own program—first in a portable classroom next to the old wooden high school and soon in the new sixth through twelfth grade building made of concrete and metal and glass. Its floors were carpeted, an economy that seemed a luxury to families who lived with bare wooden floors. The white ceiling tile was porous, and students soon discovered that sharply pointed pencils, flung straight upward, had a fair chance of remaining impaled and dangling from an unreachable height. For my room, I asked for movable tables and chairs and no teacher's desk. Students worked individually at tables against the walls and in groups at tables clustered in the middle. I bought up old magazine and card racks from the drugstore in town that had gone out of business and displayed paperbacks and magazines like *Mechanics Illustrated* that the school library didn't subscribe to. For years, I drove down my hill and along the river to school, amazed at how happy I was to be doing just this, being part of this landscape and this town.

From my students I learned that turkeys could run around after their heads were cut off, I learned about hunting and snowmobiles and chainsaws, I learned about isolated lives and about families unlike my own. I came to understand the pain, frustration, and boredom of school experiences different from my successes as a student. I wanted to learn why my students hadn't learned to read well, or at all, when they had learned other things.

The reasons I saw were neither simple nor easy to generalize. Through trying every approach I could think of, I sought ways these adolescents might learn what had so far been inaccessible.

Bill, recently moved to the area, came into sixth grade a nonreader. Reading aloud from the math text book, he read "A 7 tob of toothbest cotters 48 grants" for "A 7-ounce tube of toothpaste costs 84 cents." He couldn't read enough words to piece together a sentence from the social studies book either. I and a corps of high school students who served as tutors put together almost a full day program for him. Looking back now over some of his work and the tutors' reports I've saved, I appreciate what Bill and all of us accomplished. Then, my gaze was fixed on the gap between his academic skills and those he still needed to participate fully in classes—a gap that narrowed but didn't close.

I hoped he'd be able to learn to write and then to read his own words. I might have guessed his inventiveness from the improvisations he created when he lost his tenuous grasp on reading not a textbook but a story, especially in rhyme, like Dr. Seuss's *One Fish, Two Fish.* Based on the words he could read, words he'd read previously and the illustrations, his improvisations were rhythmic and sometimes sung, with the rhythms carrying his language forward:

TEXT:	BILL:
Bump!	Pup-pup-pup-up
Bump!	Pup-pup
Bump!	Pup-e-lee-pup.
Did you ever ride a Wump?	Do you have running feet?
We have a Wump	Ask a fish
with just one hump.	if they have running feet.
But	But
we know a man	we don't n—— a man,
	we know a man
called Mr. Gump.	c—— Mr. Gladden.
Mr. Gump has a seven hump Wump.	Mr. Gladden has six funny feet.
So . . .	So
if you like to go Bump! Bump!	if you like to go (singing) bumpety-bumpety-bump-bump-bump, bumpety-bumpety-bumpety-bump-bump-bump,
just jump on the hump of the Wump of Gump.	(speaking) go see Gladden.

Bill's inventiveness and rhythmic sense of language flourished in the long stories he wrote by hand—elaborated tales with the strong rhythms and the structural repetitions of folk tales. He wrote about the life he knew—school and the woods where his father was a logger. The characters in his stories often talked to themselves, like the boy who didn't like school and "said to himself, I will be sick the first day of school." But then he thought he might be so well he couldn't be sick even if he wanted to be; so "He said to himself, I know what I will do, I will go to school and hide under the school building and the school board will think I moved out of this town." Unfortunately, one of the students discovers him and he's caught. Then the boy said to himself, "The plan did not work." In the Paul Bunyan story Bill invented, Paul talks to himself about his logging job, telling himself, for example, that he's sick and tired of the boss and tomorrow he'll tell the boss if he doesn't like it, he can fire him. He also had fun with numbers: Paul's "light lunch" consists of 24 pancakes, 100 eggs, 40 hot dogs and 30 apple pies; and at the end of the story he sleeps for 5 years, 7 months, 2 weeks, 5 hours, 2 minutes and 2 seconds. In another story, improvised from a drawing of a woman in a rocker and a man whose head has fallen off onto the floor, the lone old lady, who had decided to build a man from a tree, talks to herself about her plans and problems. After she finally finds the right tree and chops it down, she asks herself how she's going to get it home. "So the old lady sat down on the log and started to think and think and think. Finally the old lady said to herself, 'I know what I can do. I can tie a rope to the log.'" So she got the log home and after carving it for a month, she'd created a man who not only looked real but walked into her front room. His head fell off but she put it back on and the man and the old lady lived happily ever after.

When I arranged for Bill and another student to spend a few hours a week as assistants in a first-grade classroom, his parents came to school to protest his being "put back." I, on the other hand, was glad to find a teacher willing to include these students in her classroom and able to appreciate any help they could give. While Bill still jumbled the order of letters in words or omitted letters, she reported, he was very conscientious and warm with the children and tried hard to do a good job. When he was loaned an inexpensive camera for a photography and writing project, his parents came to school with the camera they said they'd discovered in his drawer to make sure he hadn't stolen it. The father had a fearsome reputation, and jaws dropped at school when I mentioned that I'd visited the family. Perhaps his mother, in the midst of canning vegetables, had been surprised, too. One evening months later, she drove to my house, not far from hers. I think she was seeking refuge from her husband, but she only talked, then drove away.

Did I know then how much I didn't know? What did school mean to Bill and his family? He learned from his new curriculum, but how did he interpret all of the attention, and how had he survived his previous schooling? I wish I had asked more questions.

What do students do in school when they can't read? Perhaps Bill talked to himself, as characters in his stories did. An older student, looking back at his nonreading years, told me, "I just sat there and pretended I was reading. I'd always be losing my place, I couldn't follow along. I just went through every day a boring day. Torture, complete torture. The days lasted ten years for me. I couldn't wait to get home."

Most of my students read very slowly. Don, after he'd learned to read more fluently, described the experience of that slowness: "Every other sentence I day-dreamed for half an hour, just about. My mind would wander and I'd substitute words that weren't there. I couldn't read fast enough to really get anything out of it or enjoy it. I suppose it's like skating—if you can't ever learn to slide around, you have to enjoy falling down all the time." Of course these students didn't enjoy falling down in the rinks that were their classrooms. Don had accelerated his reading outside of school on some very high interest material—dirty novels. My son had learned to read on books he enjoyed. Seeing some of the lifeless textbooks my students were expected to read, as I helped them study for their classes, I felt I had to choose between helping them succeed in school or offering them material they could care about. They needed to get through school, but they also had lives ahead of them in which they would choose to read or not to read. I was torn. Creating an island within the school was not enough.

How could I create change outside my classroom? Perhaps the students themselves would help. I instituted a high school course called Introduction to Teaching, which gave students some real employment (and academic credit for) assisting teachers or working with individuals at both the elementary and high schools. The young teachers kept journals and met with me in a weekly discussion group. Some good experiences resulted for both the young teachers and their learners. For instance, when Steve played background guitar to first-grade story tellers, they suddenly became more fluent. A number of the high schoolers came to appreciate what hard work teaching was. But the discussions produced no revolutions.

I gained a creative and warmhearted high school teaching assistant who I was able to hire as my aide so I didn't lose her when she graduated. I loved having a collaborator in creating an alternative classroom. Kathy not only understood how I was trying to teach, but she knew the community inside out and helped me know more about my students' lives. She reached out to students who were on the margins at school, both academically and socially, and to the loners. Not many of our students distinguished themselves in school as leaders or athletes or performers in the arts. Benjy was one of the exceptions—he was a super basketball player in a school where basketball was the major sport, where there was a tradition of championship teams, and where the games were an important form of entertainment for the community. So although his family moved to Vermont from a very different part of the United States, he soon had made a place for himself on the court. Dyslexia knew no boundaries.

His attractive and educated mother had always sent her son to the best public schools, even selling her home so she could afford rent in the district that had the best reading program in the state. Despite that, he didn't learn to read well. Despite that, he was never diagnosed as dyslexic. She had come across the country to study in a graduate program in Vermont. I guess she'd taken her chances with the local public school after alerting us to her son's need for help with reading and writing. Knowing her concern, I loaned her a book about a mother and son, whose similarities to her own case I only learned when she returned the book with a long letter, unwinding her family history.

She looked back at Benjy's and her own and her family's history anew. I could feel the electricity of connections being made. She was a fluent and articulate writer with perfect spelling. Writing and reading were what she loved to do, and she'd been an outstanding student; it was talking and auditory learning that were hard. Yes, she saw now, that was her form of dyslexia. And then there was her confusion between right and left; just yesterday she'd turned left off a road, believing she was turning right. A five-year-old nephew who mispronounced most words and an older relative who had spelled simple words backwards in school, connected to the pattern. In the past she *had* suspected dyslexia, but said she was ridiculed for the idea at one school and never raised it again. "It was the school's attitude which was so frustrating to me: always the belittling of the 'problem'—the refusal to accept the idea that something was wrong (though Benjy was entirely nonfunctional in his classrooms), the subtle attitude that I was probably overwrought and neurotic—thus contributing to or indeed causing his problems."

I sensed she'd written this letter in a sort of white heat after reading the book, which at last confirmed the reasons for her frustrations and her son's. This understanding brought an end to some of her struggles, but she had to acknowledge now, with some resignation and sadness, that no school was good enough to make the problem disappear. Having put the pieces together, she had also found a realistic hope "that the problem can be improved on and that with great effort, he can go on to college as he hopes."

That year my own son was five years old and writing prolifically at home in invented spelling. Some of his spellings resembled ones I saw in my classroom, but his approximations were more systematic, as though he believed that there *was* an underlying system, while my students sometimes doubted that spelling made sense and thus that they could learn to control it. While I, as a parent, was there to confirm to Paul what he knew, my students for too long had been confronted with what they didn't know. As I watched Paul's intense efforts at reading and endured his tearful, frustrated outbursts at the immensity of the task, I thought of the frustrations of my students, who had learned to curb their tears. For my son, this was only a stage in his learning, not the constant accompaniment it was for some of my students.

Through Jan, my most mature and reflective student, I came to know the experiences of a child whose initial difficulty with reading had soon convinced her teachers, and they in turn had convinced her, of her inability to read. In second grade "The teacher used to tell me every day that I didn't have to read if I didn't want to because I couldn't read, and of course that caused me to be very upset. It wasn't too long after that I really, really believed I couldn't read." But she wasn't always let off the hook. In reading class, everyone had to read out loud. She was ashamed to read because she read so "choppily." She hated reading and before she knew it, she had a mental block—she just couldn't read at all. "I just didn't allow myself to, I guess."

After six years of schooling, her family traveled to a place where she couldn't attend school. It was then, with her mother as her teacher, that she started reading—that she realized she could read if she wanted to. Her mother made her believe that, just as her earlier teachers' lack of faith had made her doubt herself. Her mother taught reading by getting her books she wanted, by not asking her to read aloud unless she wanted to, by not laughing at her if she didn't read well. Her mother asked Jan about the books she'd read "and there'd always be something I'd want to tell her about—that's how she is—she makes you want to say something." Jan came to realize that more fluent reading was just a matter of time and practice. No teaching method, no reading program is as powerful as the student's experience of her teacher's faith or lack of faith in her ability to learn.

How many of my students had given up on themselves when parents or teachers lost faith? When parents themselves had struggled with learning to read, was it hard for them to believe reading could be easier for their children? There were no quick fixes I could administer as a teacher of reading. Self-confidence grew slowly in these adolescents. I experimented with teaching reading through a phonetic alphabet—a new code that gave them a second chance at reading. I scrounged up a couple of old typewriters to distance them from their own handwriting and add the appeal of a machine. We had Scrabble tournaments and played word games, some I'd invented and standard ones like hangman, in which missing letters had to be filled in until a word was complete. Cloze tests and miscue analyses indicated students weren't making full use of context cues. I urged them away from wild guessing in hangman to predicting what letters might be likely to fill in certain blanks. I asked them to spell long words that might have frightened them before they'd mastered *-tion* endings and a few other building blocks of words. They delighted in filling the blackboard with sophisticated polysyllabic words correctly spelled, just as my son at home compiled a list of "hard words," many with *-tion* endings, which he'd finally learned weren't spelled the way they sounded.

As Jan realized, new learnings required time and practice. No wonder I'd felt rushed and inadequate working with students for one semester in the Reading Lab when I was a graduate student. Two years was more like the time needed to make a real difference: time to build both faith and skill. "What I am trying to do as a teacher—above all as a student of the learning process and of my particular students in the midst of it—is to view from the inside," I wrote in my journal. "At what level of mind, of being, does one learn to read?" Jan's story revealed its depths.

Students weren't merely deficient in information—didn't just need something put into them—but needed to have their learning power released from the voices that had caused them to doubt it. Just as there seemed to exist natural healing processes in the human psyche which might only need to be freed in order to work, so I believed there were natural learning processes that must be freed to work. I could not "teach" reading in the sense of directly controlling the transaction between the reader and the page, but I tried to help students cast off old strategies and myths about reading that interfered with that transaction. Students who had been told for years to sound out words they didn't recognize and too often ended up with phonic approximations that were nonsense, needed to ask "Does this make sense?" Students who felt under a moral obligation to read word by word needed permission to move more freely, even to go ahead rather than back when they couldn't figure out a word.

Jan reflected on how her reading had improved through her work in my room. Like learning to read at home, her learning here had been non-competitive. She was able to work at her own speed and see her own progress. She didn't have to be compared to anyone else but could make herself advance as fast as she wanted, "doing it on my own free will, that's what

I loved about it. I think I learned quite fast that way." She said she was always afraid I'd ask her to take a speed reading test and she wouldn't have progressed fast enough or gotten where she should be and would feel ashamed. Instead, I asked her only occasionally if she felt ready to check her reading speed again. The last increase had amazed her. Suddenly reading had started "growing on" her, and the more she read, the better she could read, and of course the more things she read. She could see her speed was increasing and knew she was progressing because she noticed she was picking up things she'd never read before like newspapers and magazines, and reading everything on the packages when she'd buy something.

While reading had finally ceased to be a problem for her, spelling still was. But she felt better able to express herself on paper and saw that both her vocabulary and spelling had improved. Above all, she'd gained the confidence in herself as a language learner to say that someday, if she felt ambitious, she'd overcome her spelling problem, too. "I learn to spell something new every day anyway. Sooner or later I'm going to catch up with all the words."

One effect of my year of graduate work in Reading was to make me feel like a researcher in the midst of my teaching and to legitimate my role as learner. The identity of "teacher-researcher" didn't exist then. The workshops on teaching reading and spelling that I led through the community college gave me occasions to analyze and reflect on some of my students' writings and transcriptions of oral readings more thoroughly than I would have otherwise. This processing and reprocessing of what I observed in my classroom I see now was my teacher-research.

During these six years of teaching reading, I'd been watching my young son grow into language so fast I noted changes by months or weeks or even days. Before learning to say individual words, he'd vocalized wordless sentences in the shapes of statements and questions. In learning to read, he again moved from a global understanding toward specifics as he first retold stories from pictures while turning book pages and later identified words. What I'd learned in graduate school about language and literacy development was replaying like a movie on my home screen. Fascinated, I collected more tape recordings, field notes on yellow pads, and folders of writings. I was a parent-researcher as well as a teacher-researcher, and the researching brought me closer in both relationships. Eventually, researching without colleagues and mentors would not satisfy me.

6

Thinking the Unthinkable

MY RELATIVE INTELLECTUAL ISOLATION IN VERMONT— which was also my intellectual freedom—showed me my capacity for dialogue with myself and with books as colleagues. Questions, observations, theories, plans, and reading notes filled hundreds of pages on yellow legal pads. Working with children stimulated my thinking—children of farmers, granite workers, mechanics, artisans, and a college professor. I had only begun to learn what I might from them, only begun to learn to teach to all their differences. Working in a K–12 system offered the chance to teach and follow children over time. Watching my son learn to talk, to write, and to read increased my fascination with observing the learning processes of individual children. I recorded detailed observations not only of him but of several of my students, and I yearned for an apprenticeship to gain a better sense of how to go about my own research.

Five-year-old Paul had been improvising his own spellings, something I mentioned to a former high school English teacher of mine who was a student of linguistics. I learned from her of Charles Read's research on children's phonology and spelling, and so I discovered the term "invented spelling" and learned other kids were doing it and Read was studying it. Amazing! Read's thoughts about systematic learning processes operating for skills like spelling, long regarded as the acquisition of discrete items, excited me. I went on to read Carol Chomsky's "Reading, Writing, and Phonology" and I envisioned a new spelling pedagogy that would make clear the nature of our spelling system and be soundly based in a psychology of learning. I just wanted to read-read-read, and did, finally stopping in frenzied exhaustion midway through Noam Chomsky's *Language and Mind*, admitting that I couldn't learn all I so urgently wanted to within a few weeks' time. But I had learned from him that you need never lose sight of the great questions while exploring the finest details of human behavior, and I had witnessed the excitement of inquiry starting from an acknowledgment of how much we do not understand.

I applied for admission to the doctoral program in Reading and Human Development at Harvard. Now I had a reason to, whereas earlier I couldn't imagine why I'd want a doctorate.

This pull toward more graduate study had been reinforced by a year's training with other teachers from across Vermont under the federal Right to Read program. Our meetings brought me contacts with other Reading teachers and with university Reading educators. At the end of the year, we learned there would be funds to start several Regional Right to Read Centers—funds for reading materials, enrichment programs for students, inservice programs for teachers—in whatever ways the selected coordinators determined. As I wrote my application, I envisioned my center and the difference it might make to teachers and students. I saw it as a step toward a school-based learning center, a place for children, student teachers, experienced teachers, and researchers, where teaching and learning would come together as they did in my own head; a scholarly and humane place of inquiry and sharing. Here my interests in working with children and teachers and ideas could combine. I could pursue my explorations of children's reading, writing, and learning processes and provide for more discussion with others about these matters.

That spring both of my applications—for the doctoral program and for a Regional Right to Read Center—were accepted. I could delay my doctoral work, but not the funding for the Center. For myself, for my school, for the Right to Read team that had entrusted me with creating this Center, I could not refuse. The appeal was altruism and it was power.

I filled a conference room off the library, donated by my school, with materials I would want to use, and did use, as a teacher. James Moffett's exciting array of materials to support his student-centered Language Arts curriculum had recently been published, and I ordered many of them. I ordered trade books and recorded books, books for teachers, language games, and cushions for reading corners. I hired a local craftsperson to make hand puppets and a reading house. I loved being in that room, and I loved seeing the materials go out in the hands of teachers. I invited writers and dramatic artists into classrooms. I filled our auditorium with students to hear novelist Robert Newton Peck, and with people from all of the community one evening to hear naturalist Ronald Rood. I filled our school with teachers attending workshops from twenty-five area schools. I brought James Moffett to talk with teachers one glorious May weekend. I had expected my principal to feel that the Center was an honor for the school, but it was only my honor, not his. I had the money to spend and the programs to plan. Perhaps he felt inconvenienced and displaced.

Speakers came and went, teachers passed through the materials center and workshops. What remained? What difference did it all make? I seemed to have no way of knowing. My vision of a "school-based learning center . . . where teaching and learning would come together" gradually eroded. In the end, I did not enjoy acting as an administrator, as I wrote in my journal:

> Getting things done can become a substitute for living. The office model of life. The question is "What did you do—get done—today?" Answering phone calls and correspondence, taking messages, filing: transactions without meaning, efficiency without purpose except to reduce the clutter, clear the desk. For what? Whatever the next mail brings. To some extent that's how my life has felt this year with Right to Read administrative matters. The feeling of pulling strings and being pulled by strings: marionettes. Who is the marionette? Who is holding the strings? (I seem to be both.) And who is the show for? I keep coming back to that question.

I reapplied for admission to the doctoral program. The task of Right to Read coordinator had brought me into more extensive contact with school administrators, which broadened my understanding of school operations without making me yearn for political power. I had been a successful organizer, but for me the demands of the work exceed its satisfactions. I felt all the more needful of time to write, study, pursue research, and reflect.

My future didn't appear so clear to me as it had a year ago. While the past year sharpened some issues—such as the importance to me of writing and my abiding interest in the learning processes of the human mind—it stirred up questions about my continuing institutional commitments. Or perhaps the question was of my continued coexistence with the frames of reference and rhythms of a public school environment. Having taught for twenty years, I wondered how productive another twenty years in the classroom would be for me. I needed time and distance to define the questions to myself and consider alternatives. Through writing and then through continued research I hoped to find my own place to stand. "School seems too much on the surface of my life now," I wrote in my journal.

> It requires a lot of energy but does not touch me deeply. I "accomplish" in bits and pieces given to others. My deepest layers are not engaged. The sadness is that this has been true for so long. Only now I am uncomfortably aware of it and I see other options for my life. . . . I think of the kids at school. They'll survive. Some of them will miss me. Some would have a better time in school if I stayed. I would have a worse time with myself if I

stayed. I'm leaving something uncompleted, but would it ever be finished? Perhaps I'm concerned over my "changing my mind." It would be easier to just keep on going the way I'd once seen I would—enlarging my scope, modifying my direction, but all gradually and integratedly, without disruption and disconnection and uprooting and putting down new roots and daring to commit myself to something else and maybe fail.

I contemplated a writing life rather than a teaching life—although it would be seventeen more years before I committed myself to writing as a major, continuing work (and then found I needed also the human contact of teaching). When I started keeping a journal as a senior in college, it was the beginning of a long, written conversation with myself, interrupted only as I struggled with the external world in my twenties. I write to hear and keep in touch with my voice. In rereading my journals, I've discovered how far their story of my inner life was ahead of events in my outer life—sometimes dismayingly so. My journal has been a place not for grappling with day-to-day concerns but for voicing yearnings and speculations, clarifying visions and discontents, exploring multiple perspectives, and affirming partial truths.

Is there anyone except yourself to blame the bad days on when you're a writer? Not on "the kids" as a teacher may. The responsibility is frightening: You are choosing to do something *for yourself* not for a noble, altruistic reason. And not to make money. The external props are not there. As if in response to my thoughts, the sun has come out; it is warm on my back. "To feel the warmth of the sun" spoke to me as a reason, as a sign of the kind of experience and reassurance to be gained from a more free-flowing contact with the world.

I had claimed control of my classroom and chosen the limits to which I wanted to exert it. I thought of the visions of power—the superheroes and speeding vehicles that spoke to many of the boys I'd taught. I thought of the powerlessness of childhood. Of course children develop subterfuges! Those help to equalize things. But adults, with all the power, can be most ungracious in exercising it.

There were other issues I needed to face, like the question of values—

individual values, my values that I can stand on without social and institutional support. A commitment to go my own way, whatever that means. To trust in my own way. I think if I do not, I will miss joy and fulfillment. I will remain resentful, angry, under pressure, on the edge of a choice I dare not make, skirting part of my relationship with myself and my own potential.

My decision to leave school teaching was a hard and necessarily lonely one. It pulled me up by the roots, not only making me re-evaluate my life but delve back into my childhood for essentials forgotten. Back to the roots. Back home. Unexpectedly hard and nostalgic. Going backward to go forward—or go elsewhere; not simply shifting directions from where I was at the moment. Going back to my roots to anchor my new sense of direction.

And the doubts: What would come of it? Would I really change? An unsettling—a reorganization, perhaps—or rather the amorphousness of the new—before reorganization. Coming apart to come together again.

If I was not a teacher, who was I? It was a question I would return to for years. Many voices answered, as I wrote in my journal:

> This afternoon the many sides of myself seemed to be crowding in on me, urging "Now hear me," "Let me have a turn." How could I honor them at once—or even in a lifetime? Who *are* you all in there? And how can I answer you?
>
> It seems I must go back to the past to take up the threads of who I am. Back to my grandmother's hands, to the girl I was, in love with the openness and motion and freedom of the beach. Back to all that seemed too tender or fragile to endure. To a lonely childhood of imagining and writing and keeping myself company. Back through the darkness of living a life that did not feel like me because I hadn't found a way to live my self. Back to the tears and longing and impotence. The tears and longing are still there—but not the impotence. And so I have a choice now that I did not have. How exhilarating yet difficult to confront that choice!
>
> I made it—made it through—not only through the darkness but through the performance demanded by the world. I have proved myself to the world and so finally won the right to my own life. (That was part of what Right to Read was all about for me, though I didn't guess how fast it would lead me away from my "accomplishments.")
>
> To gather in the past, to love the child, and the adolescent dreams, and the parts I thought I had to let go in order to live in the world. And I *had* to live *in* the world and not as an outcast. Not hold onto the dreams in desperation, in place of life. Having life, I can now *choose* the dreams unashamedly.
>
> Returning to a home within myself is such a long and demanding journey.
>
> I need to knit together the new me with the old me, to see the changes as part of the fabric. How important is our sense of wholeness—that we see ourselves as fitting together. To feel that our life is of a piece is to be able to see a pattern in it, which is meaning. When the gap between my living

and my yearnings is too great, I am not whole. Where the parts of myself, the voices in me, are too distant to hear one another, I am not whole.

I come together to meet myself. I realize that I have changed—become something else. What I must be sure of is that I have become *me*. Else what assurance is in the change?

Soon after school closed, I immersed myself in a poetry-writing workshop.

"Returning to a home within myself" has been a more enduring process than I imagined. Fifteen years later, as I turned more toward observing and writing about the natural world around me in Vermont, I felt again as though that's what I was doing: returning home. And now, some years after that, as I work on this book, I am "knitting together the new me with the old me" and "seeing the changes as part of the fabric."

While composing this chapter, I talked with Tom, to whom I'm now married, about how my intellectual interests and research sorts of questions moved me away from teaching, yet how good it might have been if I'd been able to continue teaching while pursuing the questions arising from it. "Maybe," he said, "that's why you're so involved with teacher-research." I started to choke up, a sure sign he'd hit the mark. Hadn't I written, years ago, at the end of "What's a Teacher-Researcher?," "If teacher-research had been on the horizon ten years ago, I might still be in a classroom myself rather than having been driven to choose between knowing and doing"? But only after reliving this part of my life through these writings from my past and talking about them and hearing Tom's comment, did I truly feel the connection, grieve my loss, and know why I care so much about teacher-research.

7

Researcher AT WRK

ALTHOUGH I SEEMED TO HAVE TO CHOOSE BETWEEN teaching and researching, I didn't have to choose between parenting and researching. Researchers of child language development, like Ruth Weir who studied her son's monologues overheard from his crib, had established a precedent. What better access to children's language than through those whom we, as parents, can observe at length, interact with naturally, and know intimately? I also knew the context within which my son's language developed, though it was sometimes hard to see because I was part of that context myself. When an artist friend spoke of drawing with her children, I became more aware of the particular context in which Paul had learned to write and read. Drawing with Paul was nothing I had ever done because I myself rarely drew. While my friend seemed to attribute her children's artistic skill to talent, I wondered how much developed through their experiences drawing with her, watching her draw and being in the presence of her drawings. I tried to see Paul's home learning environment rather than take it for granted.

When I returned to the Harvard Graduate School of Education as a doctoral student, I brought with me tapes of my son talking and reading, boxes of his writings, and yellow pads of field notes and reflections. His writings weren't confined to paper. Some, for example, transformed unpainted wooden blocks into a MAL-BOX (mailbox), POST OFISS, FAKTARE (factory), and TAL.A.FON (telephone), while other writings, like newspapers and signs, were inscribed on sheets of corrugated cardboard. Paul wrote with alphabet stamps, magic markers, pencils, and typewriter.

Where did Paul or any child learn such spellings? Clearly not from imitating external models, so apparently from systems he had constructed. What were those systems? How did they change? How might they relate to developmental stages in reading? Did they parallel stages in language acquisition? Paul wrote the possessive of his name as PAULS (probably from adult information) before including it in his phonetic system and writing PAULZ. Similarly, children learning to speak may initially use an irregular past tense, like "went," conventionally but later, when they grasp the principle of regular past tense formation, say "goed." This suggests a learning structure different from that implied in classroom spelling instruction.

"With letters there's two ways of spelling some words," Paul observed when he was five. "*Cat*," he explained, "could be spelled k-a-t or c-a-t, and *baby* could be spelled b-a-b-y or b-a-b-e." A couple of days later: "I figured out two ways to spell *if*. You can spell it e-f or i-f." Such awareness that the sound-letter correspondences are not invariably one-to-one shows a grasp of some complexities at an early stage. How complex, then, may be the later stages?

How does a child know where words begin and end: How does he know where to put the spaces when he's writing? Paul wrote EFUKANOPNKAZI-WILGEVUAKANOPENR (If you can open cans, I will give you a can opener). Once he was writing relatively fluently, I mentioned that most people separated their words by spaces. At once he did so, with only a few words run together subsequently and as far as I observed no split words. Apparently the discrimination of words is something normally acquired with our native language. Since words are not invariably separated by pauses in speech (as listening to a foreign language attests), the ability must come from a deeper understanding of the language. These were some of the questions I needed to return to graduate school to pursue.

In my upstairs study in our Frost Street apartment, I spread out over my desk and floor, Paul's writings collected from several years. He studied them with me and noted his own progress. Referring to such early spellings as HAT (*hate*) and LIK (*like*), he observed, "I notice I didn't know about silent *e*'s then." He saw his early spellings as being in a kind of code, which he now had to figure out.

I came to learn what good teacher-researchers know and practice. Children aren't our "subjects," they are our "informants." We want to know what it is *they* know. Unlike experimental researchers who must devise ingenious situations for subjects to reveal what they know, teachers and parents can ask directly, although it's amazing how often we fail to do so. Usually I didn't even question my own interpretations until I voiced some in Paul's presence and he corrected me. No, he told me, he didn't read aloud so *I* could hear him but so he could hear *himself*.

I studied Paul's writings, tracked down relevant research, and wrote about some of these questions in a paper for my Reading Research seminar.

Encouraged by the interest of Carol Chomsky and Jeanne Chall, I continued with this research for my qualifying paper the next semester. I didn't have to look far for a topic for my dissertation. How fortunate I was to have professors who encouraged me rather than becoming nervous that I might be "unscientific" or harm my own child by observing him, or who viewed a case study as insignificant. When my dissertation was finished and became known, I received several distressed letters from fellow doctoral students in this country and Canada, who were less fortunate—barred or cautioned by doctoral committees from pursuing the case studies or parent research they, too, wanted to do.

Paul was eight the year we were in Cambridge. Suddenly he had friends—lots of them—within walking distance. They flowed in and out of one another's houses without needing rides from parents. No more long bus rides to school, but a network of trails threaded through several blocks of backyards, and a candy store en route. No more hilly, bumpy dirt roads for biking, but pavement, including the vast expanse of the Sears parking lot a few blocks away. And just across Mass. Avenue, the delights of the toy section of Irwin's store, as magical for Paul as the 5 & 10 my aunt took me to when I was a child. His adventures on the railroad overpass he only revealed years later.

My year in Cambridge was both stimulating and alienating. I wrote in my journal about "the surprising impersonality of the intellectual life—feeling my thoughts not as an expression of myself but as mental functioning, compounded by reading research studies that proceed from no person but from experiments and detached observations reported in the third person." The voice of the statistics text distanced me; it spoke another language, and it did not speak to me. I put this feeling of intellectual detachment another way:

> As a student I feel like a head being passed from table to table.
> I am inspected, I am instructed, I am stamped.
> They cannot see me kicking
> because my legs are invisible to them,
> they cannot hear me cry out
> because my lungs do not exist for them,
> and my eyes have only one function: to read,
> not to weep or crinkle with laughter or widen in wonder.
> May my body not disappear,
> my eyes not learn to see as theirs do.

As I stood in the book department of the Harvard Coop one Saturday afternoon watching all the absorbed browsers, I seemed to feel them substituting reading for living, and I knew that for all the stimulation and companionship books had brought me, they didn't ground my life. That experience surprised me as much as deeply inhaling and relishing the odor of cow manure spread on the hayfields when I made a brief trip back to Vermont in the spring, a trip on which I had to call my neighbor with his tractor to pull me out of the lush mud of our road. I've learned that for me, short stays in academia are exhilarating, but then I need time to incorporate what I've learned into my life and my work. My system can't digest a steady diet of scholarship. Twice graduate study has recharged me, but after a year of full-time academe, I've needed to ground myself again in my own teaching and in my vegetable garden.

When I moved to Vermont, I brought some of Cambridge along to keep me company in the isolation and unfamiliarness—the sense of an intellectual conversation extended across time and space. Back in Cambridge even years later, I kept with me visions of Vermont, like a full moon ascending Spruce Mountain as I walk through galaxies of Queen Anne's Lace, almost white in the moonlit fields. And blue layers of distant mountains at dusk. And the sounds of dry leaves underfoot in the woods, and then the silence of the snow.

I had never yearned for a doctorate nor felt quite fitted for a professorial existence, though as a Radcliffe undergraduate I'd fantasized, as I'm sure many classmates did, being married to a Harvard professor. Harvard professors then were very rarely women—I believe there were two women professors on the entire faculty of arts and sciences when I was in college, neither of whom I had contact with. But when I studied at the Graduate School of Education, plenty of professors were women. Learning from women opened some inward doors. I passed through the bias I now recognized against my own gender into greater respect for myself along with other women. As an undergraduate English Literature major, I had joined with the (overwhelmingly male) scholars in viewing women authors as minor, explicitly or by neglect.

As a doctoral student some twenty years later, I read studies by women researchers alongside of those by men. I experienced the collegiality of working on a collaborative research project with two other women doctoral students, directed by a woman professor, Jeanne Chall. We were, together, coming to understand more about what made science, history, and literature texts more and less difficult to read, as we analyzed and discussed hundreds of passages and books. We saw that both science and history could be presented as narrative or as exposition, the narrative forms usually being more accessible, as when the metamorphosis from tadpole to frog was related as a story. While the amount of technical terminology increased in higher levels of science and history materials, a more sophisticated vocabulary didn't begin to account for the difficulty of Joseph Conrad or Herman Melville. Much of their difficulty lay beneath the surface of the texts like the mass of ice below the visible tip of an iceberg. It lay in the knowledge, information, experiences with life and language that a reader needed to bring to the text to comprehend it. In developing a set of scaled passages from Dr. Seuss to James Joyce, my English Literature self was collaborating with my parent self and reading teacher self for the first time. Suddenly I saw a continuum linking the first books my son had read with literary works I grappled with in college. I was amazed at how I had kept them separate.

In June we all headed back to Vermont, where our "lawn," held in check only by constant mowing, had in our absence rampantly reverted to the hayfield it truly was. The weeds were like all the material I'd gathered in my researching that needed to be cultivated. There was so much material, so many details, I couldn't encompass them at once. I had never written anything so long as my dissertation and was astonished to find that after I'd written a substantial portion of my chapters, I forgot some of the things I'd already written. I had to reread my own writing to find out what I'd written! But getting down to writing wasn't easy. That fall I spent more time in my garden than ever before. I bless my colleague Don Graves for reassuring me I was really preparing myself for writing through this apparently distracting activity.

How to organize all my material—five years of one literate life—and various perspectives on it? The forms that any of us researchers evolve for presenting our work may appear simple and self-evident in the final paper or book, but in fact that struggle with shaping is part of the research process, is part of the work of interpreting our data and deciding what we most want to make visible. It felt almost like a physical process, as though I were a potter or sculptor forming and reforming clay. The data kept pouring in as I wrote; the dissertation discussed Paul's writings and readings from age five through nine. Another year of information was incorporated when I revised my dissertation for publication. That writing experience was a particular gift—a powerful reconnection to writing, decisive in turning me toward more writing.

When the director of the Harvard University Press asked Jeanne Chall if she had any dissertations to recommend to them, mine was one she mentioned. They accepted the manuscript but not the title *GNYS AT WRK*, taken from a sign Paul had written (GNYS AT WRK DO NAT DISTRB). It signified to me the human genius for language that I had just witnessed at work in one case among potentially zillions of others. But, I was told, no one in the editorial offices could read it, and the Library of Congress couldn't catalogue a title of nonwords, so I changed it to *A Child Learns to Write and Read.* When I mentioned the new title to my former professor Courtney Cazden, she objected that it was boring and went to bat at the Press for the original one. *GNYS AT WRK* won out. I never heard any protests from the Library of Congress or from first-grade teachers who couldn't read the title.

When the first copies of the book arrived, I gave one to Paul, who was satisfied by only looking through the facsimiles of his writings. Although I had discussed with him publishing what I considered our book and had his OK, I can't imagine that he understood what "publishing" meant until he was a good deal older and a few of his friends had read it, or until he answered the phone at our house one day and took a message for me from a caller who said she felt as though she knew him from reading the book. I stared at the surprisingly thin volume with my name on it—the final product of years of closeness with my son, of learning what I wanted to learn, and writing it the way I wanted to write. I didn't really understand what publishing meant either. Carol Chomsky saw it as a way to have a wider influence on education. John Holt saw it as a resource for parents home schooling their children. Parents told me how it helped them appreciate their own children. But for me it was finished, its life now depending on what others made of it, including their misinterpretations. I overheard one teacher admonishing her young students, "Do your invented spelling now." It was invented spelling period in her classroom.

The book stopped time for its readers who imagined that what they were reading at the moment was what I, or any author, was thinking at that moment. For them Paul will always be between five and eleven, not the bearded twenty-seven-year-old man I see. In my world, time did not stop and Paul grew up. By sixth grade, when Paul was on the brink of becoming a serious television viewer, his father wisely bought him a computer though neither he nor I had experience with them. Perhaps that was just as well. Paul taught himself how to use his computer, ignoring the instruction manual as he ignored most directions, preferring to experiment and learn for himself, as he had learned to write and read, only this time without adult models and resources. He not only taught himself to use the computer, he taught himself to program it. Doing computer work has been a livelihood for adult Paul, who also writes a column dealing with social issues arising from computer communications.

Recently, when he was home storing and reorganizing some of his possessions in preparation for a trip west, he came upon box after box of his childhood books in the closet. We were both astounded at the mass of books. "No wonder I'm such a verbal person!" he exclaimed, seeing for himself the context I'd tried to see as a researcher. It wasn't the presence of those books by themselves, but the human interactions surrounding them that mattered. Something Paul has written about computers applies to books as well: "The proliferation of computer networks gives us access to more and more computers. But what we really seem to want to connect to is each other."

8

"Thanks, Abe!"

BEFORE THE BOOK, BEFORE I HAD MY DEGREE IN HAND, I applied to teach in the Education Department of a small state college. I'd left Harvard feeling golden, but the faculty and administrators at the state college didn't know who I was. Nor did I know exactly who I would be in this new situation. I changed even as I imagined myself seen through the eyes of different interviewers, from the generous eyes of accomplished and energetic Jane Root, in search of a kindred colleague, to the inspector's eyes of Dr. C., scrutinizing my academic credentials. He asked about my doctoral research, and when I described my case study, he challenged, "What does that prove?" meaning of course one case couldn't prove anything. Proving was what research was about for him, and learning was what research was about for me, though I couldn't articulate this difference at the time. I could only be shaken by it. I knew my research wasn't worthless; I also sensed there was no way I could convince him of its value. In retrospect, I've been grateful for this question that needled me for years and finally helped me understand what research was about for me and for many teacher-researchers.

I certainly wasn't hired by the college to conduct research, however. I barely had time each semester to prepare and teach three different courses along with supervising student teachers. I don't know that anyone had time for research; teaching was what this college was about. There was no money for research. There didn't seem even to be enough money for chalk. The secret of where the chalk was hidden was passed from one faculty member to another who taught in the same classroom and hoped to use the blackboard. So this was college.

The students came mostly from small towns and public schools, some from work or marriage rather than directly from high school. The college had grown from a teacher training institute at the bottom of the hill, near the elementary school, into a full scale college ascending the hill. The Education Department still inhabited what was known as "the foggy bottom." From the new arts center near the top, I could see the village, farms, and roads spread out below against a backdrop of mountains. Although the college was a long drive from home, I looked forward to learning this countryside with its scattered, tiny towns, lakes, and one high pass with a cascading waterfall visible (if you knew just where to look) only in spring and fall when the leaves were off the trees.

Since this was my first year at the college, I hadn't been involved in the selection of cooperating teachers, didn't know any of them, and didn't know the student teachers I'd be supervising either. My first job was just to locate the schools in the outlying towns. In one elementary classroom—not a typical one—I saw a student paper red-penned with what felt like attacks on the student's character. What kind of model was this for a student teacher? I waited for her to shudder, too, but she didn't. She wasn't horrified. Or couldn't let herself feel it because she depended on the teacher for guidance and approval, a teacher sanctioned by the college. She wasn't a strong student teacher to begin with. Is that why she'd been placed here? What disturbed me about the teacher wasn't just her response to papers, but her rigidity, her lack of warmth and imagination. What was this student teacher learning? I waited for questions to come up in her journal and in seminar meetings, yet they didn't.

I spoke to a colleague on the faculty about the selection of cooperating teachers. It was a problem, he acknowledged, in a rural area. There weren't a lot of schools and there weren't a lot of volunteering cooperating teachers to chose from. Their rewards were slight enough. I wonder now what had impelled this particular teacher into volunteering, but at the time I was only frustrated and angry. My colleague's description of the problem made it seem insoluble. Even if only one student teacher of my group was placed in a classroom that distressed me when I visited, that was one too many. Here was a teacher practicing the kind of response to writing that students in my methods course said turned them off to writing. What if one of them was in this classroom next year? What would he or she do? What *could* they do? Would they end up deciding that ideals and sensitivity are one thing, but the "real" world is another?— that, as I'd heard students say, the college teachers were living in an ivory tower, promoting kinds of teaching that aren't possible in the "real" schools below? How *do* we change education, then? This was the year I decided to run for my local School Board.

I used my students' lives as one of the texts for my child development course and my course in language arts methods. In the latter, students wrote their autobiographies as readers and as writers, which were copied for the class to read (with the authors' names on them or anonymously, as they chose). For me, the autobiographies were a more interesting and grounded text than a book on methods, although we used one of those, too. I was more excited than the students, who had a hard time believing in the authority of their own experiences. I asked the students to look for individual differences as well as common threads. Coming to terms with the exceptions to almost any generalization we might draw from the autobiographies was more of a challenge than swallowing someone else's teaching philosophy and guidelines packaged in a textbook with the prickly problems removed. I wish now that I had written my own autobiography as a reader and writer and shared it with them.

Would they have been surprised that I wasn't an avid reader as a child—that my writing more than my reading transported me to other worlds? One summer, when I was perhaps eight or nine, I submerged myself in writing what felt like a novel, titled "Under the Sea," about two girls who descended into a mermaid kingdom. I devoted a whole spiral notebook to it and drew unbeautiful crayon illustrations, but I knew the gold palace set with jewels, which the mermaids swam in and out of like goldfish, was resplendent beyond what I could represent with the waxy orange crayon. When I read the pieces my mother saved from my early years, I'm amazed at how I was able to make myself into a character such as "Calamity Glenda," dramatize minor escapades like "dangling perilously out the back door" of the streetcar on my way to school during rush hour, and laugh at myself as seen through the eyes of my cat. I'm amazed at the confident and flavorful voice in which I spoke directly to my readers—all so at odds with the serious and quiet child who stares out from the family snapshots.

Through writing I immersed myself in my expanding world—eventually the intellectual world that burst upon me like a sudden shower of sparks in my early adolescence. I explored my inner world through a journal I started in college and, volumes later, still keep. Through writing I got to know myself, value my own insights, and envision where my life might move. Writing was the stage on which I could play many characters—generous, loving, funny, wise, egotistical. Through writing I became my own companion, and through that relationship I grew and still grow today.

I couldn't have recalled as many details as my students did about first learning to read, but I can still see the dark red cover with black block prints of the first and only book I remember choosing to have my mother buy for me as a child. I found it, a little natural history primer, in Brentano's Bookstore on Wabash Avenue. The writing and the illustrations were ordinary—it wasn't a book like *Heidi* that my mother would ever have chosen for me—but I *loved* the information about falling leaves and frogs and I don't recall what else. I read it again and again; it was *my* book.

I remember the old library at school, a sort of ramshackle wooden structure built over the cafeteria roof. Two gray-haired ladies, one frail and the other sour, both equally interested in quiet and order, reigned there. The spines of the books on the shelves were brown, olive, black, and sometimes navy blue or maroon. It was here where my classmate Barbara introduced me to Albert Payson Terhune's Lassie and Lad dog stories, over which we wept, and where several years later I discovered, while browsing one of those shelves, the startling illumination of the dialogues of Plato. After our biology teacher told us about the John Crerar medical library downtown, I spent hours there, researching the stomach for my biology report and feeling dizzily sophisticated. When reading meant reading books my mother chose for me, which she was invested in, I often put them aside. When reading meant opening up new worlds on my own, I rushed into them.

I asked the prospective teachers in my college class to analyze their collected autobiographies, looking at the people who influenced their reading or writing development positively and negatively, the reading materials or writing occasions they enjoyed and disliked, gender differences, and their responses to different methods of teaching. What educational conclusions could they draw from their collective histories?

In their autobiographies as readers, Dick and Jane basals came closest to being unanimously disliked; one student was neutral. Having to read aloud in class and reading graded booklets (such as SRA's) to answer a sheet of questions were close seconds as negative experiences; yet one student loved the competitiveness of SRA's and another enjoyed reading aloud. That sole student who had enjoyed reading aloud in class, however, hated listening to the other children read, especially when they weren't good readers. She also found reading aloud helpful when she was reading alone: "If I didn't understand something, I'd read it aloud and it made sense." On the other hand, many agreed on the pleasure of being read to, mostly by mothers, but occasionally by teachers, and still remembered some of those books.

Not surprisingly for a group of would-be teachers, several of them (but only girls) described how they enjoyed playing school when they were children.

> My younger brother was now four years old, I, nine. I began teaching him how to read. It started with first teaching him to write his name, showing him the sounds of the letters of his name, and led to teaching him words. He would have some of his friends over to play and I would "teach" school.

My peers would also participate and we all had a great deal of fun; I'm sure if they hadn't they certainly would have let me know in a variety of ways.

A few students who disliked school, enjoyed their own versions of it, where they were in control:

> It was more fun for me to play school at home with friends. My mother would buy some workbook-type materials at the supermarket and friends and I would play for hours with them. It was much more interesting going at our own pace and taking turns being teacher and pupil.

Most students portrayed their reading experiences in a series of scenes, as Pam did, starting with first grade and Sister Monica, whose aim was to teach her students to read the Bible. Pam remembers having many small religious passages to read and one other book she remembered well because it had her name in it. "How thrilled I was at seeing my name in print. I could read that book upside down: See Pam run. See Pam jump. See Pam do just about anything. What a treat this was for a seven year old."

Her next memory of first grade was not as pleasant. As she stood in the circle of children who would each have a turn reading aloud, her knees were knocking and all she could think of was finding a way out of reading. She whispered to Sister Monica, "May I go to the basement please." Sister Monica analyzed the situation and suggested that Pam should read right then and there because, she explained, "You will have to read out loud when you get back anyway." Pam wet her pants.

Years later, she found more interesting reading in a house where she was babysitting—*True Story* magazines—but she also enjoyed reading stories to the children. In fact, she read all kinds of things, such as letters from boyfriends, newspapers, and notes sent home by the teacher.

The summer Pam graduated from eighth grade, she had a best friend, Angela, several years older, who was such a bookworm that her parents were even trying to kick her out of the house. When Pam wanted to go to the movies or swimming, Angela would say, "I'll lend you one of my books and we can both read." Pam asked her why she wanted to work all summer when they'd just gotten out of school. Angela was amazed and told Pam reading was fun. Angela turned Pam onto the city library, where she went to be with her friend. "The first book I picked was about a saint. I got right into it and decided that I was going to be just like her and eventually become a nun. My plans changed with the start of high school."

Just as Pam recalled her pride in reading a book with her name in it, a number of students recalled the thrill of being able to write their names. Recollecting their writing histories, some described a strong urge to write before knowing how to represent letters and words. Usually they scribbled on walls and other inappropriate (to adults) surfaces. The most emotionally loaded memories of writing in school centered on the pain of being constantly corrected, the boredom of copying spelling words or "I will not talk in class" over and over again, and the joys of opening up to writing under the encouragement of a particular teacher, often during the middle school years. Many recalled passing notes as a frequently practiced form of writing. The incidents that stood out in memory and were even decisive for learning often surprised me, as in Art's autobiography:

> My feelings about writing were, and still are, exactly the opposite of my feelings about reading. Reading seemed dull and boring, but writing seemed fun and exciting. I owe a great deal of that feeling to Abraham Lincoln. Thanks, Abe!
>
> In either third or fourth grade I read or heard a story about Abe Lincoln writing the Gettysburg Address on the back of an envelope. Something about that story sparked an interest in me. I can remember going around collecting envelopes from everyone. Somehow I believed that maybe some day I too would be famous if I continued Lincoln's practice of writing on envelopes. Time went on and I became interested in poetry and song writing. It all went on envelopes. To this very day I still write songs and poetry on the backs of envelopes.
>
> Another thing I can remember writing was birthday presents for people. Back in the days when money was more scarce, I would make a coupon book and give my brothers and sisters permission to use something of mine for a certain period of time. For example one might say, "good for one day on my bike," and another, "one afternoon without me beating you up."
>
> Also, the old "what did you do this vacation" papers stick out in my mind. It always seemed that everyone else had something exciting to tell about, and all I ever had to say was that I had played or fought with my brothers. After a while I became bored with that sort of paper and began inventing things that we had done. I know I had the kids fooled, but I'm not too sure if the teachers bought my stories.
>
> The class I was in during sixth grade was comprised of sixteen girls and five boys. Needless to say there was a good deal of competition among the girls to win the hand of one of us handsome young gentlemen. That is when the notes started coming. It was great! I really enjoyed writing notes. My notes ranged from the "You're OK" type to the "One more note from you and I'll break your neck" type. I remember notes as my first way of expressing to a girl that she was OK. Somehow it seemed easier to write it and not be around when she read it.

. . . It is very easy for me to get sidetracked into writing, when in fact, I'm supposed to be doing a reading assignment. The least little thing can kindle an idea into my own fantasy.

Part of my story as a teacher is the deep impression individual students made on me. I became more interested in the dynamics of dialogue—of listening and responding—than the dynamics of groups. Working with individuals I missed the energizing highs of a whole class taking off with an idea, but I also avoided the draining lows of a classroom full of unleavenable dough. I hadn't found many opportunities to work individually with college students yet. And in this first year of college teaching, I still yearned—as I had while teaching in schools—for time and an environment that supported inquiry. I'd eagerly joined a faculty group, led by Anne Herrington and advised by Lee O'Dell, on improving student writing. This chance to revise and reflect on my teaching whetted my appetite for more.

In the spring, when I was invited to apply for the position of Researcher with the Vermont Writing Program, I felt a rush of energy. YES. Donald Graves, an enthusiastic researcher and observer of individual children, had been working with the Writing Program and suggested adding a researcher to the staff, knowing I was in Vermont. I got the job and unexpectedly vacated my office in the foggy bottom, feeling like a deserter but irresistibly pulled away. When would another chance like this come along?

9

Revision Everywhere

UNTIL I FOUND MYSELF IN THE MIDST OF IT THROUGH the Vermont Writing Program, I didn't know a revolution was going on in the teaching of writing—a revolution because this new vision and practice of teaching writing rocked the old writing classroom power structure. Teachers now sat with their students and wrote, students wrote on topics they knew more about than their teachers, students looked to one another for responses to and help with their writing, and they participated in evaluating their own progress. Had I had the support of this revolution during my first years of teaching, it could have mediated my struggles with power and authority.

While I had enjoyed writing "free themes" in school myself and had given my students latitude on topics, I hadn't formulated as a fundamental principle of teaching writing that writers choose their own topics. Nor had I articulated reasons why choice mattered—that we write best about what we know and care about, as "real" writers do. While I'd had conferences with my high school English students about their writing, these were usually *post mortems*, too late to enable students to revise. Revise? I'm sure conscientious students revised on their own, but the *process* of writing was private and unexplored. Perhaps, like me, those conscientious students suspected their revisions were a sign of their deficiencies as writers. The myth of good writers as those who get it right the first time while the rest of us are doomed to flounder was virtually unquestioned.

Papers were written for teachers as expert critics. Because I didn't know about peer conferences when I was a master teacher, I'd led a younger generation into the slavery of taking full responsibility for every word their students wrote. The revolutionaries pointed out how this narrow teacher audience limited students' writing. At least I'd been in step with them when I'd asked my college students to write their reading and writing autobiographies for each other as well as me, and when I asked them to edit these before I published them, though I and not their peers had served as editorial advisor.

The energy released as the old ways of thinking and practicing were blown apart was palpable in the cafeteria and classrooms of South Burlington High School, site of the Vermont Writing Program summer training sessions. Donald Murray, Donald Graves, and Janet Emig brought the new vision to Vermont teachers; Nancie Atwell and Mary Ellen Giacobbe brought their commitment and strategies as classroom teachers using and evolving process writing and writing workshops. Participants, including school administrators as well as teachers, were energized by their own experiences as writers in workshops led by teachers who'd been through the program its previous two years. The power of their reading aloud their pieces on the final day testified that they had not been gathered here merely to sit and listen. T-shirts designed by the teachers read VERMONT WRITING PROGRAM on the front, and on the back THE QUIET REVOLUTION. Behind it all—envisioning the program, applying for the NIE grants that made it possible, reading through the participant applications, directing and orchestrating, visiting elementary and secondary schools themselves—were Paul Eschholz and Al Rosa, professors of English at the University of Vermont. This was what I stepped into, not as a teacher of writing but as a researcher.

Being Researcher with the Vermont Writing Program for three years opened the doors to classrooms across the state—a special privilege. Rarely was I just an observer. The more a workshop atmosphere prevailed in a classroom, the more I interacted: conferring with students, interviewing them, joining in free writing and sharing sessions, comparing impressions with teachers, and sometimes discussing with a class what I was learning.

I returned one year to the junior and senior high classroom of a former teaching colleague, Susan Auld, at my local high school. Susan even collaborated with me on a piece I'd been invited to contribute to the *English Journal* on the question "Is There Life After Teaching?" Writing this helped me interpret my leaving the classroom, and see the continuity between my teaching and researching. Susan, who was not only a teacher but a Representative in the State Legislature, shared the similarities she experienced between these two roles, which I wove into my article.

> When I walked out the schoolhouse door, leaving teaching, I didn't drop into an abyss. I didn't even *see* the abyss that the phrase "leaving teaching" implies. That is the view from behind, from those who stand in the corridor and watch me walk out the door.
>
> When I walked out that door, I didn't leave behind with my plan books

all that I'd learned as a teacher. For twenty years I'd worked on the skill of questioning myself and others—a skill essential for a researcher, too. A copy of *Macbeth* dropped from my bookshelf the other day and out fell note cards full of questions I'd written for class discussions. Then there were all the questions I simply carried around in my head, like Why were the answers to that essay question so bad? Was it the topic or the way I put the question? Am I really "tearing poems apart," as some students feel? What other ways could I teach poetry? There wasn't time to think about all these questions. I had to prepare for classes, read papers, turn in grades. It was hard to hold onto what I believed was important amid the floodwaters of immediacy.

Now that I have time to reflect, I find answers lead to more questions. As I investigate the writing processes of students, I think I see a common pattern in revision: more content revisions in earlier drafts and more language revisions in later ones. But then I look at Donna's work; why is her revision sequence the reverse? Would I learn more by looking for differences rather than similarities in revision strategies? And where do those differences come from—individual styles of working? type of writing being done? comments in conferences and on drafts?

As a researcher I report on my inquiries by speaking at conferences and writing articles, teaching a somewhat different audience in somewhat different ways than I did in my classroom. But my task is the same: connecting what I know with what my audience knows and cares about. What do they need to and want to learn? What can I teach? and How? A sense of audience is part of what good teachers have as they choose material and ways of approaching it to spark a particular group of students.

An English teacher friend who is now also in our State Legislature says the skills she uses to teach her Writing Workshop are the same skills she uses as a legislator. Whether in the classroom or the House of Representatives, she sees herself as a resource person to others who want to learn something—novice legislators or citizens' groups wanting to know how to use the legislative process, or students learning how to write. It's all "how-to" as she sees it; she's just using her skills in different environments—moving around in teaching, not away from it.

What we go on to do grows out of what has been central to our teaching, such as being a resource person or a questioner. That provides the continuity between our different professional selves—the bridge across the abyss that yawns only if we equate teaching with classroom instruction. Leaving a classroom doesn't have to mean leaving teaching.

But there were differences, too, as I noted in my journal:

Being a seeker, a researcher, puts me in a very different position than being a teacher. Teachers are constantly making decisions on their feet, without time to reflect on multiple possibilities and points of view. As a teacher, I felt continually pressed to make decisions I didn't know enough to make and didn't have time to consider, much less reconsider. The external, institutional, and social pressures on me and my students were great, and it was often easier to decide in response to them than in response to an instinct that contradicted norms of curriculum or evaluation or how one should behave as a teacher. As a researcher, I check out and try to disburden myself of vested interests that would lead me to find out just what I want and expect to see. Is it possible to really *see*? I've not come to terms with these doubts about what I'm doing.

One lesson I learned as Researcher was that you can see only what a particular classroom makes visible. In one room, when writing assignments became more directed to short responses to specific questions, the individuality of the children, which had been so vivid to me when they wrote freely, vanished. Given assignments designed to elicit standard, right-answer responses, children (and doubtless adults, too) don't easily reveal the individuality that makes them interesting.

Over a long lunch in the UVM student snack bar, I compared field notes with my research assistant, Iris Estabrook, who had just left her own elementary classroom. She had similarly observed, in other classrooms, how narrow assignments reduced the visible range of students' abilities, revealing neither the extent of their strengths nor their weaknesses. When, on the other hand, students were given freer reign, their differences were magnified and multidimensional in terms of generating and sustaining ideas, vividness, vocabulary, personal style, and individual interests and information. Assignments designed to standardize and quantify student knowledge obscured at least as much as they revealed. It was a sad lesson because I knew this minimizing work was probably going on more frequently in classrooms I didn't visit, making school tedious for children and for teachers (and researchers, if any). Yet seeing the extent of individual differences in writing would frustrate teachers if they didn't have approaches for teaching that could, like what the Vermont Writing Program offered, encompass those differences.

In Linda Kinney's first-grade classroom I got to know a group of amazing individuals. Fifteen years later, as I open my file drawer, still full of their writings, and see the names on the folders, their faces and personalities reappear. The children drew and wrote every morning on their own topics, and some focused again and again on the same things: Scott's series of sharks, then handprints and then kites; Kenny's recurrent zoo stories; Margaret's daily ritual of butterflies and rainbows. While Margaret, much to her teacher's and my frustration, was merely repeating her pieces, Scott and Kenny were developing theirs. Looked at as a series of drafts rather than as separate pieces, these were revisions. In October Kenny wrote I SAW A LIEN (lion), his January zoo story included I SUO A LIN IN A CAG, and in his May story he SAW TWO LINS IN A CAGE FIGHTING. Making changes on the same page as their original writing, or even during the same time period, wasn't the way these first graders revised. My thinking in terms of the adult model of revision at first obscured what the children were in fact doing— they just weren't doing it *my* way. The child's culture is not the same as adult culture, and I needed to pull an adult-culture blinder off my eyes in order to see what these children *were* doing.

As a researcher, I had the time to become intrigued, even obsessed, with revision, searching it out in every classroom I visited as well as in my own writing. How could I pin down and see the rampant revisions quite long pieces were undergoing in Susan Auld's high school Writing Workshop? Tim's revisions, which were the most extensive, became my focus. Tim started afresh each draft of a piece he eventually called "Alone in the Woods." With the previous draft in front of him, he started over on a new sheet of paper. His way of revising allowed him a freer hand. Revision became transformation, as was evident in comparing draft one with his seventh and final draft—an evolution from a short, general piece about hunting to detailed descriptions of being alone in the woods and on a hilltop with a distant view.

DRAFT #1

The upcoming partridge season is coming and all of the hunters are getting their shotguns cleaned and getting new and more shells. I can't wait until that Saturday morning when I will get my gun and start the season off by hopefully getting some partridge. The partridge is a taking bird. It tastes like the chicken but it is a little bit smaller. I have also been practicing for bow season which starts on the second week of next month. After that I will be going deer hunting and bear hunting and after that I will go to the trapping life of a trapper. I really enjoy the life of a hunter and trapper. It is my favorite sport but this week I will be out to get the partridge.

#7 ALONE IN THE WOODS

The day was windy, the last of the autumn leaves were blowing swiftly to the ground. The woods were filled with crackling leaves. I quickly rushed out the door and sensed all of this.

The road was bumpy with rocks and small tiny pebbles. I found my logging road, it was dampened from the dew and melted frost of last night's chillness. The road had patches of grass sprouting over it, with cracked trees hanging over, where lightning and high winds blew them down. I walked up the road and heard some squirrels high up in a tree chasing each other, like they were playing tag.

The road split in half and went in two different directions. I rushed up a hill, it was bald hill. At the top I stood there searching for a view unknown to me. The wind picked up, coldness started to set in. Far in the horizon I sighted an airplane, the plane was getting ready to land at an airport. I could see bodies of water, one was miles away, the other was close-by (half a mile).

There were many houses that I could see, but it was very strange because I couldn't see any people. I was all alone. Mountains that surrounded me began to close in on me. I felt lonely but strong and satisfied. I dreamed of being a giant, and I was looking down on my kingdom. Clouds started to rise over the horizon, darkness began to fall, and I knew I had to go home.

The following day I rushed up the logging road, it was a different road, covered with moss and pine needles. I sat on a moss covered stump. Two birds gliding over some cedar trees made their landing softly and perched in a hollow elm tree. I went into cedar swamp, which is a dark, spooky patch of swamp land covered with Cedar trees. The woods became silent. All I could hear was the wind and rushing water.

I went on to some hardwoods and began to hear animals playing in trees, like little children on a swingset.

As I entered the woods the following day, I saw a fur bearing animal. It was a cottontail rabbit and he was running at his full speed. In a matter of seconds, he had vanished into the darkness of the woods. I then decided to go home and leave these animals alone, for I had all I needed from them today.

How could I trace what had happened through the five drafts in between? If only I could see Tim's changes as clearly as I saw changes in first graders' short pieces, or as clearly as revisions in art work. I'd just discovered *The Unfolding of Artistic Ability,* in which Henry Schaefer-Simmern revealed revisions his students made in paintings and other art forms. As I compared one photo to the next, I noted overall changes at a glance and could study the subtler ones by moving my eyes back and forth between photos. I could retain entire images as I couldn't retain entire drafts. If only these drafts could be like pictures!

I finally hit upon a strategy. First, I typed up Tim's drafts so I could squeeze each onto a single-spaced page of small type. That in itself showed me changes in length and paragraphing as I eyeballed the different drafts side by side. Then I placed a sheet of transparency film over draft #2. With a wide red marking pen, I traced over all the lines that remained unchanged from the original. With green I traced the new material, and with yellow, passages that had been reworded or otherwise revised. I did the same for all the other drafts, comparing each to the draft immediately before. The wordless color stripes on the visuals held the text fixed in a way that my memory for words couldn't. Laid out in a row, the transparencies told a story of successive drafts, each containing a large amount of new material, yet steadily increasing the proportion of material retained and revised from one draft to the next—a predictable pattern until draft #5. Suddenly, instead of more revised material, there was practically none; the draft was almost entirely new. What had happened here? A writing conference with his teacher, who was always looking for strengths to build on, had suggested ways to expand on his enjoyment of the outdoors. At that point, the remnants of his hunting story fell away in favor of describing the experience of his hike.

I don't know how else I could have seen his revision process so clearly. I congratulated myself on being a clever researcher and shared my discovery with Tim and his teacher, who suggested I share it with the whole Writing Workshop. Only later, as I presented the transparencies at a workshop elsewhere, did a teacher ask whether students might make their own transparencies of their revisions. Of course! The teacher in me had been submerged by the researcher.

I couldn't know in advance all the methods I'd use in my research. The technique I used on Tim's drafts was born of a problem I confronted, and I varied it as I used it to help me see what other students had done, including changes in spelling and punctuation. I kept being astonished at the number of changes I was seeing, many of which I could have overlooked in just reading through their papers. I saw how much teachers didn't have the time to see. The only ones who were fully aware of their revisions were the writers themselves, as I learned from talking with them. Sixth-grader Gerry told me she hadn't done much writing up until this year in Dot Naylor's writing process classroom. What was exceptional about her revision of her piece about learning to ski was both the shortness of the second draft compared to the first one, and her level of awareness of her own processes and growth as a writer.

Before writing anything at all, Gerry told me, she had brainstormed in her head, recalling events and eliminating "things that weren't interesting." So I was reminded that not all revisions appear on paper. Many of the revisions in her second draft were likewise based on eliminating things from the previous one. When I commented to her that the ending of the piece had changed a lot between drafts, she pointed specifically to reducing "controlling my skis and using them" to "using the skis." "Control," she explained, was like "using." "Sometimes I put in different words. Instead of dragging it out I put it into one sentence." In this and other classrooms with younger writers, I often found that revisions contained expansions, additions of detail, so I was curious about whether Gerry was finding that her revisions were usually shorter than her first drafts. She said they were. Although earlier she'd had trouble writing enough, "Now," she said, "I have so much I can put it down into shorter sentences. I used to just write it and leave it because I never really knew how to express myself." In a few months of daily practice in writing, she had increased her fluency to the point where she could afford to be selective, a real turning point in her development as a writer. At times, however, she added specifics, as when she noted that "put on my boots and fastened my skis" (draft 2) tells you more than if she'd just written "put on my skis."

Gerry's satisfaction with her own writing increased dramatically along with her sense of control. She expressed a number of times in our conversation that her writing used to be boring but she didn't know how to change it. She used to drag things out to make them long enough. Now she writes a lot and cuts down—a change since the beginning of the year, when she and her teacher were focused more on expansions. She thinks "Skiing" is the best piece she's written. Just from reading her drafts, however, I wouldn't have guessed her high level of awareness as a writer. I wish I might have observed her for several more years to see whether and how that awareness continued to improve her writing.

Steeped as I was in revision, I began seeing it everywhere—in my perennial spring urge to rearrange my living room furniture, in the changes I made in my teaching plans in response to how a previous class had gone, in ordering seeds and planning my garden from season to season, in varying a favorite recipe, in practicing the piano. And I knew these were common experiences. Where *wasn't* there revision? I saw it as scenes were replayed during drama rehearsals, I saw it as basketball players huddled with their coach, I heard it in changes to translations in French class. Why, when revision was so pervasive, so seemingly natural, hadn't it pervaded writing classrooms long before now? How had we arranged classrooms to keep revision *out*? As a teacher, I had seen how often "teaching" required not cramming in more information but identifying and removing obstacles to a student's learning and performing—releasing existing abilities. Now, as a researcher, I saw the same problem in institutional form: Writing classrooms, curricula, and teaching procedures had been set up in ways that discouraged revision, making it harder for students to show what they were learning about writing and do their best work.

A further opportunity to revise my own work and life came with the expiration of the NEH grant supporting the Vermont Writing Program and, along with it, my position as Researcher. From the beginning I had known this job would end, but I didn't know what I'd want to do when it ended. "It is a strange, unexpected time of life for me," I wrote in my journal, "deciding anew, and with a sense of freedom I never before felt, the direction of my life."

> No, not so clear as "deciding" but considering, reflecting on, feeling around for paths, looking at other people's lives as a way of considering choices.
>
> I have to discover what my work is. If I work full-time for a university, I will be told essentially what my work is. I will follow the institution's professional expectations. Teaching may be part of my work but not in a big university context. What feels right to me, what will move me along the path I'm now traveling, what are the kinds of challenges I want to face myself with, what do I want to *learn* and do in the process of, not apart from, learning?
>
> I chose to leave school teaching, I chose to leave the state college, I feel uncomfortable around the University. I have to look now to individual lives—not institutions—as sources of direction.

Although I didn't immediately see models of educators—neither Nancie Atwell nor Mary Ellen Giacobbe had yet cut loose from their public school classrooms—Vermont was full of individuals, often artists, musicians, and writers, seeking to do their work while living simply.

I would need to find companionship in my work and confirmation of its value through personal more than institutional connections. As I thought about writing, not only professionally but more broadly, I knew there was no guarantee that what seemed meaningful to me would be meaningful to an audience of any size. "The world will judge as it judges, and as I see committing more of my time to this sort of writing, I must judge it in terms of my own life: Do I feel that I am using myself fully and moving in good directions?" The question of my work, at this point, was increasingly a question of how I wanted to live. I was prepared to serve institutional time to help support my son's college education if necessary, but leaving the countryside I loved was not an option.

I never had a career plan, never envisioned ascending some desired pinnacle, never determinedly marched towards a clear, externally defined goal. My professional life chained, one thing leading to another. It also branched like a tree. Some limbs died as my sap stopped flowing into them; others sprouted new branches. Only now, as I write this memoir and have read more women's lives, have I found confirmation of what was becoming my own life pattern in those Mary Catherine Bateson described in *Composing a Life*, lives guided by "response rather than purpose, response that makes us more broadly attentive, rather than purpose that might narrow our view. . . . Our lives are full of surprises, for none of us has followed a specific ambition toward a specific goal" (1990, 234–37). At fifty, I had opened the door and was headed for surprises, or they were headed for me.

Reference

Mary Catherine Bateson. 1990. *Composing a Life*. New York: Penguin.

10

More Than I Expected

AT FIFTY, MY LIFE CRACKED OPEN. THE OUTWARD PART pushed farther out as I became a more public person, giving speeches and workshops for teachers across the United States and Canada, becoming chairman of the School Board at home, following the publication of *GNYS AT WRK* with articles for teachers and parents. At the same time I explored my inward territory more deeply through journal writing, composing music, practicing T'ai Chi, and seeking solitude in a little cabin by our stream, built in my forty-ninth year to house my spirit away from the strains of a fraying marriage. My decision, made at this time, not to seek another full-time university position when the Vermont Writing Program ended, allowed my energies to move out in all these directions.

Fifty opened into a second adolescence—a rediscovery of worlds outward and inward, of my own powers, of life as romance. But I knew now that my life was finite although what I wanted to do professionally and personally seemed more infinite and beckoning than ever. "Abundance," I wrote in my journal, "is finding wild strawberries at your feet while picking the first raspberries. Abundance is the stream still singing softly over stones in a dry season. Abundance is more than we expected."

"I've been doing what 'needs' to be done: what other people put before me as needing to be done," I journaled as I investigated research grants I might apply for. The process of fitting my vision into someone else's requirements and having to describe what would result before it resulted discouraged me. I applied for one grant to continue my research on writing and do a book about it, but I didn't get the award.

Searching for grant money is a continuation of dealing with my work in terms of what other people consider valuable and necessary. Perhaps that's why I find the grant business so depressing and distasteful now. Why should what others value and need be more important for me than what I value and need? It's so hard to turn off those voices without leaving their world and entering a monastery. How to maintain myself and my ability to reflect in the midst of all the world's voices and demands, and the need to make some kind of a living? That is the challenge—to carry one's monastery within.

I didn't have a monastery, but I had the one-room cabin I'd designed, ten by fifteen feet, the dimensions of Thoreau's cabin at Walden Pond. Mine overlooked a rocky stream running down a wooded ravine that was the northern boundary of our land. Windows starting near the floor, so I could see the stream below, were stacked up almost to the ceiling, so I could look into the treetops. It was here that I devoured Annie Dillard's *Pilgrim at Tinker Creek*, the line blurring between her creek and my stream, her experience of nature and mine. "The cabin means," I wrote in my journal then, "I have a place—literally and figuratively—that is mine apart from who I am in relation to other people: family, institutions, even friends. I do not need a grant to have this place. I do not need to fit anybody else's job description to have this place. The cabin is also within me; I carry it, knowing it is there waiting, remembering what it means to the direction of my life." It was a space in which I could gather myself, listen to myself but also listen to the wind in the trees, the piercingly beautiful song of a wood thrush at dusk, and all the variations of the stream's song—rushing or trickling or muffled under ice and snow. Here sounds changed, light changed, but the changes recurred daily, seasonally, and doubtless in cycles longer than I could perceive. The world of human work, on the other hand, was bent on moving forward, on change as progress. I was of that world, too.

Once again hoping I could make a difference in education, I had decided to run for the School Board. After all, I knew the schools from teaching in both the high school and the elementary school, I'd seen many other schools, I knew a lot about teaching and learning. Being elected felt like a further confirmation of me by the small town I'd adopted that was so different from the city I'd grown up in. I was always honored to find acceptance here by natives, not just fellow "flatlanders." (While many of us did come from places flatter than Vermont, a place like Denver might qualify as "flatland" by virtue of its distance from Vermont.) The board members represented both natives and transplants. We all cared about education, especially that of our own children. We agreed on wanting a good education, but over my years on the board I came to see how our unarticulated visions of "good" diverged, rendering that agreement almost meaningless.

An educationally minor issue—soda machines in the cafeteria—demonstrated the gulf that could exist because of different lifestyles. For some board members, soda was something everyone drank, like milk or water. If it was in their refrigerators at home, why shouldn't children have access to it at school? Others wouldn't pollute their refrigerators with soda and felt that free access to sugar and even caffeine wasn't what children who were expected to be in their seats most of the day needed. It wasn't what their teeth or bodies needed, either. I don't remember how the vote came out, but I do remember feeling how hard it was to communicate across the table about this question. I could imagine myself as someone who accepted drinking soda as a part of life, in a society that promoted it, seeing those of us who opposed soda machines in school as marginal and wacky. How comfortable it is to talk when we share assumptions about an issue; how disturbing when we don't and thus find our own assumptions challenged and needing to be articulated—without rancor, if we are to communicate.

Most everyone in this community would agree that schooling is preparation for later work. Differences come in our experiences with work and our expectations for our children's future work. Does work mean working for someone else and therefore being obedient, following directions, doing the daily tasks set out for one? Does work mean pursuing something that is of value and concern to oneself, setting some of one's own tasks and taking initiative? Some parents sent their children off to school with an admonition to do what the teacher said. Others were more like Einstein's mother, who reportedly asked her son on his return from school whether he'd asked any good questions.

Divisions had run deep for years on the board, reflecting divisions within the school district. As Goddard College, in one of the towns, expanded and as more and more flatlanders moved into the towns, tensions increased. People who didn't have their roots here, who threatened to impose their imported values—values that could also cost more in tax dollars—came closer to outnumbering those who had been born here. The board was about evenly divided during the seven years I was on it. At the same time more government regulations about education were coming down and were not readily swallowed by independent Vermonters. In the midst of these tensions, the local newspaper, in an effort to make news, highlighted conflicts in their reports of board meetings, which sometimes appeared beneath inflammatory headlines that weren't even written by the reporters who covered the meetings. When I protested to someone at the newspaper office, I was told their job was to sell papers.

While the board supported some new programs in the schools, a failure to support one proposal in my first years on the board stands out for me. The proposal came from two successful elementary teachers who wanted to combine and team-teach their classes. One objection voiced by a board member was that the teachers might not work as hard, one might just lean on the other. This view of teachers, with whom I identified, hit me in the solar plexus. I was at least as discouraged with myself that I didn't muster support for those teachers as I was distressed at the opposition. Perhaps this already should have been a clue to me that the School Board was not an environment in which I functioned at my best, yet after five years, I agreed to be nominated as chairman. There were no other nominations.

As a board member, I'd enjoyed not only being a collaborator but being a conspirator with certain fellow board members, working on committees and informally plotting strategies for change. But when you're in charge of the meetings, you have to be more neutral—not an advocate for teachers or a conspirator for change. The chairman needed mediation skills, which I didn't have and neither did the superintendent, whose demeanor failed to inspire public confidence. By virtue of our positions, we became allies. What the superintendent *did* understand was that this board needed to work together better and overcome some personal animosities. It was impossible to work on such matters during regular, public board meetings, so he proposed a couple of suppers together in a more relaxed setting. The first one, I felt, helped us hear one another. The second abruptly ended any idea of retreats.

As we ate our cake, sitting around the backyard of someone's home, several concerned community members strode irately in along with a newspaper reporter. *This meeting was illegal!* they announced. All eating and conversation stopped. I looked at the stunned superintendent. Who was going to handle this one? *Board meetings had to be public.* Clearly they—some of the towns' educational liberals, including one who much later herself chaired the School Board—suspected we were conspiring behind their backs. The good guys were raiding the secret hideout of the bad guys and I was one of the bad guys. The superintendent and I recovered enough to invite the intruders to join us. We enlarged our circle of chairs and stiffly talked about something educational. A few days later the reporter, who was actually an aspiring poet and an acquaintance of my stepdaughter, phoned to apologize. We had a nice conversation on my back porch, and one good guy and one bad guy rode off into the sunset together.

"There *is* another world," I wrote in my journal. "It is not only a dream, a longing, a vision; it also simply exists. I have enjoyed being in the world of people and actions—joining a gathering yesterday to celebrate a neighbor's high school graduation, talking with School Board members about our choice of a new superintendent, for example. I feel, finally, comfortable in this 'real' world—comfortable enough to turn toward the other, not as a refuge or escape but as that which positively calls to me: the world, again today, of T'ai Chi, of working on a Beethoven sonata, of writing a journal, and last night sleeping and dreaming in my cabin."

In the world of educational or any other kind of politics, issues become cast in black and white, but at the stream I was open to multiple perspectives and unsettling questions. I could live comfortably with my awareness of partial truths: "How can I say what the world actually looks like? I know what I see, but what does the eye of a dog see? or the eye of a bird? Why is what *I* see any more real? It is only more real *to me*. I can say only that *I* see something. Is the world so simple that it can be seen by any one eye? Even I am not fully known by any one person. Knowing is a dialogue between the knower and the known, with both sides shaping and limiting what is known." I had come to see how differently things may appear on the inside and on the outside, myself included, and come to value more the inner meanings, even of the work I did in the world.

On days when my outward activities felt like roles I was performing in other people's dramas, writing in my journal brought me back to my inner self. "A busy day being Glenda Bissex, School Board member, workshop presenter, researcher, and piano student. Also skier and cook. But I somehow feel lonesome for just Glenda, so I come to write in my journal. I wonder about writing a poem—if that would put me in touch with what feels like my self. Is Glenda Bissex, writer, closer to me than my other roles?"

Whatever our differences on the board, we were all together in knowing more than other townspeople, or even teachers, about how complicated running a school district was, and together in feeling responsible for it. The biggest and most concrete project we worked on together, one that promised a sense of accomplishment, was building a new elementary school. Looking at the designs proposed by the architects we were choosing among was exciting—the dream stage before the reality of compromise with more conservative board members, before the fact- and feeling-filled debates on alternative and conventional heating systems (we ended up with oil heat), the frustration of a defeated school bond vote, then cutting back further on the plan so we could replace our old condemned building on the next vote. Educational issues were shelved, and being on the board felt more and more like an administrative not a policy-making position. I already knew I wasn't cut out to be an administrator. The year before resigning, I wrote to a friend:

Spring is threatening to arrive. The sun and the sap running distract me. I just want to be outside working and far away from human politics. I considered resigning from the School Board after the last meeting. If I were a really good chairman we wouldn't submerge in these extended hassles, I wouldn't feel confused, I would plan better in advance, I should have known and so forth.

Before coming on the board, I'd sung with a chorus on Monday evenings, the same night as board meetings. Being on the board had felt more important than singing when I committed myself to it. But after seven years, I needed to sing. I'd lost my enthusiasm and felt I wasn't learning any longer from doing this work—at least not learning anything I valued. Nor was I changing education; my educational expertise often seemed irrelevant. I'd had more power to affect education as a teacher. Before my third term expired, I made the publicly difficult but inwardly necessary decision to resign. I had other matters to attend to.

Perennially in my journals I lament not getting down to my own work, which usually means writing. Although I wrote voluminously in journals at this time in my life, that didn't feel like enough.

The problem remains the same: I put aside the long-range for the immediate. The immediate is what is pressing and at hand, not necessarily what is important. The long-range may embody my dreams and longings that I'm hesitant to declare are immediate. But unless they become immediate—unless I *make* them immediate—they will remain lights glimmering in the distance and not lamps to see and live by. I have again put my writing aside for paying jobs and for what have come to feel like pressing School Board issues. It's all up to me; I have no obligation to write—except to myself.

When I say I want to write, I'm talking about a kind of relationship with myself and a way of using myself—using myself to explore what I think and believe, to make meanings. At other times I want to use myself to make things happen in the world, to interact with the world as constituted rather than as reflected in my mind, the world of resistances and responses.

I was being stretched both ways.

When I look at my life now in terms of what I want to be *doing*, I feel pulled in different directions—teaching, speaking, politics, and these all pulling against writing. I feel unfocused. But when I look at my life now in terms of my *being*, it seems of a piece. Its unifying direction could be described as finding my "voice"—in speaking, action, playing music, loving, as well as in writing.

I was developing new voices, both public and private.

My first big speech to educators came soon after I'd finished my doctoral work; the invitation came not so much from the University of Virginia which was sponsoring the conference, but from a professor who was unable to speak there as planned. Would I speak about invented spelling in her stead? I was persuaded and the University accepted an unknown whom Carol Chomsky had recommended. But what about the people attending the conference? I expected a sigh of disappointment to rise up from them when it was announced that I was speaking instead (the programs had already been printed with Carol Chomsky's name on them) but they were silent. I'm sure the conference organizers were wondering and praying, for I think this was the opening speech. They had been wonderfully gracious to me when I arrived but that, I explained to myself, was southern hospitality. I gratefully remember the silence. I don't remember giving the speech. Nobody walked out. In the coffee and Danish break afterwards, people— including the relieved (I imagined) conference organizers—walked up to me actually smiling. I was OK. I enjoyed the rest of the conference and being shown by Ed Henderson and others around the campus of "the capital of invented spelling."

For me making speeches was more performing than learning. Of course I was learning about performing, but my heart really wasn't in that. I learned for survival. I resisted cranking up dramatic endings to my speeches to stimulate applause. "You had them in the palm of your hand," someone told me after one speech. Yes, I could feel that and it was rather amazing that something so intangible could be palpable. Actors must be sensitive to that, strive to create it, and feed upon it. I didn't study it. My satisfactions were largely somewhere else. They came from a brief but impassioned conversation after a presentation with a previous stranger who had been touched by it. They came from getting to know, as both professionals and as people, colleagues around the country whom I wouldn't otherwise have met— Rosemary Deen, Carolyn Hedley, Angela Jaggar, Ken and Yetta Goodman, and many others. I began to feel part of a group that wasn't contained by geography or a common institutional affiliation, but loosely tied by bonds of common interests and convictions.

I spoke at a gathering of the Iowa Writing Project during the 80s, when family farms were disappearing from the landscape of both Vermont and Iowa. In one session I attended before I spoke, teacher-writers read aloud personal pieces they'd written. Again and again, their theme was the loss of a farm that had been in their families. I had watched small farms disappearing from the hills of Vermont almost as long as I'd lived there, slowly at first, then rapidly. I'd grown to love the rich smell of manure spread on the hayfields in the spring. Now the pasture just across the road in front of my house was empty and silent. The whole herd buy-out program had taken the cows I might talk to during a summer day or hear at night tearing grass off with their mouths, amazingly turning timothy and clover into milk. When I got up to speak, I felt close to these people with whom I shared not only a love of writing but, more poignantly, a grief for the farms we were helpless to stop from disappearing and with them the laborious freedom of their way of life. As I was moved to speak, first of all, of this connection, my eyes were not dry. I don't remember what I said in my prepared speech, but I'll probably always remember that unexpected feeling of connection.

Coming home to School Board meetings after speaking to groups of teachers across the country where I was treated as a distinguished guest had been a lesson in humility, reminding me how transient was my glory. "A prophet is without honor in his own country," I could say to myself. But in fact who I was on the School Board and in my little town was at least as truly myself as who I was on tour. Becoming a more public person meant learning to live with how other people saw me, even those who I felt judged me unfairly or extravagantly, misconceiving me either way. I needed to distance myself from the images of myself that pained or inflated me. Either way, too much ego was involved.

My cabin was a refuge from the excesses of the world and a grounding in the egoless world of nature. Another experience, another new voice, also distanced me from the worldly fray and the vulnerabilities of ego: creating music. Off and on during my life I've taken piano lessons. Except for my childhood lessons with uninspired teachers at my mother's instigation, I've been drawn toward the piano by my love of music and drifted away because that love exceeded my talents. My fiftieth year was one of those "on" periods. My researches on writing with the Vermont Writing Program, and especially my contact, through it, with Don Murray and his contagious fascination with writing process, suggested a research question to me. Or perhaps I'd found a safe doorway into something I didn't even know I wanted or was able to do. My question was whether composing music was like composing text; my research subject was myself.

Where would the music come from? Since I wasn't hearing any sonatas in my head, except those written by other composers, I sat at the keyboard noodling and found melodic fragments. Some I could tease out further into a line—a sentence. Paragraphs were harder, as I had limited resources for developing my ideas and limited technical skill in executing what I might envision. Still, I was amazed to see what I'd learned from all the music I'd listened to and played, for I'd studied little music theory and analysis. What I'd learned through my ears was coming out through my fingers. The melody of a song without words that I called "Love Song" spun out so easily I wondered if I wasn't just recreating a piece I'd heard, probably played on guitar. Or perhaps because it appeared so clearly, it seemed to have preexisted and I merely discovered it. I was infatuated with this song and its strange separateness from me.

My piano teacher, Susan Halligan, who also responded now to my compositions, was a concert pianist and even talked of performing one of my pieces. She heard an individual style, a clearness and simplicity. It was my voice. While I was returning from a conference, I stopped off in Chicago to visit my former piano teacher, Viola Haas. In my briefcase, along with my speech, were some of my compositions. When I worked up the courage to play them for her, she said she wasn't surprised at my composing; I was a creative person, and she would have been surprised if I'd wanted to practice eight or nine hours at the piano every day to become a performer. Why, she wondered, had it taken me so long to come to composing? Although she heard my music as string quartets, she also urged me to write for voice, knowing I loved language. She asked me to send her tickets to the first performance of my work!

She saw me as a Renaissance woman. "Perhaps I can think of that," I journaled, "when I feel in conflict about writing vs. composing vs. teaching. My feeling that these activities are at odds with one another and, I suppose, with having a professional identity, may be essentially a reflection of the age I live in with its valuing of experts."

Back home again, I wrote in my journal that the effects of that visit were just emerging: "the headiness, the deepened commitment, the excitement about nonpiano music—a Wilderness Cantata?—and the joyful intimation that my inner songs will be sung."

And two days later:

I can sing! and dance! I woke up this morning hearing in my head one of the melodies from my May 11 Piece. Went to the piano just to hear it for real—and out came more—for hours. (It's now 2:20 and I've been composing since 7 AM with only brief interruptions.) I finally hit a tough spot: The music wasn't there, wherever "there" is. (Does it gather itself in my unconscious while I'm not at the piano?)

Now I know how to play the music when it comes—the dynamics, the phrasing, the interpretation are quite clear, or soon become so. It flows. It sings. It dances. "How can we know the dancer from the dance?" Yeats's line comes to mind, one I've always remembered and never understood. I still don't.

The first sort of bouncy, light part I'd written, from an intellectual design for contrast, sounds unconvincing now. A light folksy dance emerged of itself today. It is simple and came quickly and easily; I enjoy it. I still don't know if the chorale theme is mine, although I've made it so by now. The melodies that come easily and flow and sound delicious I suspect I've unconsciously taken from music I've heard. But it may just be the sense of their coming from "outside"—outside my consciousness. And so I feel no ownership or real sense of creation, only that they have been transmitted through me, which doesn't lessen the joy and wonder.

I'm the same person I was before Chicago—but not the same composer.

Neither in composing nor in writing could I escape my limitations as a person. "I caught myself yesterday hesitating to be dramatic in the variations—too restricted by the lyrical character of my themes, too cautious, afraid of being schmaltzy. This hesitancy to express emotion still haunts me, now in a new form."

The slowness of notating my music drove me to more free improvising at the piano. And then I ran into limitations: "I've discovered through improvising that one can go on at great length musically with very little to say. I'm not interested in pursuing that course. I guess the essential question for me is whether I have enough to say through music to go on composing and find it satisfying. I know I have a lot to say through writing, and the pressure to get it said may not leave enough energy at the moment to also grapple with ideas musically."

Creating music was intoxicating and frightening. I had so much to learn if I were to continue: really study composition, notation and theory, and learn about the capacities and limits of instruments I'd never played. And how many years to do it? Both of my parents had died relatively young. I had books to write. I had to earn a living. Was this just a love affair and not a marriage? We all contain within ourselves the potential for living more than the life we are able to live. At times, like adolescence and midlife, the excitement of these possibilities stirs us up. In the face of abundance of everything except time and money, I had to make choices. Choosing to seriously pursue composing meant choosing against too much else.

For years, as a young professional, my efforts were to make my way, to prove myself in the outer world—a more problematic world for me to live comfortably in than the inner world I feared getting too involved in. The better I functioned in the outward world, the more legitimate turning inward felt, for I didn't have to see it as turning away from external failure but turning toward another part of myself. Finally I had been released into a romance with myself, with music, with the natural world around me, and once again with words. "I want to dance, cry, hug my friends—I am in love with a world in which I can be myself, know myself, and be known." In my journal, my feelings and thoughts were clearer and purer than in my daily life, and often were ahead of what I could live out. But they showed me the direction I was taking and pointed my way. They were my touchstones in choosing and valuing my outward work in the world.

> I feel as if I've started a new life—been reborn so many times I hardly know myself. I imagine that can't happen so freely when one is climbing a career ladder. I cannot say which is cause and which is effect; only that the inner freedom and the outer freedom go together. I see a consistent life direction I identify as "making the inner more outward" (through writing, composing, and personal relationships). The more what is inward becomes outwardly manifest, the better I know myself.

But movement between inner and outer work was not an easy flow. Shifting from the kind of energy and work called forth by largely external demands back toward the more self-generative work and inner energy of writing and reflecting was slow, requiring a shift into neutral, a transitional lull that felt like collapse or dissolution. I couldn't simply unplug from my inner life and later plug in again; connections to the inner structures had to be rebuilt. I needed to act in the world, and I needed to reflect and create in solitude. Constructing a freelance life that would enable me to do this was, I discovered, like designing an ecosystem. Each piece played its part in the whole—complementing, connecting, or throwing other pieces out of balance. Recurrently I had to make adjustments to keep the system in productive harmony with itself and with the changes in me.

11

Designing a Freelance Ecosystem

I NEEDED A STABILIZING MIDDLE GROUND BETWEEN the ego inflations and puncturings of being a more public personage, on the one hand, and the joys and despairs of exploring more deeply my inner worlds, on the other. Teaching in an alternative degree program for adults provided some of that stable ground. It was even familiar ground, for I had earlier taught part-time in this program for four years while I was teaching Reading at the high school. As my school commitment had increased, something had to go—the adults or the children? I could be replaced with someone more like myself in the Adult Degree Program, I thought, than at the local school, where I imagined I made more of a difference. And so I'd left the Program.

Then, I had been happy to be a specialist in Education. Now, eight years later, the faculty was too small to be strictly departmentalized, which allowed my expanded interests to extend my teaching; in addition to education studies I took on many studies in writing, including writing about nature, and occasional studies in music. I had women colleagues who were constructing freelance lives, too, and I was returning to the kind of teaching I liked best—working individually with students. Every study was different, designed by the student together with her or his advisor during intensive residencies and carried out over six months through written dialogue once the students returned to their lives and jobs all across the country. It was the way I myself would have liked to study. I felt a renewed appreciation for this kind of educational mentoring, for working with adults, for being able to manage my own time and do more of my work at my desk at home, where I could look out the window at the mountains and take a break to walk or cross-country ski.

I felt good because I was learning—learning about teaching, learning to listen long distance. As I told students at one graduation, "I am learning to read not just the papers that you send me, but the processes by which you produced those papers—to try to imagine how you work, because I am teaching you, not your papers. What and how much might you have censored? Who were you trying to please or impress? What gave you the greatest freedom? What touched you most deeply? Where are your heads at odds with your hearts or souls? Although the papers are silent, if I listen hard—not just with my mind, but with some inner resonator—I think I can hear. At least this is one thing I'm learning as a teacher, or learning to trust. And then you let me know in the next mailing if I've heard right."

I was free to present myself to students as a whole person, not just an expert in a particular field. In one faculty self-description, I wrote of "my life on a small hilltop in Vermont, where I grow vegetables, forage with a passion for wild berries, and question whether animals and plants are inferior to humans, wonder why our standard of living is considered higher the more we depend on the labor of others to sustain our lives, and try to escape from the intellectual closet of cause and effect thinking with its prizing of control." In another self-description, I mentioned books that were important in my life: "When I'm in other people's homes or offices, I'm always drawn to their bookshelves to find out what they choose to occupy their minds with. If you scanned my study shelves, you'd see some of my important companions: Annie Dillard's *Pilgrim at Tinker Creek*, Abby Whiteside's *Indispensables of Piano Playing*, Martin Buber's *Between Man and Man*, Joseph Conrad's Preface to *The Nigger of the Narcissus*, Rhoda Kellogg's *Analyzing Children's Art*, Tillie Olsen's *Silences*, Henry Bugbee's *The Inward Morning: A Philosophical Reflection in Journal Form* and Loren Eisley's *The Night Country*."

I identified with many of my students—women who had come here to college because they were at transitional and growing times in their own lives. Debra—creative, artistic, and full of strong convictions—who had enjoyed working with children outdoors, was struggling with becoming a public school teacher. In one of my letters to her I wrote:

> My head is still spinning from your papers and journal, from all the thoughts your teaching and reflecting and reading have generated, and from the exciting sense that this past month has been a real breakthrough time for you. The breakthrough was most explicitly announced by your concern with developing your own teaching style, but a change was evident in your writing from the very first page I read—your mind was clearer, your voice was stronger. I'm sure you know what I'm talking about

because you must feel different yourself. It's exciting to be on the other end of our conversation.

One thing that is very evident in your journal is your constructive problem-solving approach to issues of classroom management—your ability to reflect on and learn from decisions that led to kinds of behavior you don't want in your classroom. You're also resourceful in thinking of new approaches, like the reading aloud that immediately quieted the kids. And because you have a clear sense of your own values and beliefs, you're not just casting around for *anything* that works; you're searching for ways of teaching that enable you to be yourself (not the ogre of the social studies lessons) and to respect the children. All of this makes your work more difficult but, of course, more worthwhile. . . .

You suggest that teachers should re-examine their role as educators. I'd like to see you do such a re-examination. It's an issue I'm very concerned about, too. I tend to see classroom learning and teaching as incredibly inefficient. Instruction can get in the way of learning. Children can be seen as blank slates and their minds not respected. Competency exams for teachers stress their role as possessors and givers of information—not their importance as role models of learners and of caring human beings. Your essay was one way of beginning to state your beliefs as they relate to education. Actually, beliefs about human nature, the soul, the purpose of life, and other fundamental philosophical questions undergird the whole educational system. I'm coming more and more to see that it's at this level where my basic questions about it lie. The particular practices and attitudes that disturb me are reflections of its fundamental assumptions, and these assumptions are rarely challenged.

Sally was working on her own autobiography while as a therapist she led a workshop on writing as healing. Her writing, reinterpreting her early years from an adult perspective, was a work of healing as well as writerly crafting. She was a gifted but very careful writer. Could I move her to take more risks?

I'm glad you mentioned in your journal Natalie Goldberg's encouragement to go deeper and take risks. Your autobiographical writing is so well done—clear, vividly detailed, interesting, in language that is flowing and polished—that I have little to comment. Having achieved this level of competence, perhaps it's time for you to push further as a writer. While you're clearly continuing to grow and learn *as a person* from the autobiographical material, you may be ready for some further challenge to stimulate your growth as a writer. If you have a sense that this is true, do you also have a sense of how to go deeper and take risks? Or does Goldberg provide suggestions? I've been trying to think of what I'd suggest, and a few things come to mind:

One is not sending me your rough drafts (which don't seem very "rough" to me) so that you can feel freer to mess around and experiment without my looking over your shoulder. I have a pretty good sense now of the kinds of revision you do on paper. I think the main work goes on in your head, anyway. But how to temporarily silence your inner critic? Perhaps you could have a dialogue with her in your journal. Who is this critic? With whose voices does she speak? What does she want from you? What will happen if you don't do it? Are there other parts of yourself that can confront rather than placate this critic? Read the first chapter of Peter Elbow's *Writing with Power*, in which he talks about intuition and conscious control—how they can complement or undermine each other. They can't be running the writing show at the same time or they get in each other's way.

There might be episodes in your autobiography to stretch you as a writer. I think, for instance, of the scene of you locked up in your bedroom for over a week, which was not re-created or dramatized. You handle dialogue very well—a gift other writers would envy. What about interior monologue or images reflecting inner states? Or just describing what you did and what your eyes saw in such a way that a reader infers your state of mind without your labeling any emotions?

In response to your question, I don't really have any comments on journal writing in general, except that a journal should serve the purposes of the writer. It's a place for talking to oneself or making notes rather than writing for others. At the moment I'm keeping three journals: a dream journal, which also contains my reflections on the dreams, on dream images and on my inner life; a music journal, where I record my weekly music sessions with my stepson's six-year-old, my own experiences with music, and my reflections about learning music; and a journal-journal which, before I started the dream journal, was more personal but now is more intellectual, including germs for possible pieces of writing.

The amaryllis bulb Sally gave me has multiplied over the years; each spring the flowers flame from several pots around my house. In less tangible ways, too, former students continue to be present in my life because I learned so much through our work together. At its best, we shared something of our lives as well as our minds.

While I was trying to nurture my students, I was in turn nurtured by the supportive atmosphere of the Program during my fifties explosion. I dared go public with my composing—first giving a presentation on the creative process, in which I talked about it, then playing some pieces and finally agreeing to play for the intimate, personal graduation ceremonies. I wrote in my composing journal:

> I had set aside composing in order to get through the Program residency, School Board budget and divorce negotiations. But tonight—after telling myself clearly yesterday that if I were asked to play for graduation I'd have to refuse because I had no piece to play—tonight I looked through my compositions and fragments and found two pieces I *wanted* to play. After modifying the two pieces, three bass notes I'd tried in the ending of the chorale became a boogie bass pattern to a different rhythm and dissonant harmonies in the right hand. I don't know where it came from, that mode and the energy and the joy. Perhaps it came from my joy at making music again. I can have good relationships with people, as with my students now, but that is no substitute for the love and joy of making music. I cannot be without it. Making music is a form of making love.
>
> The relationship with a piece I am creating, in words or music, follows much the same course as any love relationship: spontaneous attraction to some particular aspect of the yet unknown creation, then a pursuit of it and its unfolding as I become intoxicated with it, and then settling down to living with it—crafting, revising, knowing it.

A colleague in the Program to whom I'd lamented the lack of women's nature writings on the shelves of the best local bookstore asked me why I didn't find those writings and gather them for a book. Every city and university where I went to speak, after taking up her suggestion, offered a site for searching through libraries and bookstores, the secondhand ones being more fruitful. I talked with nature lovers, scholars, feminists, scientists, friends and relatives, librarians and bookstore owners, and some of my students. Their knowledge and, above all, their interest in my project encouraged me. When I was at a conference in Washington, D.C., I visited the Library of Congress and was overwhelmed by the number of nature books written by women— books about gardening and books of nature study for children, books within women's traditional sphere of home and family. This wasn't what I had in mind. Where were the adventurers, the naturalists, the homesteaders, the farmers? I collected only a handful of their writings from anthologies of nature essays. Yet I was sure those women were out there—in the woods, on the water, in deserts, on coasts, on farms, in backyards, in the Arctic—not only living in nature but writing about it. Were they out of print? or had they never been published? After a couple of years I had gathered enough well-written pieces for a book. Now, what did I make of them all? Were women's experiences with nature different from men's?

Two kinds of perceptions stood out as characteristic of how women, more often than men, described their experiences: the observation of living creatures as individuals and as family members rather than as representatives of a species and, related to this close study of individuals, a quality of empathetic imagination that enabled both the women and their readers to enter into the lives of other beings who share this earth with us. I was more interested in tracking down these women writers and trying to see what distinguished them as women than I was in organizing and getting permissions to reprint the pieces and seeking a publisher. If I didn't publish my collection, I knew someone else would publish one (and several years later, they did). Warning myself of this wasn't enough to push me to do it. The choice became one of putting my energy into my own nature writing or into editing this book. Having a sense of the companionship of other women nature writers—a long shelf full of them in my study—eased my way into my own writing, serving a purpose I didn't recognize when I started the project. *Beyond Her Garden* (my proposed title) joined several other books, on teaching reading and writing, and on researching, that existed only in my journals and file cabinets.

After teaching five years in the Adult Degree Program, I felt I wasn't doing my own work—a recurrent theme and discontent expressed in my journals over the years. I couldn't define what "my work" was, but I knew when I was doing it and when I wasn't. I knew I was doing my work when I felt focused, productive and true to myself, when I felt one with the work so there was no space to doubt its worth. For several years this teaching had felt like my work. Then I saw all the letters I mailed off to my students as taking energy I could otherwise spend writing nature essays and writing about learning. Teaching in the Adult Degree Program had nurtured me as it nurtured students, when we needed it. I left thinking I might want to return again.

For five years I'd worked hard at teaching and speaking and writing, spending the energy my fifties rebirth had released. I not only needed to balance the ecosystem of my freelance life, but attend to its seasons, its rhythms, as well. Speaking to the graduates the autumn of my last residency in the Adult Degree Program, I acknowledged my need now for dormancy:

> The week before you came for your residency, we had a snowstorm. Rain of the day and the night before turned to wet snow and kept up until everything was plastered white, and the trees with their colored leaves still on held the snow until the trees bent or broke, and many of us ate supper and went to bed in the dark because power lines were down everywhere. Walking around after the snow had finally melted, I found my paths blocked with bent and broken trees, and I came to appreciate again, as I

often do, the wisdom of nature. Of course the leaves usually fall before the snow does or the trees would be destroyed. Broad leaves shed rain but not snow. And so I should rejoice not just in the colors of autumn but in the falling of the leaves, in the bareness that spares the trees for another season.

Perhaps I identified, too, with those burdened trees, trying to hold too much, though accumulation seems to be a peculiarly human problem. The older we grow, the more stuff can accumulate—the peeling paint around the windows that has been neglected for years, the cartons of papers waiting to be sorted out and thrown out (horrors!) or filed away in the file cabinets I haven't bought yet, the unanswered letters, the address book that showers scraps of paper when I open it, the paths overgrown with brush, the cellar, the garage. . . . When Lorna [one of my students] in one of her papers discussed Erik Erikson's notion of "moratorium," I latched onto the word. He thought that adolescents needed moratoriums—but I knew that middle-aged folks needed them too. Why must we always be doing, moving ahead, improving? Nature knows better; she sends us winters and dry seasons. Nature imposes moratoriums. Dormancy. The buds of next spring's lilac leaves and flowers are already formed, but they're waiting. Waiting is hard for human beings. There's always the expectant little voice in the morning asking, "What are you going to do today?" and calling you to reckoning in the evening with "What did you accomplish today?" Would I dare to answer "Nothing"? I hope I'm headed for something of a moratorium as part of my growing and being.

For these graduates, many of whom had completed a demanding culminating study simultaneously with a full-time job and family responsibilities, I hoped the notion of "moratorium" might be useful, too. I put it a little differently talking to myself in my journal:

I need to stop. Stop what? Stop the busyness that masks my dis-ease, or perhaps even my happiness. Stop the pressure to get things done, to move ahead. Stop the pile-up. All the stuff that is loading my study and closets and sheds and barns seems a reflection of the inner pile-up, as do many of my crowded dreams. There is something impersonal I want to move away from—or something more personal I want to move toward. Sometimes it feels like preparing for death, and that scares me. But I have to learn how to unburden or I'll sink in the mire. Let go—of the stuff, of the obligations, of the ties and tugs that render me momentarily needed but leave me essentially ungrounded. What *is* the ground of my being? Where do I belong?

12

Enter, Ducks

WHEN I LEFT THE ADULT DEGREE PROGRAM, WHEN I resigned from the School Board, when I closed my classroom door, it was to open other doors. Where they would lead was clearer in retrospect, but leaving allowed me to move into other rooms. Sometimes I started to open one door before I'd closed another.

While I was still teaching in the Adult Degree Program, I had started teaching in Northeastern's Institute on Writing and Teaching. I'm immensely grateful to Tim Perkins for his invitation to lead a yearlong teacher-research course that combined my love of one-on-one, individualized teaching with my interests in research, in learning, and in writing. The first year was a big experiment for all of us, full of doubts and fears, but in the end exciting and energizing, as we reconvened that second summer on the island of Martha's Vineyard. The teachers shared their findings and their experiences not only with one another, but with those who were just beginning the course. And with a wider audience through *Seeing for Ourselves*, thanks to another nudge from Tim Perkins and the collaboration of my colleague Richard Bullock. When I opened this door, I'd walked into a room that led to other rooms I hadn't envisioned.

The questions asked by the first group of teacher-researchers demonstrated how little teachers knew about qualitative research then, only a dozen years ago. In planning their inquiries, many thought they needed "control groups" but weren't sure how they could set them up in their classrooms. I couldn't imagine their doing that either. Such assumptions and paraphernalia of experimental research designs had to be cleared away before they could plan inquiries that would support, not distort, their teaching. Their questions also tended to fit the mold of traditional research: "Is method X better than method Y?" rather than "What happens when . . ." or "How do students respond to . . . ?" They were set to test hypotheses about teaching writing, seeking the confirmation of yes or no answers rather than the richer, more context-dependent information that open questions produced. Initially, they felt they had to ask "new" questions and come up with "new" answers, thus contributing to a general fund of pedagogical knowledge, rather than valuing the questions they wanted to ask as teachers.

As spring approached, worries about not coming to "conclusions," not arriving at monumental discoveries, increased. Never having led a group of teachers through their own inquiries, I hadn't anticipated this. What *did* I expect them to come out with? Well, I didn't really know myself. I seemed to have been operating on faith that if they observed and reflected, they would learn. I saw learnings in their letters to me. How to reply to their disappointments now? Why were they feeling let down when I wasn't? I met with as many as could come to a restaurant somewhere along the New York State Thruway—at a geographical midpoint for the teachers who lived in the northeast. I hope they drove away from our lunch and several hours together feeling as relieved as I did. More baggage from experimental research had been unloaded: the expectation that research must lead to new generalizations of lasting and universal import. I began to be explicit about the audience for their research; it was not primarily the world of professional educational researchers, but themselves as teachers, each other as fellow teachers, and their own students, who were also collaborators in their research.

Through confronting the shadow of experimental research in teacher-researchers year after year, I came to understand more and more about the ways it was inappropriate for us. I came to a greater consciousness about research methodology and assumptions, and became passionate in my defense of observational case study. "The case study is not so much an instance of something general as a *different* view than one that generalizes," I wrote in my journal. I came to see the roots of my conviction about the value of cases in my literary training, in all those "cases" I'd studied and taught—*Lord Jim*, *Antigone*, "My Last Duchess." No one had asked what these lives "proved." I finally had a stockpile of responses for the interviewer who'd asked what my doctoral case-study research had proved.

Each year of the course I spent less time confronting traditional research methods and assumptions because qualitative research was becoming more familiar and accepted in education, because word was passed along among participants in the Vineyard program, and because I was learning ways to head off the old expectations. I asked that "yes/no" questions be rephrased as "how" or "what" questions, and that research questions, and hence their answers, be understood as pertaining to a particular classroom. As I write this, I've just received a letter from two coresearchers in my current course who won't be disappointed in their results because they've realized that "as we approach the question 'How do portfolios and portfolio assessment affect students as writers?', we will be telling the story of what happened to us, our classrooms, and our students based on one particular model that fit our purposes." Ending reports with "learnings" rather than "conclusions" reduced expectations of earth-shattering discoveries and focused on the value of the inquiries to the particular teacher, not to some demanding and vast audience of researchers beyond.

In traditional research, students would be seen as "subjects"—actually more like objects—whom the researcher seeks to understand through ingenious experiments. But teacher-researchers cannot keep an antiseptic distance from their own students. How strange that we think we must distance ourselves from situations and people to "know" them! "Science" seems to invalidate knowledge through love and familiarity and reflection—though not for Annie Dillard and Loren Eiseley. We think we know the most from the largest sample, which tells us the least about individuals. Statistics show that occurrences are *mathematically* significant. Their intent is to enable us to *predict* and thereby *control*—diseases, the growth of crops and, supposedly, the learning of students. The aim of teacher-research, on the other hand, is to *understand* in order to teach more effectively.

I had in my head an expanding gallery of images of researchers to replace the traditional man in the white lab coat: a naturalist in a salt marsh observing wild ducks, a parent carefully recording a child's monologues, an ethnographer experiencing and observing life in another culture, a teacher listening to tapes of her own writing conferences. My readings about nature had added the support of ethologists like Michael Fox and Konrad Lorenz, whom Fox quotes: "Konrad Lorenz, at the opening reception of an international conference on ethology, shocked some 'objective' scientists present by stating with characteristic zeal that 'you must first love your animal before you can study it.' I would rather rephrase this by saying, 'You must first love your animal before you can learn from it,' and by love, both Lorenz and I mean openness, sensitivity, and empathy, which is the key to intuition, clarity of vision, and understanding. It is therefore the key to our humanness" (1980, 119–20).

When, in their letters to me, the teacher-researchers wondered aloud or speculated about what their students were thinking or feeling, I'd respond, "Did you ask them?" It seemed so obvious, and yet I caught myself sometimes not asking my students when I should have. My defensive solution when I sensed things were not going well was to talk faster and lay on more material rather than pause to ask what was happening and what suggestions they might have. I didn't want to hear any bad news, but I learned courage from teacher-researchers like Pat Fox. She started out investigating why some of her junior high students wrote very good papers in English, for example, but not in History. She asked her class under what conditions each of them wrote their best and each of them wrote their worst. Etai's hand shot up: "Best or worst according to whose standards, yours or ours?" This question wasn't part of Pat's research plan, but she responded to the challenge: "That's an interesting question. Is there a difference?" Etai's question—or rather, her openness to his question—changed the direction of her research. She studied students' criteria for evaluating their own writing, and learned the nature of that difference. She had to continue to ask her students—as informants, not mere subjects—in order to learn what she needed to know. Instead of distancing teachers from their students-as-subjects, their research was bringing teachers closer to their students as sources of information and as research collaborators.

As a student of literature and a writer, I had found the impersonal, jargoned, and reference-laden sentences of educational research publications highly indigestible. I saw my approach to both the doing and writing of research as humanistic. After reading one scholarly journal, I acknowledged to myself how much I didn't want to write that way. I didn't just want to report on "studies"; I wanted to write artistically and persuasively—I wanted to show individuals not statistics. I didn't want to say, "Here are the numbers, you better believe this." I'm usually not convinced by numbers or by logic (though I may be momentarily overwhelmed or put off by them). I didn't just want to argue a way of seeing, I wanted to make people *experience* a way of seeing. To do that I had to know very clearly how it is that I did see. Writing helped me know that.

Since I experienced writing up research as part of the research process—as the final act of interpreting, of seeing—I had many writing conferences with my Case Studiers by mail and by phone. An unfocused draft (as many first drafts were) reflected a vision that needed sharpening, data that had not yet been fully digested. The ultimate question of any inquiry—"so what?"—had not been addressed. Writing and thinking were inseparable. One researcher who had been highly involved with her students and passionate about the intercultural curriculum she was teaching and researching, finally achieved distance by writing about herself in the third person. Each researcher had to find her or his own form, for the formula for traditional research reports didn't fit. More and more that form emerged as story and, to the researchers' surprise, one of the main characters turned out to be themselves as learners. Once in a while the papers were shaped as dialogues or as images embodying the essence of the researcher's discoveries, which were then unfolded in their various dimensions. And the teachers wrote in their own voices, not in impersonalese.

These papers didn't just sit in my file cabinet: They were packed into cartons and loaded into the trunk of my car each summer as part of the required reading for the new Case Studiers. I now have three cartons full—a veritable library of models of teacher-research that also offer a fund of insights and strategies for teaching and for learning from teaching. Teachers have more than "tricks of the trade" to learn from other classroom teachers. They can learn ways of seeing and thinking as well as doing; they can find comradeship and courage. I envision schools of education where teachers are learning from the writings of teachers along with writings of university educators, and where volumes of teacher research sit on the shelves alongside the other books.

When Ann Gere and I, who were both involved with teacher-researchers, happened to be Trustees of the NCTE Research Foundation together in the early 80s, we conspired to initiate grants for teacher-researchers in addition to those previously awarded university researchers. Teachers weren't likely to need large grants for research assistants and such; what they really needed was time, which we couldn't give them, but we could give them recognition. For me, that seemed the most important gift. The trustees' discussion of what sort of application form would be used raised questions about exactly what teacher-research was and what should be expected from a teacher-researcher grantee. More than a decade later, teacher-research is still defining itself. I hope it never defines itself down to a single definition.

I was finding a new answer to my nagging question about how I could best effect educational change. Through the work of teacher-researchers, I saw changes happening in many classrooms and in many teachers, not because of directives from me but because teachers were willing to risk looking and questioning. As they became more aware of what was going on, they also became more aware of choices they had made and of other choices they could make as teachers. Rather than teaching them how to teach (an authority that felt less and less comfortable for me with any group of teachers), I supported, questioned and prodded them, and taught them how to look closely and learn from their own classrooms. Long after they'd finished my course, they continued to observe and question and change. Each of us is the educator we're in the best position to change.

As I was teaching the Case Study course, my journals each year became more filled with my observations of the natural world around me. For several days one spring I wrote up the "news" of the natural world, to see what that would be when I decided not to listen any longer to the radio news—the distant and massive disasters and agonies I felt powerless to affect.

The news is that a blustery, wintry northwest wind blew today, and I saw the snow showers, like white veils, moving across the mountains toward me.

The news is that two beige moths were found floating dead on the surface of the last quart jar of maple syrup left open under the spigot in the sugarhouse.

The news is that it was warm enough to hang the laundry outside for the first time, so warm I had the sliding door to the living room partway open. I came into the house to find Tom's cat, Roo, munching a bird (goldfinch by the few colored feathers that remained) on the Turkish rug. She did a clean job—only some grey down was left drifting around and a bit of wing with a few feathers attached. No feet or beak. No blood.

The news is that below the woods trail, I saw a spot of snow as well as small dark pools of water. The soggy brown leaves were soft under foot and fragrant with a warm earthy smell that winter had locked away.

The news is that at eight o'clock, when it was nearly dark, frog voices sounded from the pond—first the burbling of the wood frogs, soon joined and overpowered by the shrill peepers, each frog seeming to keep its own distinct rhythm in the chorus.

The nature news made days seem rich though unmomentous and allowed me to let go my sense of self-importance. I needed that, as I also wrote in my journal: "I'm not allowing space in my life for silence, for the terrible uselessness of doing nothing and not being important. I need to sit with that—to look at it directly—or my life will be run by people who ask me to do things, like speaking or serving on boards, that make me feel important."

My journals became filled, above all, with ducks. Not that I sought them out; they simply landed in the small pond in my backyard, so I watched them and became engrossed in their stories of courtship, jealousy, even rape, and their sociabilities and hostilities. Since ducks were largely what I researched and wrote about for a few years, I found myself talking about them to the teacher-researchers I worked with. As I talked and they intently listened, I realized that my pond watching was more than an interesting byway; it was part of my being a researcher. Since ducks moved very fast, couldn't be interviewed, and didn't leave behind artifacts I could examine, I had to invent new research techniques. Identifying individuals was essential for interpreting their social interactions; I began to realize what the field books don't tell—that the characteristic movements of individuals can be more distinguishing than visible markings. While I wanted to slow down the ducks in order to see more of what was happening in chases, battles, and rapes, I wanted to speed up the turtles, when they appeared, so I could see that anything at all was happening. Although I do not draw, I found myself at intervals sketching turtles in various positions on logs so I could trace their movements. For the first time as a researcher, I wished I were a fly on the wall, completely nonintrusive. I didn't want to know how these creatures behaved in the presence of human beings, but how they behaved in their own society. Was I disinterested? Hardly. Comparisons with human society frequently came to mind, and observations, as of dragonflies emerging from their nymphal shells, became images in which I recognized my own experiences of giving birth to my son and of my own rebirth.

Re-searching—observing and reflecting—became a habit. I not only observed almost any form of life around me but I now observed myself as an observer. Watching ducks and songbirds, I recognized the same process at work as when I observed in classrooms or had long ago observed my son. I saw more clearly how questions I hadn't yet articulated shaped my observations, how my observations were directed to answering questions I didn't yet know I was asking. I first became aware of this while watching four mallard ducks on my little pond one October. As a sequence of facts, my observation isn't particularly interesting. The facts were interesting to me, I discovered, as evidence of social interaction patterns. I first noticed a tight group of four mallards, one male and three females, foraging among the cattails at one end of the pond. Their bobbing up and down in unison reminded me of a wooden toy I'd had as a child of chickens feeding on a round board. Pull the strings under the board and the circle of hens raise their heads. Release the strings and all the necks lower, beaks clicking down on the board to feed again. The image embodied my sense of the gregariousness of these mallards.

> A wood duck, who has kept to herself, swims out toward the middle of the pond, where she takes off. 2 mallards move out into the open water as though considering taking off, too. The other 2 remain foraging in the cattails and soon the wanderers rejoin them.
>
> The 4 stand in a row on the west edge. The drake swims out to the middle and waits until others move out, too, then swims farther as the others catch up with him. Snow falls. All return to cattails.
>
> Snow stops. Male again leads group out into the middle of the pond, where they preen—but I don't believe he's always the leader. They all head

over to the west shore, where they continue preening. Soon the female with the darkest bill and brightest orange near the tip and cheeks, leads them into the cattails. She is joined by the male as the lead pair.

A different female leads them out and then back again into the cattails.

I see that one question I'm observing for is who makes the decisions about where the group is going? How are these decisions arrived at if there's disagreement?

My research process seems to be: observing what intrigues me and eventually uncovering—that is, bringing to my awareness—the questions driving the observations.

On another occasion, I was watching evening grosbeaks at the feeder—a small, round one, big enough to hold only two such large birds, but two pairs were in the lilac bush eager to feed. As I watched, I became aware of my guiding yet often tacit questions and hypotheses. I was curious to watch who would bump whom. Would the males be more aggressive? Would they bump females or the other male? Would a female yield her place more readily than a male? At the moment I was observing, all I was aware of was a compelling desire to see what would happen next. I was in the midst of reading *Lifting the Veil: The Feminine Face of Science* so gender issues were on my mind. Someone else might have been curious about other questions—or not curious at all.

Observing wasn't enough; I wanted to write about what I was seeing in some form beyond my journal, and so I began a new apprenticeship in writing. I worked on shaping journal entries into stories, finding their themes, battling the literalism of the researcher, reading and talking to people to learn more than I could from just my own observations—yet valuing my seeing for myself. The point was not to learn as much as possible about mallard ducks, or whatever, but to learn what I wanted to learn through observing because I loved the questioning and the discoveries of that process. Fortunately, my writing group enjoyed the ducks and encouraged me. I allowed myself the luxury of being a student at two Wildbranch outdoor writing workshops. I had much more to write than I had time for and finally, facing that I would never have time to write until I *made* time, I cleared away as many activities as I could afford to and switched to the smallest date book I could find ($2\frac{1}{2}$" x $3\frac{3}{4}$"). More than would fit into that book was too much. Proud that I'd made this commitment at last, I sat down to write.

After a while, I felt lonely. What had I done? Wasn't I a writer after all? Was I deceived about my capacity for solitude? Most days, I wrote at home, looking out over fields and woods and mountains, with my dog and cat for company. If I wasn't writing nature essays, I was corresponding with my Case

Study students. I made lunch dates with friends. Thank goodness, I had a writing group though we met only monthly. Still, my ecosystem felt out of balance. Around that time, nearby Goddard College had called me occasionally to advise them about students who were struggling with reading or writing and to work with a few of these students. As I sat at my solitary desk one day, another call came from Goddard, asking if I could be on campus part-time for such students. It sounded like moving backwards to the kind of teaching I'd chosen to leave years before. I'd found the special education community's view of teaching and learning narrow and unimaginative, focused on deficits and isolated skills. But here was an opportunity for human interaction, while doing something useful and getting paid. Goddard wasn't the traditional public school I'd taught reading in years before; its holistic view of education would support mine. And I wasn't the same teacher; all I'd explored about learning as a researcher, especially the diverse paths that individuals travel, would help me move in new directions, not backwards. I loved working with adults, but how would I feel about undergraduates, and how would they feel about me?

Gradually the students ventured into my office, students who had come to this college because it didn't have tests and language requirements, because classes were small and experiential and students shared in planning the curriculum. They came to me when they weren't able to avoid writing any longer, when they couldn't remember what they'd read, when they couldn't get down to studying, and when they were caught between their needs for novelty and for structure. They even came to learn about grammar, punctuation, and spelling, and their exhilaration when they mastered such skills suggested how this knowledge represented success in an educational system they felt had earlier rejected and failed them. They were erratic, frustrated, angry, exuberant, and endearing. I met with them not only sitting in my office but on the lawns, in the cafeteria, and even, in the case of one very active young man, walking the trails through the campus woods. I felt freer than ever to teach by intuition as well as design, to trust the dialogue between us.

Intuition was all I could go on when Nick came to me bearing a thick packet of test results and interpretations about his discrete auditory and visual processing abilities and such—generally positive results from which the evaluator could conclude only that he had some kind of "learning disability." What was going on when Nick tried to read? Why was he so frustrated? Why was holding onto meaning so elusive? I searched for some successes that might give a clue to what could work for him. He spoke of two books he'd read without a struggle, books that had stayed with him—*Black Like Me* and a collection of stories ostensibly about learning to sail but at the same time about learning to navigate life. In the one he recounted to me, a novice sailor was becalmed on his small sailboat in a foggy harbor. No matter how hard he pulled on the rudder to turn the boat so his sail could catch the wind, the boat did not move. Finally an experienced sailor saw his plight and yelled to him, "Let go of the rudder." At once the boat turned itself enough to catch the wind and move forward.

What was Nick trying too hard to do that cut him off from the flow of reading? Trusting for the moment in the wisdom of the story he had chosen to remember and to tell me, I probed his reading process and found rigid old habits of word-by-word reading, of stopping to look up unfamiliar words in a dictionary, of regressing in his reading when details slipped from his mind. He was holding so tightly onto the words that he missed the flow of meaning. Seeing this didn't translate into any more precise label for his problem but did portray it in an image that suggested a solution and implied hope. The wind *was* blowing; he needed to learn how to use it. Instead of trusting in tests to inform me about Nick's difficulty—although the test results helpfully ruled out severe dysfunctions—I searched for what he knew about himself that he wasn't aware he knew or that he didn't see what to do with.

When I had taught remedial reading, the diagnosis of choice was dyslexia. Now it was attention deficit disorder. I learned what I could about A.D.D. but had doubts about its reality until students started describing in themselves the same list of symptoms I'd read about. And they hadn't read the books! I saw the diagnosis of A.D.D., like that of dyslexia, as essentially context-dependent, arising from a mismatch between certain characteristics of some persons and the demands of our linear, print-oriented culture. While I don't recalling having read any positive views of dyslexic traits, some researchers on A.D.D. saw the flip side of distractability, disorganization, and difficulty in following directions, for example, as constant alertness, flexibility, and independence. The more I read and worked with students, the more I appreciated that the organization, purposefulness, patience, carefulness, and goal-directedness that students with A.D.D. lacked, could also be seen— doubtless *were* seen—less favorably by these students with a different kind of energy. I caught a glimpse of myself through other eyes as I contemplated appearing narrow, obsessive, inflexible, overcautious, plodding, and unimaginative. At that moment I realized how I needed and valued the kind of spontaneous energy some of my students were overwhelmed by, and I recognized why I found them appealing as well as frustrating.

More than frustrating. A long conversation with one student, which I felt had resolved a problem, turned out not to have resolved anything. What had I spent so much time and effort for when it unraveled so quickly? I began to realize that for this person nothing might be "settled" for very long, and she might not even see this as a problem. Students' work might not be done on time as something else had captured their attention, appointments with me got lost in their whirl of activities, and I grew angry. Sitting in my office alone one morning when a student hadn't shown up, I saw how much of my anger was ego. Clearly my time was more important than his. How dare he not show up! Then I saw I could either learn a lesson in humility or continue to waste my time in indignation. As a teacher-researcher, I keep trying to learn (even though I'm a little proud of this lesson in humility).

By the end of the year I was thirsting for more continuous days to work on writing this memoir. Several interpretations of my decision to give up some of my hard-won writing time for teaching presented themselves to me. I was copping out or acknowledging after a brief trial that although I loved solitude, I couldn't take what felt like the isolation of a writing life. A long-standing interpretation of my difficulty in committing more of my time to writing was that in our culture and in my family it has been acceptable for women to work, even to be committed professionals like my mother—so long as that work involved serving others and not asserting one's nonserving needs and gifts. Maybe I just couldn't free myself from culture and family. Or maybe the explanation wasn't just personal but had to do with the length of time required to evolve a writer's life, like the years required to become the kind of teacher I could become. Or part of me needed human contact and yearned to teach, while another part needed solitude and the fulfillment of creating, and I was just recognizing my destiny, my ecology, as it sought its own balance. Perhaps this was not a contradiction and a conflict but the straining of a self-regulating mechanism in a complex system.

The tension between serving others through teaching and political involvement and, on the other end of this tug-of-war, creating and contemplating through writing, music, and my love of nature has defined my life. I cannot resolve that tug-of-war by lopping off one end of the rope or the other any more than I can resolve the tension between living a linear professional life and moving around through the various lives I carry within me by severing part of my self. Above my desk is a painting of a woman holding between the fingers of her outstretched arms a long thread with weights tied on either end of it. She gazes calmly ahead of her, this figure of Libra, on a birthday card my husband gave me.

A seminar on the Lifespan by Patricia Carini that I'd participated in long ago had made me aware of a limitation of the developmental perspective, namely its assumption of progress: that as we mature we come to know more and more, better and better. A developmental perspective implies that children's knowledge, the most partial and least valuable, is superseded by superior adult knowledge. Carini had listened to too many children to believe that—and so had I. She knew their knowledge was *different* and their wisdom, for all its lack of experience, was still penetrating. She helped me to see a life's journey as moving through different ways of knowing and being, exploring in turn possibilities that couldn't be explored all at once. G. Gordon Rohman spoke of our not knowing *more* about things but knowing about things *differently* as we move through our lives. Carl Jung described the goal of maturation as wholeness rather than perfection, moving around rather than ahead. There is no definitive interpretation, no single explanation that explains everything. The price of seeing something is not seeing something else. As we move through our lives, we learn different partial truths.

For over twenty-five years now I've lived in the country; I'm immersed in the life of the earth and water and sky and rocks around me. It fills my senses as well as my spirit. I enjoy solitude. Nature is not better than students and teachers, one kind of student is not more worthy than another, reflection is not better than action. They are all different; they have their own seasons in my life. The seasons cannot exist simultaneously in one grand truth about life. It's like the coffee can I kept on top of the steam radiator in my bedroom when I was a child. I dropped into it stubs of crayons, always hoping they would melt into a fantastic swirl of color, yet always finding a muddy brown mass. Perhaps the whole truth would appear muddy brown, too, unless it was too blindingly iridescent to see at all.

Reference

Fox, Michael W. 1980. *The Soul of the Wolf.* Boston: Little, Brown.

Part II

Essays

Growing Writers in Classrooms

1981

I LIVE ON A HILLTOP IN VERMONT, THREE MILES ABOVE A town of a few hundred souls. Living with nature while being engaged in education has shaped my understanding of learning, and so I write about learning as growth.

Organisms, whether plants or animals, bean seeds or tadpoles, grow through orderly processes toward internally determined forms. Growth occurs through interactions between an organism and its environment. The organism provides its growth processes and its structure; the environment provides the nourishment to activate and sustain those processes, enabling the organism to grow to its potential form.

Manufacture is different from growth. A manufacturer takes inert raw materials and imposes upon them an externally determined form to fulfill the manufacturer's purposes. Children are not raw materials, teachers are not manufacturers, and schools are not factories, although some people talk and act as though they were. The industrial model of schools can be seen, for example, in a striving for the uniformity of mass production—homogeneous grouping, all children reading "at grade level"—and in an emphasis on the technology of teaching rather than on educative relationships.

Studies of how children learn to speak have shown us some growth processes of language, processes children bring to their subsequent literacy learning. Without benefit of programmed text, even very young children learn systematically, not randomly or by mere imitation. This is evident when children overgeneral-

103

ize rules, as in regularizing past tenses ("They goed away") and plurals ("He has four foots"). Preschoolers' invented spellings, which are unconventional but consistent across children, are likewise rule-governed. For instance, nasals before consonants are unrepresented (DUP = *dump*) since the *m* is not articulated as a separate speech segment. Without instruction in sound-letter relationships, these young spellers abstract relationships from the letter names they know, leading them to many conventional consonant spellings but also to such inventions as H for "ch" (PKHR = *picture*).

Children learn to talk by interacting with an environment that provides rich information about language: They learn by speaking, being spoken to, asking questions and listening to speech; they receive feedback, support and encouragement. The first of three principles of language growth I will describe and relate to learning to write is that *children learn to talk by talking, in an environment that is full of talk.*

Some people believe that children all learn to speak because speech is somehow "natural" for us as humans while writing (and with it, of course, reading) is not "natural." But children who have grown up in isolation from human society—the wild boy of Aveyron in the last century and Genie most recently—have not grown up speaking. The capacity for speech may be innately human, but it develops only in a speech environment.

Although written language arose later than speech in the history of mankind and is not yet universal, it was preceded by drawing, another form of writing down meanings, of representing graphically what we know. Our use of an alphabetic writing system may lead us to forget that there have been in human cultures writing systems that did not represent speech sounds but were closer to drawing. Children in our culture remind us of this connection as they take one of their first steps toward literacy, differentiating writing from drawing.

I was taught much about the naturalness and forcefulness of the urge to write among children growing up in a literate society by my undergraduate Education students. I asked them to write their autobiographies as writers, reaching as far back into childhood as they could. The earliness and vividness of their memories astonished me:

> I started writing as soon as I could hold a pencil. I can remember sitting up in my high chair with the tray up, working on my homework, like my brothers and sisters. I would yell to mother, "Is PTO right?" And she would say, "Yes, I guess so." I would say, "Yes, PTO is right," and go on pretending to do my homework. The only word I thought I could spell right was PTO, which I later learned wasn't even a word.

I can remember wanting to learn to write so badly! I would watch my brothers and sister as they scribbled nonsense on paper. They looked so official, so grown up. I would imitate their grandeur. I quite often played "restaurant" where I would "write" orders on paper and hand it in to the "chef."

My writing career began at an early age. When I was a preschooler, I would study my older brother's school papers. The thing that intrigued me most was the letter *C*, which the teacher used to indicate that the paper was correct. I worked on making my own *C's*. I practiced them in orange crayon all over the bathroom walls in our house.

I remember, before school years, doing a lot of scribbling, although this scribbling meant nothing to my family. I can recall being able to read the whole thing. As the family giggled and thought how "cute" it was, I would sit in my chair and read my scribbles.

Since I can remember, I wrote. I remember taking crayons and writing on the walls and my mother would yell at me because it was scribbling. But would it be funny if I wrote a word; she probably wouldn't have yelled at me then. I really remember wanting to express with my pencil, pen, or whatever, but I couldn't, no one understood!

When I became aware of letters I was amazed, and I learned to write words. I remember my teachers making me always write in pencil because I'd have to erase my errors. I always wished it could have been in pen so I could just keep writing without stopping.

Just as children learn to talk by talking in an environment that is full of talk, children learn to write by writing in an environment full of writing and writings. In the classrooms of Vermont Writing Program teachers, children of all ages are learning to write by writing every day in environments that are full of writing in progress as well as finished products. Teachers write, often at the same time as their students do. They share their writing problems or drafts with their students and may ask for their help as critical listeners or readers. Through writing conferences, modeled and guided by their teachers, students become eager to share their writings with one another. They know they are writing to produce reading, not exercises for the teacher or "dummy runs." They come to understand, through the power of their own experience, that text conveys, above all, meanings.

Which brings me to a second principle of language development that also holds true for writing: *Children learn language among people who respond to their meanings before their forms.* We are eager to attach meanings to babies' first speech sounds. We do not immediately correct a beginning speaker's misarticulations; in fact we sometimes imitate them. We do not insist that beginning speakers talk in complete sentences, but we may expand their one- or two-word sentences to check if we have understood their unverbalized meanings. How differently some beginning writers are treated in classrooms!

One youngster had his own "dictionary" in which the teacher recorded words he needed to have spelled for his writing. He had been writing at home for over a year and was already spelling a good many words conventionally, so I was surprised to find the word *dog*—one of the first words he'd learned—in his dictionary. When I asked him if he didn't know it already, he said, "Yes, but I didn't know how to make the *g*." While at home he had written at length and in a variety of forms, at school he wrote one sentence on the few lines beneath his picture the way the other kids did. As he must have seen it, writing at school meaning writing correctly formed letters in correctly spelled words on the lines. Instead, he spent much of his time elaborating his drawings, for which there weren't expectations of correctness.

In contrast, beginning writers in Vera Milz's classroom (1980) write notes to their teacher, to each other, and to penpals—all of whom respond to their messages. They write journals whose content their teacher responds to in writing at the end of each week. They write books that their classmates read. They know they are writing messages—meanings—and their skills grow through constant practice within a literate environment rich with information about print and through the genuine motivation of being understood.

Children learn language—written or spoken—among people who respond to meaning before form. That is the principle of writing conferences such as this one from a primary classroom in Vermont. Tiffany reads her story aloud to Amy. The story tells about mice chasing another mouse. Echoing a question her teacher asks in writing conferences, Amy leads off with, "Tiffany, where did you get the idea?"

> *Tiffany:* I just thought about it. I got it from writing some stories on a piece of paper.

> *Amy:* Why don't you tell what happened to the other mice?

> *Tiffany:* That's a good idea.

> *Amy:* 'Cause how would I know that? They ran after him. What did they do after that?

Tiffany: I guess they just ran back 'cause they knew he was too far away to catch him.

In a high school classroom, Jeanne is finishing reading to Martha a draft of her piece about someone in a hospital:

> ... This was the toughest part of the visit because there wasn't much to say, and everything they did say was due to the fact that they forced their words out. Very soon the talk would die and her visitors would stare at the ceiling till someone suggested that they leave. A procession left the room, and just like everyone and everything else at the hospital, it too traveled slowly.
>
> Now satisfied with their departure but joyed with the thought that they cared enough to visit her, she looked around her dull brown cell and wondered when she could get out, back into the real world.

Martha asks, "Are you talking about your own experience?" The writer, Jeanne, answers, "Slightly my own experience, and then a couple of weeks ago my mom was in the hospital and a lot of my own feelings came out just walking down the hall to visit her. I didn't like it at all."

> *Martha:* I kind of think you have two purposes: one being how different people change when they talk to people in the hospital, and then that it's a really scary thing—that they want to get it over with fast. Well, I'm trying to decide which one is the purpose. Which one do you mean?
>
> *Jeanne:* I don't know. Maybe a little bit of both. I was looking mostly at the personality changes 'cause when I went down you just sit there and you're really quiet. You try to say something and it's always, you know, "Well, how's it going?" and you really don't care. You're just down there to be nice and polite.
>
> *Martha:* Do you mean to say—is your focus on the patient or on the visitor?

These writing conferences did not just "happen"; they were guided by teachers who put first things first and trained their students to do the same. Once Jeanne and Tiffany have revised their pieces in response to their readers' questions about content, they are ready for an editing conference where they will work on form—spelling, punctuation, and such.

Good writers have been found to focus first on meaning, while poor writers, conceiving of good writing as correct writing, focus from the start on correctness and neatness, on avoiding errors. Their premature corrections, according to Sondra Perl (1979), break the flow of their writing and thinking without making substantial improvement. Of course correctness is desirable, but placing it before meaning confuses the means with the ends of writing—like hitting the right notes but missing the music.

Good writers, seeing personal value in writing, write spontaneously outside of school and thus get additional practice. At home or at school they have models of writers and an interested audience that responds to the content of their writing. Poor writers, on the other hand, view writing as an externally imposed task. They do not see adults writing, and their teacher audience at school corrects their writing rather than responding to its message (Birnbaum 1980). Children can be taught to be poor writers or good writers. The role of the teacher is crucial, especially for children who have less opportunity to learn to write at home.

Finally, *language grows from being telegraphic and context-embedded toward being elaborated and explicit.* Children do not start speaking single words but one- and then two-word sentences. "Car" may mean "I hear a car"; "sweater chair," "My sweater is on that chair." Generally the most concrete and significant words are stated, while the rest of the meaning may reside in the context shared by the speaker and the listener; for example, they both hear the car. Soon after children begin using telegraphic sentences, more and more of the deleted elements appear on the surface—are stated rather than assumed.

We see the same process as children begin writing. In invented spellings, more and more of the omitted speech sounds become represented: from H to HS to HAOS for *house.* Text often develops in the same way, as seen in some writings by first graders in September:

Jamie drew a monster (labeled MSTR) standing beside his cave (CAV). He chose the most important and concrete words to write; the deleted words emerged when he told his teacher his paper said "This monster lives in a cave."

On the first day of school Jennifer drew a house and wrote H. The next week both her drawing and writing were elaborated: a house (HS) with a smoking chimney and a lawn in front on which stood two smiling figures, Mary (M) and ME. She told her teacher it said, "I am at my friend Mary's house."

An eight-year-old with a learning problem who is also in this classroom shows the same pattern of development. The first day of school he drew a square green wagon with a large wheel (labeled WE) and dictated, "My wagon has wheels." The next week he drew a pelican (PLEN) in wavy water (WTR) with a dock (DC) at one edge of it: "I saw a pelican in Florida near the dock." Toward the end of September his sentence was fully represented in writing: THE FIS IS IN THE WTR.

Teachers who grow writers in their classrooms also regard pieces of writing as growing things to be nurtured rather than as objects to be repaired or fixed. These first-grade writings were nurtured by a teacher who provided an hour every day for children to write on subjects they chose, who listened to each child read what she or he had written and then responded to it, who repeatedly encouraged children to figure out spellings for themselves, who typed their favorite writings into books for other children to read and for the authors to see their own words in conventional spellings, who collected each child's writings in a folder so the parents, the child, and she—the teacher—could see the child's progress.

Once their sentences become explicit and elaborated in writing, children need help in making explicit their meanings on a larger scale, as happened dramatically through a third-grade whole-class writing conference. Tanya chose to read to the class the first piece she had written in September, when in order to minimize interruptions during writing, the teacher had told her students to put down the letters they knew in a word if they didn't know the spelling or couldn't figure it all out; thus "h,n" represents Hunger Mountain.

> I went on a hike to h,n, and I had a picnic the food was fruit and meat and I like it and it was fun my frend Jenny went with me. We camt out. The end

Her classmates and teacher asked questions and commented about what she'd written: "Which Jenny?" "You should say where you camped out." "It doesn't make sense 'the food was.'" "What was the weather like?" "What did you have to drink?" "Did you walk from your house to Hunger Mountain or did you drive there?" The teacher then asked Tanya, "If you went back to work on it, what parts would you work on?" "I think I need to work on all of it," said Tanya. And she did. The next day she wrote her second draft, a much fuller version:

> I went on a hike up to hongger montain. I went by car. I had fun climming up hongger montain. When I got up on top I met my freind Jenny Adams. I ask what was she doing here. She said "That her father drove her" I was glad she was here. We had supper and after we went to bed in the morning we had breakfast and after that are parnets came and pit use up and took use home. I ask Jenny's Father and mother if she could stay other night her parnets said 'yes' I was glad that she could The end.

The writing problems of adult literacy students as well, Elsasser and John-Steiner (1977) observe, come from failures to transform compact inner speech into elaborated written language that is comprehensible to readers who do not share the writer's context.

Language—both spoken and written—develops from being telegraphic and context-embedded toward being elaborated and explicit. It is learned among people who attend to meaning before form. And it is learned in a language environment, not merely by imitation but by re-creation—by constructing and testing rules. That is, children learn language not just as little mimics but as little scientists. Each child needs to make sense for herself of how language works. That seems to be how language grows.

When we try to manufacture what must be grown, we are in trouble. The self-regulating systems of growing things, interacting with their environments, create the energy for growth. Manufacture requires new, external energy. When both teachers and learners are cut off from their natural energy sources, we have to "motivate" learners and combat teacher "burn out"—acknowledgments of our educational energy crisis.

When teaching is seen as control rather than nurturance, it is not surprising that students are seen as and become "irresponsible," for they are not being responded to; they are being "made into" something. They are raw materials for our educational technology—materials to be ground down to uniformity so they can be "efficiently" processed according to the designs of publishers, test makers, and curriculum committees.

As Robert White has said,

> the task of rearing and guiding children can best be represented by the metaphor of raising plants. This should be encouraging, because raising plants is one of mankind's most successful activities. Perhaps the success comes from the fact that the husbandman does not try to thrust impossible patterns on his plants. He respects their peculiarities, tries to provide suitable conditions, protects them from the more serious kinds of injury—but he lets the plants do the growing. He does not poke at the seed in order to make it sprout more quickly, nor does he seize the shoot when it breaks the ground and try to pull open the first leaves by hand. Neither does he trim the leaves of different kinds of plants in order to have them all look alike. The attitude of the husbandman is appropriate in dealing with children. It is the children who must do the growing. (1952, 363)

References

Birnbaum, June. 1980. "Why Should I Write? Environmental Influences on Children's Views of Writing." *Theory Into Practice* 19: 202–10.

Elsasser, Nan and Vera John-Steiner. 1977. "An Interactionist Approach to Advancing Literacy." *Harvard Educational Review* 47: 355–69.

Milz, Vera E. 1980. "First Graders Can Write: Focus on Communication." *Theory Into Practice* 19: 179–85.

Perl, Sondra. 1979. "The Composing Processes of Unskilled College Writers." *Research in the Teaching of English* 13: 317–36.

White, Robert W. 1952. *Lives in Progress.* New York: Dryden.

The Child as Teacher

1984

IN CONVERSATION WITH MY NINE-YEAR-OLD SON PAUL, I once spoke of his having read aloud when he was very young so that I could tell him if his reading was correct. I was wrong, he explained to me: Rather, he had read aloud so *he* could hear and judge himself. How presumptuous I felt. But I was a teacher and I "knew" that learners—especially those just starting out—needed adult feedback to keep them on course. Reflecting on his first-grade year, Paul remarked, "I taught myself how to read in my head [i.e. silently]. I remember a lot of the kids couldn't do it." Since that conversation I have seen more of children's abilities to manage their own learning. Not all children are as conscious or as outspoken about this self-teaching as Paul, but they have demonstrated it again and again.

Anthony Weir was two and a half years old when his mother recorded his language in the crib (Weir 1962). Alone in bed, he clearly was not speaking for the ears of any adult when he corrected his own pronunciation and grammar or when he practiced minimal phonetic pairs and made substitutions in his own sentence frames. Holdoway (1979) has shown us children as young as two and a half making self-corrections while they reconstructed texts, page by page, from familiar books. Harste, Burke and Woodward (1981, 143–44) found that "whether in the midst of writing their names or forming certain letters children often as young as three would say, 'No,' hesitate, and then cross out, proceed along or change to another communication system. They knew not only what they knew, but what they did not know and needed to work on." The researchers comment:

> We found this phenomenon particularly interesting in that it

112

flies in the face of current pedagogy, which assumes that corrective feedback must come from an obliging adult; that errors, if not immediately corrected by an outsider, become reinforced habits of some consequence to the acquisition of literacy. Children in our study seemed well aware of their literacy decisions, changed their perceived errors and capably self-selected a set of things upon which they knew they needed work. (1981, 144)

This essay considers the role of the child as his or her own teacher, particularly with respect to the development of writing. I will argue that children mediate between the structures of their minds and the information available in their environments, that they carry on several kinds of dialogue with both outer and inner voices, and that this teaching-learning process is guided by certain principles (very probably innate) that organize human learning. Finally, I will reflect on the relationship between such a view of "child mind" and some assumptions and practices of traditional classrooms.

Two Children

Paul and Scott are two self-teaching children. Paul is a preschooler I observed in his home, and Scott is a first grader I observed in his classroom. Paul comes from a middle-class, highly educated family, and Scott from a working-class, modestly educated family. Compared with others his age, Paul was advanced in his literacy skills while Scott was behind. Paul did much of his early reading and writing in a very quiet home environment, where he worked undisturbed for stretches of time. Scott, on the other hand, worked in the midst of his classmates, with whom he talked a great deal, and he concentrated on his work for briefer periods. Both boys were in the early stages of learning literacy and both were teaching themselves, organizing and monitoring their own learning.

Paul

Before he was much of a reader, Paul was a writer, inventing his spelling according to the principles that Read's research (1971) has illuminated for us. Read argued that children, without instruction in sound-letter relationships, taught themselves a spelling system based on using letters to represent their letter names (as in DA for *day*), on abstracting sounds from letter names (as "ch" from ay-ch = *h*), and on categorizations of sounds in terms of place of articulation in the mouth. Representations of short vowel sounds are not evident from the letter names children know. The spellings that Read found among preschoolers for short vowels—unconventional but consistent across children—seemed to be derived from letter names closest in place of articulation to the short vowel sounds.

Like other inventive spellers, Paul at five years old represented the short *e* sound with the letter A as in TADE for *Teddy*, his dog. When he changed the spelling to TEDE, he pointed out the change to his father. A week later, as he read the print on a red raspberry yogurt container, he observed that he had spelled *red* RAD, which he now understood was not right because, he explained, RAD said *raid*. Thus, at five years old Paul was aware of his own learning, was able to note differences between his own and the conventional spelling systems, and was able to explain why his was incorrect.

In a case where the conventional spelling did not make sense to him— the spelling of the -*tion* ending—Paul did not master the spelling for three years, despite direct instruction. The evolution of Paul's spelling of *directions* shows the evolution of his understanding of our spelling system:

DRAKTHENS	(5 years 7 months)
DRAKSHINS	(5 years 8 months)
DIREKSHONS	(7 years 5 months)
DIRECTOINS or DIRECTIONS	(8 years 1 month)
DIRECTIONS	(8 years 7 months)

That particular word, or any word, could have been corrected earlier but might have stood as an isolated item to be memorized. When Paul finally mastered *directions*, he wrote lists of what he titled "hard words," including many ending with -*tion*. His spelling reflects the learning of a principle, not merely a word.

In Paul's spelling of *Teddy*, the modification of his letter-name strategy for spelling the long *e* sound was gradual. Paul started, mostly with proper names, to use Y rather than E for a final long *e* sound. After his friend Toby corrected Paul's spelling of her name (TOBE), he had written KANDYS but also TADE. The next day he questioned the spelling of his father's name, Henry. "Is it an E at the end?" he asked. Two weeks later he wrote TEDY. Twice he overgeneralized the Y for a final long *e* spelling, writing FRY for *free* and SEY for *see*. Paul's ability to generalize and even overgeneralize such spellings reveals his search for principles rather than for isolated correct words.

As he finished writing a song about Teddy, TEDY O TEDY WIL U KAM BAK O PLES WIL YOU KAM BAK SUN (Teddy, oh Teddy, will you come back. Oh please will you come back soon), Paul observed that SUN, intended for *soon*, said *sun* instead. He had not been taught to read *sun* (that is, he was not taught to decode or to recognize the word on sight), yet here he was applying to his own spelling the knowledge he had gained through reading and he was noting discrepancies between the two systems. Three weeks earlier, his reading knowledge had called another of his own spellings into question. While writing a friend's last name, Potter, which Paul had written PATR, he realized, "p-a-t spells *pat*. So what would that be?"

Thus Paul was able to keep taking in information about our writing system from the world around him and modify his system accordingly. He did not take in at once all the information that was present in the world around him—that is, all the words he read that were spelled differently from his invented spellings. Often the new information was not fully incorporated into his system until several confirmations had established that something, such as E to represent "eh," was indeed part of the conventional system. Paul's spelling, like his language acquisition, was a process of active learning and experimentation, hypothesis making and testing, and incorporation of new information from his environment through the processes of assimilation and accommodation, as described by Piaget. In doing this, Paul was not unique. He is simply one carefully observed example of a preschool literacy learner. As Söderbergh has argued:

> Now if a child learns to talk at a certain age without formal instruction, solely by being exposed to language, and if written language is to be considered as an independent system, why cannot a child learn to read *at the same age and in the same way* as he is learning to talk, solely by being exposed to written language? He would then be supposed to attack the written material, forming hypotheses, building models, all by himself discovering the code of the written language. (1971, 15–16)

Söderbergh's study documents this in detail, revealing her daughter's spontaneous induction of word analysis—first morphemes, then phonemes— from words learned by sight. Literacy learning, like language learning, is not merely imitative but systematic and creative, in the sense that the child constructs (or reconstructs) the rules for himself or herself.

Schools appear to assume that children do not learn from direct interaction with their environments but that this interaction must be initiated and mediated by the teacher. The teacher selects, organizes, and calls children's attention to information they need to learn. As we have seen, children's search for the rules governing the systems of spoken and written language powerfully organizes their learning. Children also have been seen to structure their learning in ways strikingly like textbook or workbook exercises. Weir's son Anthony, at two and a half years old, practiced making substitutions in his own sentence frames: "What color. What color blanket. What color mop. What color glass." Paul at five years old, devised his own phonics exercises: "You spell *book* b-o-o-k," he commented after writing one day. "To write *look*, you just change one letter—take away the *b* and add an *l*." While lying in bed one evening he mused, "If you took the *l* out of glass and pushed it all together, you'd have *gas*" and "If you take the *t* and *r* off of *trike* and put a *b* in front, you have *bike*." After a conversation about Daedalus and Icarus, Paul observed, "If you put an *l* in front of *Icarus*, you get *licorice*." Yet Paul had a difficult time completing workbook exercises the next year when he was in first grade. The playfulness and sense of discovery were gone, and he was not interested in merely demonstrating what he already knew.

In addition to selecting and organizing information for children and giving them corrective feedback, the teacher's role includes asking questions. Usually these are questions to test children's knowledge rather than questions to which the teacher is truly seeking an answer. Sometimes teachers' questions are designed to help children think further about a topic. In any event, the classroom is seen as a place where teachers generally ask the questions and children answer them. Yet children are full of questions, about written language as well as about many other aspects of their world.

When Paul started to spell inventively, he asked questions about how to represent sounds: "What letter makes the 'uh' sound?" or "How do you spell 'sh'?" The questions reflected his concept of writing as the transcription of speech sounds. Only later did he come to ask for the spellings of words. At the start of his invented spelling, Paul asked a great many questions. Several months later, when he had incorporated this information into his system, he wrote independently. When he needed instruction, he sought it, and then he learned it by practicing because it was information he needed to use.

Torrey has reported the case of an unlikely self-taught early reader—a child who, on the basis of currently accepted predictors of reading success, might have been expected to fail:

> John had no more than average tested verbal ability and perhaps even less than average cultural stimulation in the direction of reading. The key factor in reading therefore must be something else. Large vocabulary, sophisticated thinking, accurate articulation of standard English, active encouragement and instruction in reading skills, may very well help a child to learn to read. However, even a single case like John's shows us that they are not indispensable. (1973, 156)

What Torrey sees as crucial was John's ability as a learner: "He appears to have asked just the right questions in his own mind about the relation between language and print and thus to have been able to bridge the gap between his own language and the printed form" (1973, 157).

Children's attention may be focused on specific information they want rather than on the broader questions that guide their search for specific facts. Ferreiro's research (1979–80) has shown us the fascinating journey children take in their search for understanding the relationship between print and meaning or speech, and the theories the children did not articulate but demonstrated in their responses to print by selecting, for example, longer words to represent larger objects.

Paul reflected on the relationship between reading and writing. When he started spelling inventively, he announced, "Once you know how to spell something, you know how to read it." However, as his reading advanced and he became more aware of conventional spellings, he commented on words he could read but could not spell. At six years old, he commented, "*Hate* is about the only word I can read but can't spell. I always spell it *hat*." Three months later, Paul observed that "Sometimes you can read a word and you can't spell it—like *dinosaur*. I can read but I can't spell that." Spelling now meant to Paul conventional spelling, which he did not see as preceding or enabling reading. He articulated a broader question at about this time, a question he compared to the chicken-and-egg riddle: "Which came first, reading or writing?" He decided that writing came first because you had to have letters, or even a picture, before you could read it.

The dialogue of question and answer and of reflection seems to be a natural part of the learning process. Dialogue is carried on between children and the sources of information in their environments, and it is carried on within children's minds as they hypothesize and reflect. Dialogue is essential to learning but the classroom is not essential for the creation of dialogue. Perhaps more genuine dialogue occurs outside classrooms than within them.

Scott

Scott was another self-teacher, a child I knew in his first-grade classroom, where he was given space and support to explore writing. Each morning the children had up to one hour, as they needed it, to write and/or draw on topics of their own choosing. After the children finished a piece, they took it to their teacher and read to her what they had written or told about what they had drawn. In the first week of school, Scott drew roughly representational pictures, dictated action-packed stories that accompanied them, and wrote only his name, copied from a placard on his desk, and the date, copied from the blackboard. In the third week of school, Scott started what was to become a series of shark drawings and stories. Focused as I was on his writing development at the time, I overlooked what these drawings showed about Scott as a learner. Only later, when reviewing his writing folder for the year, did I see them as remarkable evidence of Scott's ability to teach himself and as forerunners of the approach he was to take in working on his own literacy skills.

Scott made his series of six shark drawings (Figures 2 through 7) within a two-week period. Although he was not receiving instruction in drawing or, as far as I know, referring to other pictures of sharks, his shark evolved from what looked like a small, grinning, bobbing toy to a huge, fierce creature rising from the ocean depths. (In the picture reproductions, other objects Scott drew on the page have been excluded to concentrate on the shark's evolution.) Without instruction or immediate models, how did Scott learn to draw a shark? Possibly he received some comments from peers that led to changes, since the first graders wrote at tables and often talked and commented on one another's work. More compellingly, the stories Scott dictated after drawing each shark indicated his clear intention from the start to portray a fierce creature.

Scott's revisions of his shark drawings move steadily in the direction of expressing this intended fierceness or "sharkness," and the story itself becomes more coherent and focused as he reworks it. His most important teacher must have been his own eyes—his ability to measure the work he had produced against what he intended, to clarify that intention to himself, and gradually to find the means of realizing it. Art educator Schaefer-Simmern has documented many such cases of artistic unfolding among untutored adolescents and adults, arguing that "The ability to create artistic form by means of visual conceiving is a natural attribute of the mental existence of man" (1948, 198).

Although Scott did not work on his drawings and writings for extended periods on any one day, his writing folder shows how many different times he worked further on a particular subject, such as his shark, by starting it again and again, not to repeat but to learn and improve. In November, he began a series of tracings of his hand that involved also spelling and numbering. I have selected for discussion only certain tracings from this series, which was made over several months' time, to illustrate Scott's approach to his own literacy instruction.

In his first piece on the hand, Scott wrote a string of letters (KinHeL) not corresponding phonetically to what he said aloud about the piece ("This is my fingerprint"). Approximately two weeks later, he wrote above the tracing of his hand another letter string (ASFA), but on the palm he wrote HND, corresponding to his oral statement "This is my handprint." In January Scott

Figure 2
"The ship shark comes and the ship goes away because the shark was too slow for it and finally the shark bited into him. Inside was cold so the man put the heat on."

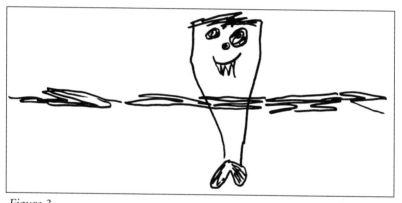

Figure 3
"The sailboat was floating for days and days and this old shark come and it was heading right for the boat and it got mad it was getting sunny. It was all clouds. He was going to Hawaii."

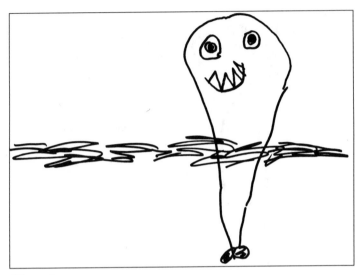

Figure 4
"The shark was gonna attack the boat."

Figure 5
"The sun was coming out. Then the clouds were getting shady. Pretty soon a shark came. Then the boat was heading for it. Then the shark was looking at the clouds."

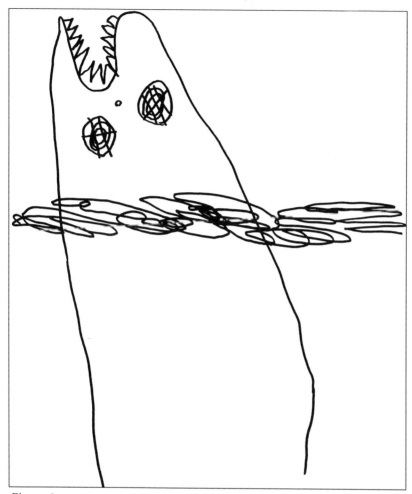

Figure 6
"The shark's gots to get to the sun. The shark's trying to get something.
The shark's trying . . . "[The rest of the story is lost.]

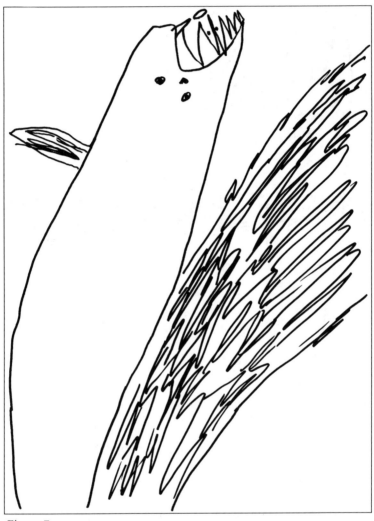

Figure 7
"Once a time there was a shark and a whale fighting. And the shark stopped 'cause he saw some boats coming down from the sky. He ate them."

was able to represent *handprint* much more completely as HDPRIT, and in another month he wrote a full message: ImaDafgrprnt/[line break] it is mIfig print/afigrrint (I made a fingerprint. It is my fingerprint. A fingerprint). His spelling was not entirely conventional but would be readable if his letter formations and use of space were more conventional. He had come a long distance from the letter strings that did not represent sounds to a phonetically, occasionally conventionally, spelled out message.

In another similar example, in April Scott worked on elaborating both his drawing and his message and on making them correspond more accurately (Figures 8–10). The first piece in this series (Figure 8) shows a person with kites flying up from both arms. Scott wrote, "I am fiingg [flying] a Kite." In the second drawing (Figure 9), the person is more completely represented and the kites have faces and ears. "I am flin A Kite," Scott wrote and then, more accurately, "I am Flin 2 kites." In the final piece (Figure 10), Scott includes more information in his writing: "I em fline A Kite in the Felb it is A mikemas Kite" (I am flying a kite in the field. It is a Mickey Mouse kite.)

Figure 8
"I am flying a kite."

Figure 9
"I am flying a kite. I am flying 2 kites."

Figure 10
"I am flying a kite in the field. It is a Mickey Mouse kite."

His drawing focuses on the juncture between himself and the kite, detailing the fingers of his hand as it holds the kite string.

Scott persistently rotated letters, sometimes continued his writing above rather than below what he had just written, and was in the least advanced reading group in his room. Having these difficulties, Scott might, in a different school, have been removed from his writing time to do special exercises so he would be "ready" to write later. Instead, Scott directed his own learning. He gave himself his own exercises, he learned a great deal about written language, and by the end of second grade he was reported to be reading at grade level. As his shark drawings demonstrated, Scott was both a learner and a teacher.

Reflection

Scott learned from many teachers in his classroom: from his own self-criticism and persistence, from the talk and writings of his classmates, from the books he read, and from the instruction and support he received from his first-grade teacher. Learning is part of what the human mind does; it is hard to stop it from learning. We do not need to go to school to learn, except to learn those things we cannot learn through association with the people and the world around us. In a literate society, literacy is not one of the things for which we need schooling. As Smethurst, who surveyed the history of teaching young children to read at home, stated:

> A first grade classroom is by no means the only place for a child to begin reading—and maybe it is not even the best place to begin. Throughout the five thousand years or so that people have been reading, many children have been taught to read at home. Their teachers have been parents, siblings, relatives, servants, masters, governesses, tutors, or playmates. In some societies this sort of teaching has even been commonplace. Perhaps reading is, as Margaret Mead suggests, an apprenticeship skill. (1975, 3)

The same argument could be made, of course, about learning to write.

We have *chosen* schools as the places to teach literacy, a decision that is more political than educational. This being the case, research on preschool literacy learning may have as little impact on teaching as has research showing that instruction in formal grammar does not significantly affect the language use of students. The issue may not be how children learn but why schools teach as they do.

Until fairly recently, research on learning to read and write focused on school settings, reinforcing our society's identification of literacy learning with schooling. However, during the past fifteen years, beginning with Durkin's (1966) study of children who read early, preschool literacy has received some research attention. Steinberg and Steinberg, having taught their son to identify letters and words before he could speak, argued that "readiness" meant readiness only for formal instruction in a school setting, and not necessarily readiness to begin the process of reading in itself (1975). Based on her study of early fluent readers, Clark remarked that "Certain characteristics may appear crucial because of the particular approach used in learning to read and the fact that learning to read normally takes place in a group situation—in school" (1976, ix). Early readers often were discovered to be early writers as well (Durkin 1966, Clay 1975). Read's (1971) study of preschool inventive spellers dramatically revealed the power of child mind, as have the subsequent studies of children's encounters with print by Harste, Burke, and Woodward (1981). And yet schools operate as though children were empty vessels to be poured full of information about literacy.

Child mind asks questions, seeks order, and monitors and corrects its own learning. These are natural functions of human mind. However, these are also functions that teachers have regarded as their own special domain, functions that teachers have so preempted that children often abandon them when in classrooms. Such distrust of child mind in the classroom is but one manifestation of the school system's distrust of the learning ability inherent in human mind. Distrust of both teachers and students is manifest in the increasing control of curriculum and teaching methods by the "outside experts" in publishing companies, which Smith (1981) has decried, and in the proliferation of administrators in proportion to the teachers they supervise and make decisions for.

To look closely at child mind is to take it seriously. Children are small; their minds are not. Child mind is human mind. Its contents are different from adult mind because it has had less time to gather information, to gain knowledge from experience, to develop certain kinds of thinking and means of expression. And, probably because it is not yet completely acculturated, it is more of a world mind in the sense that it is open to trying options that other cultures have developed, for example, in their writing systems (Ferreiro 1979–80; Harste, Burke, and Woodward 1981; Bissex 1980). Although these options, whether conventions used in writing (such as dots rather than spaces between words) or principles (such as letters representing syllables rather than sounds), are discarded as part of the child's literacy learning in our culture's system, exploring them may function to define for the child the characteristics of the system he or she eventually adopts. These options not only reflect the scope of the child's intellectual explorations but make possible those explorations and the asking of those unarticulated but overarching questions about the nature of written language.

Children reconstruct their language systems, both spoken and written. You cannot reconstruct a system by accumulating bits and pieces of information; you reconstruct it by discovering, through all the specific information you know about it, what its principles are—the rules by which it works. Children, in searching for order, assume order exists in the world. *Independently* they all invent virtually the *same* systems—for syntax, for example, or invented spelling—which bespeaks something more at work than immature minds in isolation. The immediate context in which learning takes place has been attended to in recent ethnographic research, but there exists also a broader context of historical and universal dimensions, which somehow is internalized. Or we could say that child mind possesses structures isomorphic with historical and universal ones. This is not surprising since human intellectual history has been shaped by the same human mind in which child mind participates, and because language universals *are* universal by virtue of their greater cognitive simplicity.

Slobin has formulated such a principle about language: "Forms which are late to be acquired by children are presumably also relatively difficult for adults to process, and should be especially vulnerable to change" (1977, 194). This is true for spelling acquisition in the greater regularity and stability of consonant sound-letter correspondences than of vowel sound-letter correspondences. It is the consonant representations that preschool inventive spellers master first; the vowels remain a problem for many of us into adulthood. The salience of consonants for representing the language can be seen in the development of Speedwriting, a shorthand system that essentially omits vowel representations yet remains readable. Historically, the greatest shifts in spelling and pronunciation surround the vowels.

In describing the acquisition of phonology, Jakobson stated that at the beginning of language development the child possesses only those sounds that are common to all languages of the world. The last sounds to be acquired are those occurring comparatively rarely in the languages of the world. Pointing to studies of phonological development in children of many different countries, Jakobson observed that "The relative chronological order of phonological acquisition remains everywhere and at all times the same" (1968, 46).

> In all parallels between child language (or aphasia) and the languages of the world, what is most conclusive is the identity of the structural law which determines always and everywhere what does or will exist in the language of the individual and in the language of society. In other words, the same hierarchy of values always underlies every increase and loss within any given phonological system. (1968, 66)

Thus it appears that there is a force outside a society's educational institutions, including the family, which guides the language learning of children.

To understand child mind in its engagement with written language, we need to be not only psycholinguists but comparative and historical linguists and cultural anthropologists. Harste, Burke, and Woodward, in their study of three- to six-year-olds, noted the range of conventions the children explored:

> It is as if, among the 48 children studied, every convention that has been adopted by written language users worldwide was being reinvented and tested by this group of very young language users. Some tried writing right to left, others bottom to top, and a not surprising majority, given the culture they were in, wrote left-to-right, top-to-bottom. The use of space in relationship to placeholding individual concepts posed difficult problems for these children. Some used space and distance freely about the page, others drew dots between conceptual units, some drew circles around sets of markings, others wrote in columns to preserve order, while still others spaced their concepts using what we would see as the conventional form for this society. . . . The symbol system itself proved no less interesting. Children's markings, while having many English language features, ranged from pictorial graphs to symbol-like strings. (1981, 137)

Schaefer-Simmern has observed a similar phenomenon in the artistic development of children and adults who are permitted to be self-teachers: "In the organic development and realization of visual conceptions, definite corresponding stages of artistic configuration in works of art of various epochs and races are reexperienced" (1948, 199). Kellogg, in her analysis of children's self-taught art, argues that "a comprehensive documentation of the Gestalts found in child work and a consideration of the possible bearing they have on the adult art of all times and places would enhance human self-understanding" (1969, 218).

When we speak of children's development in writing, we mean development toward those forms selected and refined by our culture. Often we do not appreciate the forms, used in other times and places, that children independently re-create but must unlearn as part of their schooling. We tend to see our writing system as a given and children as developing toward it. Yet if we step away to gain a broader perspective in time, we see the writing system itself developing; we see that the child's literacy learning is cut from the same cloth as mankind's written language development.

The child as teacher is child mind interacting with the information and structures provided by its immediate environment, and guided and supported by the enduring structures of human mind and language which, like a great net, protect it from falling into the abyss of nonlearning. Children have demonstrated their power to abstract, hypothesize, construct, and revise. Given this view of children, surely one role of education is to affirm each child's inner teacher.

References

Bissex, Glenda L. 1980. *GNYS AT WRK: A Child Learns to Write and Read.* Cambridge, MA: Harvard University Press.

Clark, Margaret M. 1976. *Young Fluent Readers.* London: Heinemann.

Clay, Marie M. 1975. *What Did I Write?* Auckland: Heinemann.

Durkin, Dolores. 1966. *Children Who Read Early.* New York: Teachers College Press.

Ferreiro, Emilia 1979–80. "The Relationship Between Oral and Written Language: The Children's Viewpoints." In *Oral and Written Language Development Research: Impact on the Schools*, ed. Y. Goodman, M. Hausler and D. Strickland. Urbana, IL: National Council of Teachers of English.

Harste, Jerome, Carolyn Burke and Virginia Woodward. 1981. *Children, Their Language and World: Initial Encounters with Print.* National Institute of Educational Final Report. Bloomington: Indiana University Press.

Holdaway, Don. 1979. *The Foundations of Literacy.* Sydney: Ashton Scholastic.

Jakobson, Roman. 1968. *Child Language, Aphasia and Phonological Universals.* The Hague: Mouton.

Kellogg, Rhoda. 1969. *Analyzing Children's Art.* Palo Alto, CA: Mayfield.

Read, Charles. 1971. "Pre-school Children's Knowledge of English Phonology." *Harvard Educational Review* 41: 1–34.

Schaefer-Simmern, Henry. 1948. *The Unfolding of Artistic Activity.* Berkeley: University of California Press.

Slobin, Dan. 1977. "Language Change in Childhood and in History." In *Language, Learning and Thought*, ed. J. Macnamara. New York: Academic Press.

Smethurst, Wood 1975. *Teaching Young Children to Read at Home.* New York: McGraw-Hill.

Smith, Frank. 1981. "Demonstrations, Engagement and Sensitivity: The Choice Between People and Programs." *Language Arts* 58, no. 1: 103–12

Söderbergh, R. 1971. *Reading in Early Childhood.* Stockholm: Almqvist & Wiksell.

Steinberg, D. D. and M. T. Steinberg. 1975. "Reading Before Speaking." *Visible Language* 9: 197–224.

Torrey, Jane W. 1973. "Learning to Read Without a Teacher: A Case Study." In *Psycholinguistics and Reading,* ed. F. Smith. New York: Holt, Rinehart & Winston.

Weir, Ruth. 1962. *Language in the Crib.* The Hague: Mouton.

Watching Young Writers

1985

WHEN A CHILD WHO IS JUST BEGINNING TO TALK REFERS to water as "wa-wa," parents are thrilled that the child has successfully identified the name with the thing and come close enough to adult pronunciation to be understood. When a child who is beginning to write puts down DRAKTHENS for *directions*, adults see an error and may worry that the child will form a wrong habit if it is not corrected. The focus is on what the child does not yet know (conventional spelling) rather than on the knowledge the child has demonstrated of the alphabetic principle of our writing system, of specific sound-letter relationships, and of letter forms and sequencing.

Adults seem to have faith that children will develop accuracy in speech without constant corrections—how many ten-year-olds do you know who still say "wa-wa"?—but we respond differently to beginning writers (and readers). Because an error is in writing, it may appear permanent and thus in need of immediate erasure and correction lest it become established. Yet the child who wrote DRAKTHENS did not regard that spelling as permanent, for a month later he wrote DRAKSHINS, two years after that, DIRECKSHONS, and in another year spelled the word conventionally. Although the child had correctly copied several -*tion* words two years before mastering *directions*, this spelling had not made sense in terms of what he understood about sound-spelling relationships and so he had not learned from the instruction.

Is learning to write such a different process from learning to speak that we must take a different approach to it, that we can have faith children will learn to speak correctly yet believe they need constant instruction and correction in order to learn to write? How much of the difference lies in the different conditions

131

under which speaking and writing have generally been learned, that is, the home and school environments? At home, children hear speech, are spoken to and practice speaking frequently; they have adult models, functional as well as emotional motivation to learn, and a tutorial relationship with at least one accomplished speaker of the language. If we enlarge the notion of "instruction" to include not only explicit teaching but also the availability of information in the children's environment and the presence of reasons for them to engage with it, then we see that children are indeed "taught" to speak at home. We see also that children may learn to write in school through means other than formal instruction: by writing every day and for reasons that are real to the child, by being written to, by seeing writing and writers, by asking questions and receiving requested information about print.

Studies of child language development show us that children do not learn merely by imitation since they use constructions and forms of words that are not spoken around them. For example, after children become aware of plural and past tense endings, they tend to regularize all plurals, as in "mouses," and past tenses, as in "goed" or even "wented." Children certainly have not been taught these words nor the rules for forming plurals and past tenses; rather, they have overgeneralized rules learned from their observations of the speech around them and through their own reasoning. Children do not regard these learnings as permanent. Continuing to listen critically to the language around them, they find they have to revise such "rules," and the over-regularized forms drop out of their speech. Like little scientists, they are constantly making and testing hypotheses about language, among other things.

Observing Emergent Writing

Children in a literate society start learning about written language long before they enter school. They learn from television, they learn from cereal boxes and toothpaste tubes, they learn from road signs—they learn from the print in their environment and from the adults they see using print. Before they can write conventionally, they write in their own ways but with the knowledge that writing communicates meanings and words, as these early recollections from young adults suggest:

> I remember, before school years, doing a lot of scribbling. Although this scribbling meant nothing to my family, I can recall being able to read the whole thing. As the family giggled and thought how "cute" it was, I would sit in my chair and read my scribbles.

Since I can remember, I wrote. I remember taking crayons and writing on the walls and my mother would yell at me because it was scribbling. But wouldn't it be funny if I wrote a word—she probably wouldn't have yelled at me then. I really remember wanting to express with my pencil, pen, or whatever, but I couldn't; no one understood.

From looking closely at scribbles and scribblers, Harste, Burke, and Woodward concluded that

> Children as young as three, regardless of race or socioeconomic status, differentiated writing from drawing. . . . Generally the children's art was characterized as being global, centralized and connected. Children, prior to the product being particularly representational to the adult eye, usually drew a large figure in the center of the page having a unity or cohesiveness of lines converging about this point. Their writing, on the other hand, was typically linear, spaced, and located off center. (1981, 127–28)

When children first write, Ferreiro's studies of three- to six-year-olds show us, they will represent an object by a single letterlike shape (1982). Then, moving closer to our writing system, they will use a combination of several varied shapes to represent a name. For some time, the number of letterlike forms required for a word corresponds to the size or quantity of the object names: more letters for *horse* than for *chicken*, and more for *carrots* than *carrot*. Only after trying out this theory do children discover the correspondence between writing and speech, first reasoning that letters represent syllables and, finally, sounds. Children puzzle over the relationship between print and meaning or speech before schooling compels them to do so, and their understanding evolves through a series of hypotheses about that relationship. Many of the theories they try out and the conventions they invent (such as syllabic writing, dots to separate words, and writing from left to right) are or were used in other written language systems (Bissex 1980; Harste, Burke, and Woodward 1981). Children do not leap from illiteracy to an understanding that our writing system is alphabetic when they receive their first phonics lesson.

> Children go a long and complicated way before discovering that the writing surrounding them is alphabetic in nature. They explore other hypotheses, some of them not being adequate for the alphabetical system, although they would be appropriate for other systems of writing
>
> The writing that precedes that alphabetical period is far from unstructured: It provides evidence of children's efforts in the search for an understanding of the laws of the system. (Ferreiro 1982, 56)

Once children have grasped the alphabetic principle (that our writing system is based on letters representing speech sounds) and know the names of at least some letters, they invent their own systematic spellings—a further stage in their active search for the laws of our writing system. Read has shown us how these young spellers reason (1971). Consider how the spelling FEGR (*finger*) might have been invented. Without benefit of phonics lessons, the young writer could have abstracted the sounds "f" and "r" from the letter names "eff" and "ar," thus arriving at the first and last letters of FEGR. The G, whose sound cannot be derived from its letter name, could have been derived from the child's name, Gary, or was perhaps supplied by an adult. The nasal (*n*) before a consonant is typically not represented by inventive spellers because the nasal sound cannot be heard or felt in the mouth as a separate segment. The jaw and tongue remain in one position for -*ng*. Since the *e* in *finger* cannot be heard or felt as separate from the *r*, it is not represented by children who are spelling by ear or by mouth, using everything they know about the spoken language they have already mastered in order to figure out written language. Many very young spellers, Read found, represent short *i* ("ih") with the letter E, as in FEGR. Why? Either because the place of articulation in the mouth for "ih" and "ee" are closely related, or because the letter name "E," when pronounced slowly ("ih-ee"), starts with short *i*. As well as abstracting sounds from letter names, inventive spellers use letters to stand for letter names, as in DA (*day*) and AGRE (*angry*).

In sum, children use their knowledge of speech sounds and of the alphabet, combined with some information requested from adults, to devise a spelling system. Read stresses the systematic nature of invented spellings; children's judgments about how to represent sounds are consistent and rule-governed and, as subsequent research has confirmed, amazingly uniform across the different groups of children studied. Yet this immature system is not fixed but is in a constant state of re-evaluation and change, moving increasingly toward more complete and conventional spellings.

Knowing that writing has meaning and functions, understanding the alphabetic principle of our writing system, and establishing rules for representing speech sounds are not all a child must have accomplished in order to write. Clay reveals the many graphic and spatial principles children master as they move into writing (1975). They learn that writing is linear and that in our system it goes from left to right and top to bottom of a page. Before children represent speech sounds in their writing, they learn not only about directionality and the use of space but about patterns, for example, the "generating principle"—that letters recur in variable patterns—so that with knowledge of only a few letter shapes a child can produce strings of print that resemble conventional writing.

Observing Writing Development in Schools

Children often spend several years learning about print *before* they enter first grade. The start of schooling marks the beginning only of formal instruction in writing, not the beginning of children's learning about written language. What does this mean for first-grade teachers? It means they need to find out right away what children *already know* about written language in order to tell where effective instruction can start. By the end of the year, if writing folders are kept for each child with pieces accurately dated, the children's progress will be clearly visible.

This is one way first-grade teacher Mary Ellen Giacobbe found out what her children could do as writers. Each day during the first week of school she introduced five or six children to journals (books containing forty pages of unlined 9" x 12" paper for them to write in). These children worked at the writing table while the others were assigned elsewhere in the classroom. Giacobbe circulated around the classroom observing and talking with the children: "Tell me about your building" or "Why do you think the sand goes through this strainer faster than through that strainer?"

> Someone tugged at my sleeve and I turned to see Mark standing by my side with his journal. "Tell me about your drawing, Mark," I said. He pointed to each part of the drawing and said, "This is the ocean and this is a sailboat and this is the anchor. These are clouds." He had written BD for *boat* and KLD for *cloud*. (1981, 99)

If Giacobbe had not asked Mark about his drawing, she might not have understood his writing. She then watched Ellen write: THE TRCE WAS TACAN A WEC (The turkey was taking a walk).

> She read it to herself, crossed out the T in TACAN, changed it to a W and on top of A WEC, she wrote D THE HALL. Her message now read THE TRCE WAS WACAN D THE HALL (The turkey was walking down the hill). Already Ellen knew that she could change her message so that it said exactly what she wanted it to say. She was rereading and revising.
>
> My attention was drawn to the tap, tap, tapping of the black marker on David's page as he was creating a snowstorm. He wrote: I SO SO (I saw snow). David said, "This is a big snowstorm. A real blizzard." As he touched

each word, he read "I saw snow." I asked David, "What do you notice about the words *saw* and *snow*?" He replied, "They both begin with the same sound." (1981, 100)

Giacobbe found out that David understood what a written word was and already knew some phonics.

As the blank pages in their journals came alive with drawings and words telling of their experiences, I could see these children had entered school ready to engage in the active process of writing. They were writing their own workbooks. They were showing me what they knew as well as what they needed to know. There were no errors to be red penciled. Just information showing me what the next step of instruction should be. (1981, 100–101)

Other teachers ask the whole class to write at the same time, using single sheets of paper, while the teachers circulate around the room to observe how the children are writing: Are they sounding out spellings? Which children are not yet using letters to represent sounds but rather are showing a more visual knowledge of print by writing strings of letters or other symbols? Are children writing from left to right and from top to bottom of the paper? Are children asking for and giving one another information about spellings or letter formations? Are some children able to read back what they have written? (In the early phase of invented spelling it is not unusual for children to have difficulty reading their writing.) Do some writers make self-corrections and revisions as they work? Have children already memorized the spellings of some words? Did someone at home teach those spellings, the teacher might inquire, or were the spellings picked up from reading? The teachers need not instruct at the beginning; they are essentially finding out information about their children's learning by observing, listening, and questioning.

Teachers will learn much about their students' concerns and interests as they draw and write if children generally choose their own topics rather than respond to assigned topics. First graders usually have no trouble taking this initiative, especially if they start out by drawing. As they share their writings, in small groups or as a class, they gather more ideas. From observing children writing and from talking with them about what they write, teachers will come to know their students' lives as well as their skills. Teachers will find that ground, between their own lives and their students' lives, where they can meet, and they will find that ground, between their own knowledge and their students' knowledge, where they can truly teach.

When teachers ask children to show what they know, teachers are faced with more diverse responses than are revealed through filling in worksheets or following assignments. Having evidence of how children are not the same at the beginning of school, teachers will not expect them to be at the same, standardized place in their writing development by the end of the year. They will expect children to grow and learn, and will see their essential role as being responsible for that *learning* rather than for *teaching*, in the sense of covering a curriculum and correcting errors.

Two Young Writers

In another first grade room, near the end of the year, we could see these two examples of writing:

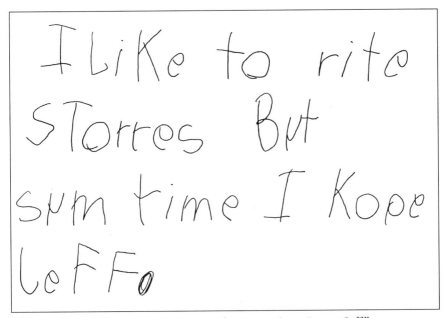

Figure 11 Scott. "I like to write stories but sometimes I copy Jeff."

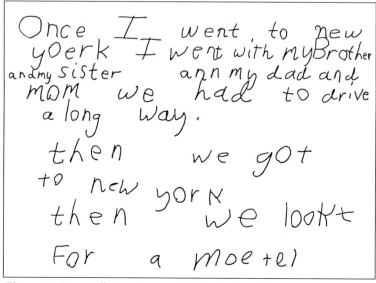

Figure 12 Kenny. "Once I went to New York . . ."

We might conclude that Scott (Figure 11) and Kenny (Figure 12) had learned a very different amount, especially since this is only one of six pages Kenny wrote while Scott did his sentence. Leafing through their writing folders, however, we see what different places they started from and the different paths their learning took—information that standardized tests could not give us.

The first few weeks of school, Scott's writing was largely in the form of drawing. When his teacher asked him to tell her about his picture, he told elaborated, action-filled stories that sounded vivid and exciting but appeared somewhat incoherent when written down, such as this one from the second day of school: "The rocket was starting to take off and the people got in. They saw treasure on the ground. The people jumped out. The rocket was starting to blow up." The only writing on his drawing of the rocket (Figure 13) was his name, copied from a placard on his desk, and the date, copied from the blackboard.

The first week of school, Kenny drew a detailed picture of three pigs standing in front of three houses and the big bad wolf approaching. He wrote (not copied) his name and APBBW (*a pig, a big bad wolf*). "A pig made a house of straw and then a big bad wolf came," was what he said about his writing. The influence of children's literature on both the content and form of Kenny's writing was clear from the start. Many of his pieces the first weeks of school began "Once upon a time . . . ."

Figure 13 Scott's drawing of a rocket.

Scott, two weeks after his rocket drawing, made a house with a door, a window and a face in the window—a sort of revised rocket (Figure 14). Starting with the bottom line and working upward when he ran out of space, he wrote two strings of letters, many of them reversed. When asked about his piece, Scott told this story:

> It was getting sunny and he was thinking about his old friend named Puff the Magic Dragon. He wished he was here. He was watching if he would come. He writed a letter to him. He wanted to sail away with him. Finally he got there. Puff the Magic Dragon says go home because he had the sneezes. It was so sad that he comed back that boy because the big man poured some soup to make the sneezes go away.

Although Scott's teacher worked with him on identifying and writing letters to represent a few of the sounds in his dictated stories, he did not move readily into invented spelling but rather seemed to need more practice with letter forms first. Two months later, he wrote a solid page of letter strings (Figure 15) and "read" what he had written: "This is Sheldon. He is a big dog and he jumps on the man. He goes to bed and he sleeps for one hour

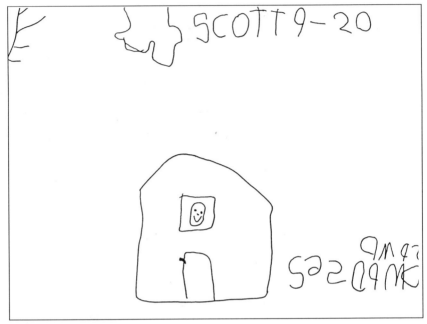

Figure 14 Scott's revised drawing.

and a half and I got a pony with him. My dog hunts for rabbits." While his letters did not seem to correspond to sounds, the amount he had written was much more in proportion to the amount he told.

Ten days later, he invented his own phonetic spellings, such as "Rkht" for *rocket* in Figure 16, although he was still writing strings of letters that did not represent sounds.

Thus, after nearly three months of school, Scott approached the point of writing development Kenny had reached before any first-grade instruction: writing labels for drawings and using accurate representations of consonant sounds. Figure 16 is one page from a seven-page booklet Scott wrote that day. When he read the booklet to his teacher, he expanded the labels he had written into complete sentences: "This is my rocket," "This is my donkey," and so forth. Two months later he wrote out the full statement behind the labels, as in Figure 17: "This is my little house."

What had happened to Scott's imaginative tales and vivid language? Like some other storytellers in his classroom, Scott had limited his language to what he could write. When they started spelling inventively, and even shortly before—as if in anticipation of the limits of their own ability to represent language in print—they reduced their stories to simple, repetitive sen-

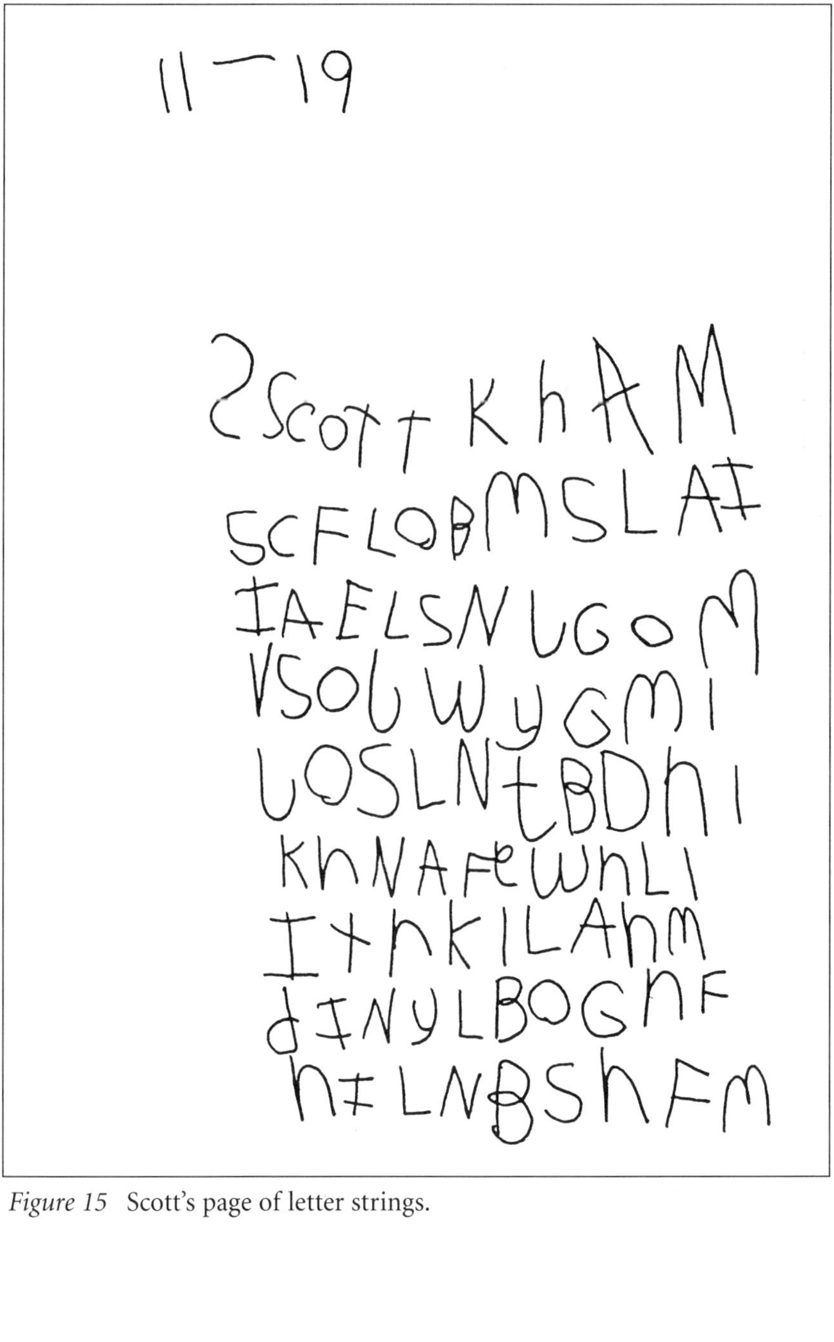

Figure 15 Scott's page of letter strings.

Figure 16 Scott's invented spelling: "Rocket"

tence patterns such as "This is . . ." and "I see . . . ." These formulas could be kept easily in mind while the children labored to sound out spellings and recall correct letter shapes. Scott's early action narratives tumbled out so fast even an adult writer could barely keep up transcribing them. Just as children start reading at a level far below the level of oral language they comprehend, children start writing at a level far below the language of their own speech. Transcriptions by the teacher preserve the vitality and zany charm of children's oral stories, and may help to develop basic reading concepts and skills,

Figure 17 Scott: "This is my little house."

but keep the power of writing in the hands of the teacher. Scott's written language was less interesting than this oral language—but he had done it all himself!

In February Scott wrote four solid pages of print—no drawings at all. Looking at one page of this unusually long story about his dog (Figure 18) we can see what, in retrospect, he was rehearsing with his letter strings almost three months earlier, before his writing represented sounds (Figure 15).

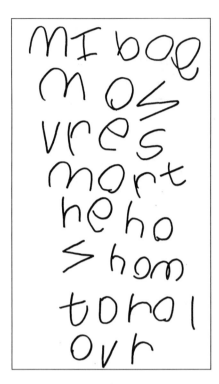

Figure 18
Scott: "My dog was very smart. He knows how to roll over."

Scott's last first-grade writings (Figure 11, for example) and one of his earliest (Figure 13) show the full course of his writing development. It no longer appears that he has learned little about writing during first grade.

Scott was not pushed to copy writing beyond what he could produce, nor was he removed from his writing classroom to do directionality and readiness exercises. His teacher gave him time and faith and encouragement to continue to learn from his own writing. And he did. "Children have shown to us that they need to reconstruct the written system in order to make it their own. Let us allow them the time and the opportunities for such a tremendous task" (Ferreiro 1982, 56).

Reflection

When we appreciate the depth of children's understanding—how they start from the most fundamental and difficult questions about literacy, when we understand how much they need to know and do manage to learn beyond what is in our textbooks and worksheets and lesson plans, we become more aware of the many ways in which we teach. We teach by allowing children space to ask their own questions, to guide their own learning, and to inform us of what they need to be taught. We teach by surrounding children with a richly literate environment which evokes their questions about print and draws them toward using print. We teach by confirming what children know—the knowledge they can grow on—as well as by supplying new information.

Children come to see themselves as they are seen by others. Do we see our students as learners or as mistake-makers? Do we see ourselves as nurturers of growth or as correctors of errors—as gardeners or as animated red pencils? We teach by what we see as well as by what we say.

References

Bissex, Glenda L. 1980. *GNYS AT WRK: A Child Learns to Write and Read.* Cambridge, MA: Harvard University Press.

Clay, Marie M. 1975. *What Did I Write?* Auckland: Heinemann.

Ferreiro, Emilia. 1982. "The Relationship Between Oral and Written Language: The Children's Viewpoints," In *Oral and Written Language Development Research: Impact on the Schools,* ed. Y. Goodman, M. Haussler, and D. Strickland. Urbana, IL: National Council of Teachers of English.

Giacobbe, Mary Ellen. 1981. "Who Says Children Can't Write the First Week?" In *Donald Graves in Australia: "Children Want to Write . . . .",* ed. R. D. Walshe. Rozelle, Australia: Primary English Teaching Association (Distributed by Heinemann).

Harste, Jerome, Carolyn Burke, and Virginia Woodward. 1981. *Children, Their Language and World: Initial Encounters with Print.* NIE Final Report. Bloomington, IN: Indiana University School of Education.

Read, Charles. 1971. "Preschool Children's Knowledge of English Phonology." *Harvard Educational Review* 41 (February): 1–34.

Remapping the Territory

1988

WHEN I DRIVE FROM MY HOME IN VERMONT INTO OTHER
states, I see "Welcome to Massachusetts" (or wherever) signs but
no black boundary lines painted across the highway as my road
map shows. The pavement isn't red, the countryside (except in
winter) isn't white, and the cities aren't yellow the way they are on
my map. If I had a topographic map, I would envision hills and
valleys. A geological map would show the rock underlying the
vegetation and pavement and buildings. But what map would
show the first splashes of brilliant foliage in the north and the still
lush September green of Connecticut?

The map is not the territory, as general semantics reminds
us, and the map never represents all the features of a territory.
Thus it's possible to make different maps of a territory, each corresponding to some characteristics, each incomplete.

Why worry about maps—literal or figurative ones? Because
we follow them. We act according to the way we see things, the
way we understand them to be. If the map you draw to guide me
to your house isn't accurate, I won't get there or I'll get there late.
If I'm told to teach grammar to improve my students' writing, I'm
being given an inaccurate map. The bridge between formal grammar and better writing—if there ever was one—is out. You can't
get there from here.

"On a visit to Leningrad some years ago," E. F. Schumacher
tells us in *A Guide for the Perplexed*,

> I consulted a map to find out where I was, but I could not make
> it out. From where I stood, I could see several enormous
> churches, yet there was no trace of them on the map. When
> finally an interpreter came to help me, he said "We don't show

churches on our maps." Contradicting him, I pointed to one that was very clearly marked. "That is a museum," he said, "not what we call a 'living church.' It is only the 'living churches' we don't show."

It then occurred to me that this was not the first time I had been given a map which failed to show many things I could see right in front of my eyes. All through school and university I had been given maps of life and knowledge on which there was hardly a trace of many of the things that I most cared about and that seemed to me to be of the greatest possible importance to the conduct of my life. I remembered that for many years my perplexity had been complete; and no interpreter had come along to help me. It remained complete until I ceased to suspect the sanity of my perceptions and began, instead, to suspect the soundness of the maps. (1977, 1)

The territory of education has its maps—its official descriptions and drawn boundary lines. But we are teaching in an exciting time when some traditional boundary lines are being redrawn, often through the vision and energy of writing projects.

One map showed two separate sovereign states, of people who teach writing and of people who write. But as writing projects got teachers writing themselves, the boundary lines blurred and parts of the once sovereign states overlapped. This new zone was populated by teachers who also saw themselves as writers.

On another map, the territory peopled by teachers of teachers was both separate from and north of—that is to say, superior to—the larger state peopled by teachers. Then writing projects came along and asked teachers to teach fellow teachers, so there grew up a whole new group of dual citizens. The boundary opened up.

Another map established the separate domains of teaching and learning, the former occupied, of course, by teachers and the latter by students. But teachers in writing projects and then more broadly in teacher education programs discovered that they could observe and study what was going on in their own classrooms. They could even enlist their students' help as co-researchers and interpreters. Teacher-research changed the map of teaching and learning. As teachers asked the research questions that were most important for *them* and found answers from which they and other teachers learned, they became empowered as knowers and crossed the once formidable border into Researchland.

Yet another map showed each subject area as an island in the Sea of Curriculum. Although students were required to write during their visits to most of these islands, the teaching of writing occupied a separate island.

That is, until writing-across-the-curriculum projects rebuilt the causeways that had washed away between these islands. Writing teachers, traversing them, became more aware of how written dialects varied from island to island, and subject area islanders came to share responsibilty for teaching writing in their dialects.

Now, in that curricular sea was the island of Reading and the island of Writing. But the more teachers themselves wrote and learned to confer with their students, the more they saw that writing needed to be responded to as reading—that writing *was* reading. And students and teachers started to look at reading materials as having been written by someone and therefore as open to the same questions that were being asked in writing conferences. So the map changed; Reading and Writing weren't separate islands any more. It is this particular change I'd like to look at more closely now.

Once you start looking for connections between writing and reading, they pop out at you. *Of course* reading and writing are closely connected; how could we ever have considered them otherwise? Where did we get that old map? Well, if you treat the published books we teach in schools as sacred texts and students' writings as defective exercises, there doesn't seem to be much connection between the two. There's a boundary wall between them. By "sacred text" I mean a book treated as having one interpretation of its meaning which is known to and taught by an authority—the teacher. Students may analyze the text to learn how good it is, in the case of a piece of literature, or may be expected to absorb the information presented by the text, in the case of, say, a science or social studies text. The book is to be approached as a text to be learned from and valued. This is hardly the way student papers have traditionally been approached by teachers. Students wrote papers as practice, "dummy runs" as James Britton calls them. Teachers read students' papers to evaluate and correct them. We assumed the papers were faulty and industriously hunted out the faults (apparently presuming that the students were quite blind to them).

When asked why she had turned away from further academic study, Pulitzer prize–winning historian Barbara Tuchman replied:

> One incident that confirmed my turning aside was the comment on a history paper I had handed in for Professor E. A. Whitney's History II (History of England during the Tudor and Stuart periods). The paper contrasted Thomas More and Machiavelli, as two voices of the renaissance. I poured into it all my enthusiasm for research, and my rather unpolished literary talents, and felt I had delivered myself of a shining product. It was returned with a stingy mark of A-, followed by the comment, scrawled in

large handwriting on my title page, "You spelled Philip with two *l*'s;" not a word about the content or composition or ideas, if any. (1986)

Children know that writing is to be read when their teachers respond first to the message and later to the mechanics of their writing—later, not never. Children know that writing is to be read when their writing is shared with other students—through conferences, oral readings, and classroom-published books. I've been amazed to find out how most children *love* to read their writing aloud to a group once they know that what they're trying to say, and not their errors, will be the focus of response. The parents of a fifth grader who had had such an experience with conferences commented that their daughter "loves to read aloud to us and her *reading* has increased tenfold." Children know that writing is to be read when they write letters to their teachers and their classmates, and these letters are answered in writing as part of the curriculum.

When writing is seen as reading material, and when reading is seen as having been written by someone, the boundary wall crumbles. Writing conferences treat students' pieces as reading materials. A teacher might receive pieces by summarizing them back to the student and asking if she had understood what they wrote. Peer conferencers might tell what they particularly liked about a piece and what they'd like to know more about or what confused them. These are reader responses, not corrector responses.

Some students I've observed have absorbed conference questions so well that they started applying them to the texts they were reading. One suggested Hemingway might have used more specifics in a passage in *The Old Man and the Sea.* In other classrooms, teachers started making the connections. A sixth-grade teacher said to her students as they were discussing a textbook, "You know, somebody writes every word you read." One student's eyes widened as he responded, "I never thought of that." How may his reading be changed now because he *has* thought of that? This insight may be the beginning of critical reading, for texts no longer appear as anonymous voices of authority. If he once believed—consciously or unconsciously—that anything in print must be true, he can begin to question that belief. He doesn't automatically believe everything people *say*; now he can see books as people saying things through print.

When Mary Ellen Giacobbe was teaching first grade, I visited her classroom, which contained shelves of books written by the children themselves. They had selected from their writing folders the pieces they considered their best, and after final editing conferences, Mrs. Giacobbe had typed them up in standard spelling and bound them in cardboard covers. These books—

most of them written at a higher reading level than first-grade basals—were a central part of her reading program. Her children knew these books had been written by someone.

In a third/fourth grade classroom I saw students make a list of all the things a favorite author, Bill Peet, must have known about in order to write one of his environmental stories. As writers themselves, these children had made lists of things they knew about in order to help them pick topics, so they were becoming conscious that the writing they read, like the writing they produced, was based on the author's knowledge.

Several years ago six schools participating in the Vermont Writing Program committed themselves to teaching writing schoolwide by a process-conference approach. Administrators as well as teachers participated in Writing Workshops. Many parents of children in these schools commented on changes they'd seen in their children's *reading*: the children read more, were more interested in reading, and were better readers, which was supported by their standardized test scores. The mother of a second grader in a tiny rural school noted that her child now "appreciated an author's ability." All of these schools held Young Authors' Fairs at which books written by students were displayed for parents and for students in other classes to read. I noticed custodians and secretaries reading too. Some schools invited a children's author to talk about his or her work. When this happened, students had lots of questions to ask on the basis of their own experience as authors, like "When you write, do you make a lot of revisions, too?" All these students, and their teachers, know that reading materials were written by someone.

Perhaps the ultimate sign that the boundary line between reading and writing has vanished will be the day a teacher returns a paper to a student to revise because it's boring for her to read. For years—forever?—we teachers have obediently read all student writing that came our way, fighting down our natural instincts as readers. What have we been saying to students by doing this, by putting ourselves in the role of correctors and evaluators rather than readers? Have we been collaborators in meaningless writing? Why haven't we expected better?

Part of the answer lies with the conditions for writing in schools. As long as teachers told students what to write about, when to write, and for how long, we felt obligated to read what they had been obligated to write. Or, I should say, we felt obligated to grade it, which involves reading of only a very narrow kind. Now that students participate in decisions about topics and about when a piece of writing is finished, teachers are freed to respond as real readers. The more students become real writers, the more we teachers can become real readers, interested in learning about our students and what they *do* know, through their writing.

We know that real writers revise, that good writing doesn't just spring full blown out of talent and inspiration. Real readers also revise, as anyone who's read a book or a poem more than once knows. A good reader isn't necessarily someone who at first reading fully understands a piece of writing—not if that writing has richness. Two readers who confess to revising are a Harvard professor and a first grader. Chris's first-grade teacher, Carol Avery, reported that

> Just as Chris reread his draft and made revisions to enhance the meaning, he also reread commercial materials and expanded and enhanced the meaning he generated from the printed page. A favorite book near the end of the year was *Hill of Fire,* the true story of the birth of a volcano in a farmer's field. One day Chris said, "The first time I read this book I was thinking about the volcano growing over the village but this time, I read it again, and I was thinking about volcanoes and how they begin. Like this one just started in a field." (1983, 33)

Dr. Lester Grinspoon of the Harvard Medical School said in a review of a book by Andrew Weil: "Like good cheese, *The Natural Mind* gets better with age. I learned more reading the book fifteen years after its original publication than I did in 1971."

To speak of revising in reading means we are seeing reading in some sense as composing. The meaning is not simply there in the text to be transferred to a reader—the same meaning to every reader or on each successive reading of the book. Because of what he'd learned the first time he read *Hill of Fire,* Chris was able to think about a different aspect of volcanoes when he read the book a second time. Dr. Grinspoon is surely not a poor reader or a poor learner. Things he'd thought about and learned in the fifteen years between his readings (which included what he'd learned from *The Natural Mind* the first time through) enriched his second reading.

Writers who revise know how long it takes to write something well—or even to be clear about what we want to say. We don't feel like failures if we don't get it right the first time. Readers need to know how long it may take to read something well and not feel they are failures because they didn't understand everything the first time, as standardized tests and perhaps teachers' questions seem to demand. As teachers, we need to be models of revisers for our students, showing them how to learn and improve, showing them that revising isn't just for kids who don't know as much as we do about writing and reading.

Now that we've opened up the boundary between reading and writing, now that we're looking for connections, we're seeing differently and so are our students. They're learning more because they can put to use in writing what they learn about reading, and use in their reading what they learn about writing.

Perhaps I've made the process of remapping sound easy and filled only with excitement. It is not easy. When we question old boundary lines, we are left with confusion, anxiety, and chaos until we see the outlines of a new map. Remapping is exploring, and facing the unknown takes courage for we may lose our way and even perish. Redrawing boundary lines may dispossess some citizens while leaving some countries scrambling to house new residents. New maps are not made overnight any more than good writing is.

Maps are not sacred texts though some people may treat them as such. Maps are composed and revised by human map makers. The map is not the territory but represents certain aspects or a certain view of it. The boundary lines that are drawn—the categories through which we conceive reality—are not themselves reality. Without the "Welcome to Massachussetts" sign, I wouldn't know I'd left Vermont. As Ken Wilber has said, "The ultimate metaphysical secret, if we dare state it so simply, is that there are no boundaries in the universe" (1981, 31).

References

Avery, Carol. 1983. Young Writers Learning to Read. Unpublished paper. Northeastern University.

Schumacher, E. F. 1977. *A Guide for the Perplexed*. New York: Harper & Row.

Tuchman, Barbara. 1986. *Radcliffe Quarterly*. 72(1): September.

Wilber, Ken. 1981. *No Boundary: Eastern and Western Approaches to Personal Growth*. Boston: Shambhala.

On Learning to Read Nature's Writings

1991

UNTIL RECENTLY I SEEMED TO LIVE TWO LIVES. FOR almost twenty-five years my home has been on a Vermont hillside where I've watched the sky for signs of weather, the mud around my pond for prints of deer hooves, the snow in the woods for records of creatures who disappear before I arrive on skis. At the same time I've been a teacher of reading and of writing, and an inquirer into the nature of literacy and how it's learned (or not quite learned).

That view of my life as double-stranded was changed by stones I picked up on a walk along an arroyo, a dry gully, in New Mexico. Some stones were pale grey with fine lines and wrinkles on them, others were light green embedded with little rods of deeper green—stones I could easily hold in the palm of my hand and later slip into my pockets. They weren't particularly beautiful, but I felt at once that the lines and wrinkles and rods were writings that told the histories of the stones, or would tell them to a more knowledgeable reader than I was. The writing beckoned me, yet I was literate enough only to sense I was in the presence of texts, not literate enough to read them.

At home, beside my rocky stream that never dries up, I sat under a huge hemlock tree. Looking at its bark, I realized it might also be a text to someone who could read it. The bark fibers had been pulled apart as though the wood growing inside over-stretched the stiff skin. The tree was not just a physical object any

153

more than a book is, except to an infant who chews on a corner of it and then casually drops it. Once the child learns that the marks in the book say something, she looks at the book differently and starts asking questions about what the marks mean. In the same way, being aware that the hemlock could be a text was my first step in becoming its reader.

The trunk of the hemlock was ringed with dead branches, black quills, skeleton arms with the fingers broken off. Once feathered with green needles, these bare bones were the tree's past borne into the present. Scars spotting the smooth birch trunks nearby were the only signs that they, too, once bore lower branches. I understood then why hardwood is clear and softwood is knotty. I'd never even wondered about it before I started reading these trees—never wondered why clear pine boards and cedar shingles were scarce or why maple and oak aren't knotty. The hardwoods prune themselves while dead evergreen branches stay in place, knotting each year's new layer of wood. So knots are older than the rest of the wood in a board—are old bones carried forward in time by the new growth built up around them. Perhaps carpenters are readers of boards.

When I dug holes for footings for a cabin high on the stream bank, I uncovered a golden layer of sand beneath the sprinkling of brown needles on dark woods' soil, and beneath the sand, clay as far as I could dig. Clay and sand are laid down by water. I tried to imagine the stream that I could cross on a few stepping stones, flooding this entire valley. How would it be long after I'm gone? A dry ravine like the arroyo in New Mexico?

To a digger who is a reader, the holes tell a story—an old story about flood and rebirth that carries me beyond this moment. Without a reader, there is no writing, either in nature or in print. "The unread story is not a story," says fantasy writer Ursula LeGuin, "it is little black marks on wood pulp." It is just a stone, a tree trunk, or a hole. "A novel, poem or play remains merely ink spots on paper until a reader transforms them into a set of meaningful symbols," says Louise Rosenblatt. "The literary work exists in the live circuit set up between reader and text."

In these woods in winter, the patterns of animal tracks recorded in the snow are writings as much as the straight tracks of letters across a page. I'm learning to read the pointed hoofprints of deer who share my trails, the chains of asterisks mice string from tree to tree, and the widely spaced, clustered ovals of leaping hares' feet. As I ski, I know that the woods, cold and silent as they seem, are full of life and stories. Writings are tracks; reading is the art of tracking, of re-imagining the movements of an animal or a river, of recreating the thoughts and images that traversed a writer's mind. For a reader, writing is visible evidence of the invisible. On a whale watch I learned about whale footprints that appear on the water after a whale has surfaced and resubmerged—round, slick spots caused by the turbulence of the vanished whale's movements.

On the beach at Plum Island I watched an arcing blade of beach grass—a green curve, twisted twice, that narrowed to a brown point. The wind, pushing against the blade, swept its tip around, inscribing arcs in the soft, dry sand. Then the wind, straightening the blade more upright, made it cut smaller figures—*m*'s and *w*'s, and tight little coils when the blade pivoted on its tip, driving it deeper into the sand. Inside a large arc was a decorated border, like an ornate Louis Sullivan arch. As I watched the brown stylus in the hand of the wind inscribe curves and angles—the basic shapes of our alphabet as well—I might have said, "You are not writing because you do not use the letters I know." But the grass has its own repertoire of shapes, defined by the length and sharpness of its blades, by the direction and strength of the wind, and by the texture of the sand.

Canoeists and fishermen read the water. Farmers read the sky for weather signs. Hunters and loggers read the woods, each for their own purposes. Geologists read rocks. We all read faces. When I see how many texts I might read, I realize my illiteracies and know how narrow my notion of literacy has been. For those who can read them, texts hold through time the momentary motions of wind and water, of plants and animals, and of the human mind. Reading, in one form or another, is what we all do to survive in and understand our worlds. It knits my life as a teacher together with my life as a learner in the woods.

How I Read Is Who I Am

1994

AS A READER, I USUALLY AM AWARE ONLY OF THE TEXT before me, not of the processes by which I transform those marks on the page into meanings in my mind. As a writer, my processes are more visible; their tracks flit across my computer screen and linger in my notebooks and discarded drafts. Writers like to talk about *how* they write, which is helpful to apprentices, while readers generally talk about *what* they've read. So how are students struggling, for example, with the demands of first-year college reading, to see what real reading looks like? It's not what's described by the traditional injunctions, implied or explicit, to start at the beginning and read to the end, getting every word in between correct and remembering every detail.

In the 1920s psychologists traced the eye movements of readers, revealing many forward leaps and regressions that reflected non-word-by-word mental processes. More recently, miscue analysis has opened a window onto the strategies of the reading mind as it searches for graphophonemic, semantic, and syntactic cues to making meaning from text. In preparation for visiting a colleague's class and talking with them about reading different kinds of material, I decided to observe and describe my own usually transparent reading processes as I read their textbook. I found myself, instead, looking through the textbook into a mirror: a startling and yet, on reflection, not at all surprising discovery. How I read is who I am. How else should I read? What had I expected? Something more impersonal and more directly text-driven. I believe that how I *write* is who I am. I value my voice in writing— but in reading? Well, there it was, all over someone else's pages!

I started near the beginning of the book, as the students had, with the chapter on how to write a summary, which triggered a

156

long-dormant association. As a high school sophomore, I'd struggled with the *Junior Précis Practice Pad,* under whose vile green cover lay pages of passages followed by blank lines—never enough lines to contain my summaries, in which I tried to say everything the original did but in fewer words. This frustration, remembered for over forty years, accompanied my reading of the chapter. So did the more positive, immediate memory of Ken Macrorie's voice, challenging impersonal authority, for I'd just come from re-reading the beginning of his *I-Search Paper.*

I soon found myself in difficulty with this chapter on writing summaries— a lecture from an impersonal authority to an impersonal audience on a topic not dear to my heart. Furthermore, the lecture format set up for me an expectation that I should receive and remember all the information delivered—more than I could digest at once. Some things I recognized as things I already knew how to do, but the authors couldn't know that so they threw the book at me.

How many times have I urged students to take control of the text rather than let it control them? Yet here I am, frustratedly playing victim. OK, it's up to *me* to sort out what I know from what I don't know rather than going along with the authors' assumption that I don't know much of anything. I don't have to stick with this page. Flipping through the chapter, I see that farther on the authors describe how to write a summary through examples, not just rules. That's more my learning style; I'll skip the rules. Somehow I've got to cut down on the information overload.

That feels better until I hit what for me is a bump that almost derails me. I'm asked to determine the author's purpose (for any given piece of writing) and to judge whether he has achieved it. How presumptuous! I've always choked on this one, and I do so again. I can't listen. I'm sure there's a way of asking readers to think about the point of a text without sounding as though they must be mind readers. It's hard enough to know the intentions of people we confront face-to-face.

I quit this chapter and scan the section of articles on gender issues, the section these students had chosen to read now, expecting I'll be more interested in both the topic and the presentations. I dip into several articles that are moderately appealing until "Ralph's Story" holds me. I keep wanting to know what's going to happen next in Ralph's unfolding, self-inflicted tragedy of postponing again and again what he truly wanted to do with his life for all the socially acceptable reasons like career advancement and financial security. I think about how the phrase "and then I could live my life the way I wanted to" builds pressure as it's repeated, like a refrain in a folk tale. I like it but suspect Ralph didn't repeat it nearly verbatim so many times as he told his story to his men's group. But that doesn't bother me; it just adds the dimension of speculating how the piece was constructed from the actual events. I think about my son, leaving for San Francisco to find more meaningful and challenging work in journalism but parting from his girlfriend to make the move. Is he driven by such disastrous ambition? No, that doesn't ring true. The story also connects to my life in terms of my own career choices, my stepping off the career ladder to take my own detours yet occasionally envying colleagues who have climbed it. I remember Ralph's story—the feeling of it, some but not most of the details, and its message for me about how we—women as well as men—can be driven to postponing our real lives in order to achieve a career goal to satisfy others whose love we may lose in the attempt. I don't remember much about how to write a summary.

So what does my reading experience mean? Has reader response theory released me from expecting reading to be transmission and myself a receiver? It hasn't released the students I talked with who were concerned about being distortion-free receivers. But what if we, as readers of nonfiction, start not from such expectations but from the notion that we are primarily persons rather than impersonal receivers? In my imagination I hear a chemistry professor colleague exclaim in distress, "But there are *facts!*" Yes, but I'll never remember *all* the facts in this chapter, and selecting the "important" ones isn't an entirely objective matter. Their sticking has something to do with the glue inside my head, not just with how the author has emphasized them. My reading of informational text seems just as colored by my nature and experiences as my reading of personal narrative. So how do I receive information when I can't be a blank receiver, when I can't avoid reacting to the material and to the way it's presented, when I inevitably filter it through my self?

Maybe when I start on a book I can give up the struggle to be an "objective" reader or the illusion of being one. I am not a reading machine. I'm full of preferences and prejudices, memories and expectations, information and ignorance. I choose what I want to learn from the books I choose to read. Or what I learn chooses me. How can I, as a Learning Specialist, help students receive what they're "supposed to" from their reading? Maybe they have to try to become someone else as readers—role-play being the readers they're "supposed" to be. But then who will be doing the learning from the text? All of us are doomed (or privileged) to live in our subjectivity. And what besides that subjectivity makes meaning out of the words on the page and drives me to read in the first place?

As often happens, an insight leads me into a thicket of questions. The more I live and read, the more I'm unsure what reading is. But I'm pretty sure it's as different from what we've traditionally taught it *should* be as the five-paragraph essay is from real writing. The students with whom I shared my experience as a reader confirmed this with confessions of their own wayward reading processes and the likenesses and contrasts among them. Hopefully we all felt a little freer to be ourselves as readers after the discussion. While this may make reading more liberating in life, will it serve them as students needing and wanting to be informed, even in their nontraditional college?

Confronting myself as a reader of student papers is even more disturbing. As I've become more aware of the individuality and variability of my own readings, I've tried to read papers a second time a day or two after my original reading to check up on myself. I've done this, too, with manuscripts I've reviewed for journals and publishers. Sometimes the papers appeared the same, and sometimes they didn't; papers I'd had an initial negative response to were the most changeable. (In fact, in the process of writing this essay, I reread that chapter on writing summaries and found the authors' voice considerably less dictatorial, and I noticed they addressed me at least as "you.") In the face of reader response theory, how can I still treat my students' papers as simple texts and myself as an all-knowing reader? There is no single complete reading, as Thoreau knew: "If you are describing any occurrence . . . make two or more distinct reports at different times. . . . We discriminate at first only a few features, and we need to reconsider our experience from many points of view and in various moods in order to perceive the whole" (Cameron 1989, 6).

As I've watched myself read and evaluate, I've thought more deliberately about how I want to respond. I've tried to write my responses to student papers as *my* responses rather than as proclamations from an impersonal and omniscient authority. But what do I do about grading, which is decidedly not construed as personal response? Fortunately my students will also be graded by other teachers who are different persons, and therefore different readers, than I am. But my greater awareness of myself as a reader makes me agonize in more different ways than I ever did before about assigning grades. Evaluation was simpler as long as I focused (so I imagined) on students' texts.

To grade student papers, Yancey and Elbow suggest in a recent article on holistic scoring, is to become a nonreader:

> The [real] reader brings multiple schemata to the text, and that's, we think, when we get a "rich" reading. . . . In holistic scoring, however, these multiple schemata of the reader are replaced by—and reduced to—the unified schema articulated in the guide. So the reading process of rating seems, more and more, unlike reading. (1994, 97)

I read eagerly, grateful for their corroboration of my experience.

Much of our system of education and evaluation, both lower and higher, assumes that texts can be transmitted simply and directly to readers, whether those texts are books or lectures or piles of student papers, and whether those readers are students or their teachers. The impersonality of reading is a myth, as students who challenge teacher interpretations and fairness may recognize. As more teachers question the myth, we can begin reconstructing relationships among teachers, students and nonliterary texts, talking with one another in ways that enlarge the meanings of learning and knowing.

References

Cameron, Sharon. 1989. *Writing Nature: Henry Thoreau's Journal.* Chicago: University of Chicago Press.

Elbow, Peter & Kathleen B. Yancey. 1994. "Holistic Scoring." *Assessing Writing,* vol. 1, no. 1.

What's a Teacher-Researcher?

1986

TO DISPEL SOME TRADITIONAL ASSOCIATIONS WITH THE word *research*, I'll begin by saying what a teacher-researcher *isn't.*

A teacher-researcher doesn't have to study hundreds of students, establish control groups, and perform complex statistical analyses.

A teacher-researcher may start out not with a hypothesis to test but with a "wondering" to pursue: "I wonder how much my students think about their writing outside of class. Vicky mentioned today that she mentally revises compositions on the bus coming to school. What about the others now that they're writing on their own topics?"

A teacher-researcher does not have to be antiseptically detached. He knows that knowledge comes through closeness as well as through distance, through intuition as well as through logic.

When a teacher-researcher writes about what she's discovered, she need not try to make her writing sound like a psychology textbook. Her audience is herself, other teachers, her students, their parents, her principal, maybe even the School Board—none of whom is likely to be upset by plain English and a personal style.

A teacher-researcher is not a split personality with a poem in one hand and a microscope in the other.

So what *is* a teacher-researcher?

A teacher-researcher is an observer. "Research means looking—and looking again," says Ann Berthoff. "This new kind of REsearch would not mean going after new 'data,' but rather REconsidering what is at hand. REsearch would come to mean looking and looking again at what happens in the classroom. We do not need new information; we need to think about the information we have" (1981, 31).

Marie Clay notes that "an interesting change occurs in teachers who closely observe. They begin to question educational assumptions" (1982, 91). One assumption that has been questioned by observers of children in classrooms (and of children before they enter school) is that learning to read precedes learning to write. Young children have been seen learning to read *while* they write.

A teacher-researcher is a questioner. "Why is Terry unwilling to read?" "How are poor writers and readers different from good ones? Do they have different concepts of what writing and reading are all about?"

Problems can become questions to investigate, occasions for learning rather than lamenting. Everything that happens in a classroom can be seen as data to be understood rather than causes for blaming or congratulating ourselves or our students. Teachers are constantly making evaluative judgments, but that evaluative frame of mind narrows our vision. "I really enjoyed asking questions of my students," one teacher-researcher told me, "because it gave me more insight into those students."

New approaches to teaching are no longer just risks but opportunities for learning. "What would happen if I had a reading workshop in this class and we shared and discussed books everyone chose to bring?"

A teacher-researcher is a learner. In my ideal school, principals ask teachers, "What did you *learn* today?" not "What did you *teach?*" Teacher-researchers have plenty to respond. (In this ideal school, principals are researchers, too.)

It's no accident that the notion of teacher-researchers grew out of writing projects that actively engaged teachers in *doing* what they taught. And whatever our subject matter, isn't it *learning* that we teach? Just as classrooms become writing workshops, they also become learning workshops, where both teachers and students see themselves as learners, where teachers are learning from children (as Lucy Calkins did in *Lessons from a Child*), where teachers ask questions of themselves as well as of students, where teachers are models of learners.

Finally, a teacher-researcher is not, as I have said, a split personality but *a more complete teacher.* Teachers have asked whether it's possible to teach and do research at the same time. The very question reflects the separation we feel between knowing and doing, and the division within our educational systems between those who "know" (such as college teachers, who have classrooms yet are not considered "classroom teachers") and those who "do" (the teachers who are not trusted, and often do not trust themselves, to know what and how they should teach). "I can't tell you how much difference researching has made to me," one teacher who had received some criticism of her teaching methods said to me. "I knew I was doing the right thing because I'd done the research." If teacher-research had been on the horizon ten years ago, I might still be in a classroom myself rather than having been driven to choose between knowing and doing.

References

Berthoff, Ann E. 1981. *The Making of Meaning*. Portsmouth, NH: Boynton/Cook.

Calkins, Lucy McCormick. 1983. *Lessons from a Child*. Portsmouth, NH: Heinemann.

Clay, Marie M. 1982. "Looking and Seeing in the Classroom." *English Journal* 71 (February): 90–92.

Why Case Studies?

1987

ABOUT TEN YEARS AGO I DID A CASE STUDY DESCRIBING five years of my son's development as a writer and reader. I had set out not to do a case study as such but simply to understand more about his learning in the only way I could see to do it. At the time I was a remedial reading teacher and had been for many years before that an English teacher. As a teacher and as a parent I was often, though unsystematically and sporadically, observing and thinking like a case-study researcher. Of course I was not conscious of this; it was simply the way I looked at individuals learning. Although I had not deliberated a choice of method in observing my son for what eventually became my doctoral research, I was soon enough confronted with professional opinions about my case-study approach that provoked me to become more aware of the meaning of the choice I had tacitly made. In my first interview for a teaching job in a college education department, my description of my case study was challenged with, "And what does that prove?" Yet to a faculty member at another college my work sounded "Wonderful—just like Piaget!"

After my study was published, I received letters from beleaguered doctoral students in need of support for their own case-study research. Some wanted comradeship and confirmation; one had been warned of the dire effects observation might have on her own child; another's proposal had reportedly been rejected because observation and description of events in a natural classroom setting was not considered rigorous research. It was clear

This essay was originally published in *Seeing for Ourselves: Case-Study Research by Teachers of Writing*, edited by Glenda L. Bissex and Richard H. Bullock. (Portsmouth, NH: Heinemann, 1987). The work of the teacher-researchers referred to here appears in that volume.

that the way people went about their research was a political issue, and one I felt increasingly responsible for understanding. I began to see how much was attached to that little matter of methodology—how it was related to what you researched and why you researched, to the kinds of questions you asked and the kind of answers that would satisfy, to the kind of relationship you felt with the subjects or objects of your inquiry, to your assumptions about knowledge and control, and even to your gender. The more I understood, the stronger the commitment I felt toward the implications of the research path I had been drawn to as a graduate student: observation of individuals in their normal environment.

It is not difficult to see why teachers have felt excluded from the world of traditional research. In the roundtable discussion among teacher-researchers, Peggy Sheehan recalls how the term *research* used to make her think of statistics and control groups, which "turned me off completely." These have been part of the accepted methodology. A researcher formulated a hypothesis—for example, that students who had worked on sentence-combining exercises would write sentences with more subordination than students without such training. The study would be designed around two equivalent groups of students, differing only in that one had no experience with sentence combining. The researcher would specify what was to be counted (in this case the number of subordinating constructions per sentence of student writing) to measure the effect of the training. A statistical analysis of these figures would indicate the mathematical probability that the differences found between the two groups could exist by chance. If the probability was slight, the researcher could conclude that the sentence-combining practice made a difference. Finally, a report would be written, reviewing other research as background, describing how the study was done and on whom, and presenting the results and interpreting them.

The language of such reports usually signals that they are addressed to other university researchers, not to classroom teachers. Listen to the beginning of an article reporting a study of some effects of audience on writing:

> Recent inquiry into the nature and process of writing reflects the influence of cognitive developmental psychology (Barritt & Kronn, 1978). As the field of rhetoric describes the rhetor as accommodating message to purpose and occasion (Perelman & Olbrechts-Tyecca, 1969), and as sociolinguistics portrays the language user as switching among alternate codes in order to express social or pragmatic meaning (Blom & Gumperez, 1972), so does the cognitive developmental model postulate that the course of communicative development is marked by growth in social cognitive acuity enabling communicators to adapt messages to the internal states of

their receivers (Flavell, Botkin, Fry, Jarvis & Wright, 1968). The study of audience awareness in written composition draws from these foundations (Britton, Burgess, Martin, McLeod & Rosen, 1975). (Rubin & Piché 1979, 293)

Now listen to how Nancie Atwell begins her account of research she conducted in her eighth-grade classroom:

> One afternoon last September five things happened within one fifteen-minute period that made me aware of a change at my school.
>
> Bob Dyer, principal at my school, put a Bette Lord novel in my mailbox with the note, "I think you and your kids might enjoy this."
>
> Underneath Lord's book was my copy of Francine Du Plessix-Gray's *Lovers and Tyrants*. Susan Stires, our resource room teacher, had returned it with the note, "God, can she write. Thank you for this."
>
> Under Francine was a message from Nancy Tindal, a kindergarten teacher: "Do you have some afternoon this week to respond to my Open House speech?"
>
> When I went back to my classroom, I found another note on the chalkboard from a former student who'd borrowed a novel the week before: "Hi. I was here, but you weren't. I love *Portrait of Jenny*. Who *is* Robert Nathan? Your favorite freshperson, Amanda."
>
> And finally, Andy, another freshperson, came by with a copy of an interview with Douglas Adams that he'd promised me over the summer.
>
> It was only because these things happened so one on top of another that I noticed and considered what was going on here. (1984, 240)

Atwell goes on to show us how her study grew out of reflections on her experience as a teacher rather than out of previous research studies. She speaks in a personal voice, as one individual to another, rather than in the impersonal tone of one authority to another. She describes what she has seen in her classroom, not an experiment she has designed. Her observations focus on the reading development of two of her students, and as she shows us some of the letters they wrote her about the books they'd read, we see how their individual character, and not just a particular kind of training, shapes their learning. Her description of their growth takes the form of a story, because it *is* through narrative that people are revealed in action, learning and growing. The significance of two students' development cannot be measured statistically; the meanings Atwell sees emerge from her understanding about learning.

The opening paragraphs of these two articles announce that their research has been conducted in different worlds for different audiences. But, you might ask, is a study that describes what a teacher has seen in his or her classroom really research or just a slice of life?

There are many ways of *re*-searching—of looking again at something. While the term suggests the existence of a single process (commonly known as the scientific method), the reality of researching is not so monolithic. The experimental, statistical approach was handed down to psychology through the physical sciences. Psychological research (which includes educational research) is being influenced today by methods from field studies of human cultures (ethnography) and studies of animals in their natural settings (ethology), methods that emphasize describing rather than counting, and observing rather than experimenting. Yet psychology has its own alternative research tradition: The work of Piaget and Freud originated in case studies. Piaget's first cases were his own three children, whom he observed as they played with household objects. Parents who recorded their own children's early speech and who were trained in linguistics pioneered our understanding of children's language development.

A research approach appropriate in physics, for example, may not be appropriate to the study of human beings. "No individual is exactly like another. . . . Here is a fundamental difference between living individuals and atoms. Two atoms of the same kind are identical in every respect—they are completely alike. Two living beings of the same species never are completely identical" (Weisskopf 1966, 218). Research methods appropriate to the study of living beings have struggled for respectability in the scientific community. As nature writer Sally Carrighar tells us,

> the field workers have had some handicaps in winning respect for themselves. For a long time they were considered as little better than amateur animal-watchers—certainly not as scientists, since their facts were not gained by experimental procedures: they could not conform to the hard-and-fast rule that a problem set up and solved by one scientist must be tested by other scientists, under identical conditions and reaching identical results. Of course many situations in the lives of animals simply cannot be rehearsed and controlled in this way. The fall flocking of wild birds can't be, or the homing of animals over long distances, or even details of spontaneous family relationships. (1965, 38)

Nor can the complex interactions in a classroom. Because living beings are unique, there are limits to the extent research enables us to predict and control the behavior of individuals, limits to the replicability of studies on living beings, and limits to the generalizability of the findings from such research.

Traditional research, even on human beings, has sought to make generalizations based on similarities in behavior. Large numbers of people are studied in order to wash out the effects of particular individual differences. Case studies, by contrast, enable us to see individuals as individuals; and when several individuals are compared, common traits as well as differences become apparent. "And what does that prove?" The challenge reasserts itself. Perhaps nothing to a scientist. But case studies can be seen to have their roots in the humanities as well as the sciences. As novelist Marjorie Kinnan Rawlings said, "A man may learn a deal of the general from studying the specific, whereas it is impossible to know the specific by studying the general" (1942, 369). Through the lives of literary characters, we come to know other people in a way that is different from the knowledge gained through abstraction and generalization. Literature assumes that the lives of its characters partake of human universals; if not, why should we feel engaged with its characters? While case studies do not provide the generalizability of large numbers or of experiments that can be readily duplicated, they are more true to life in their revelation of individuals in action and their reflection of the complexities of those individuals and actions.

Traditional research in education has tried to isolate and measure the effect of single factors, such as practice in sentence combining, over a large population of subjects. Case studies, by looking intensively at individuals, encompass *many* factors that influence their behavior. When a researcher's attention does not have to be directed toward identifying and counting a few predetermined items (such as subordinate clauses), it can be informed and guided by all the available data as they are gathered. Researchers can attend to information that is humanly significant though not mathematically measurable; they can, for example, ask a young writer what led to her choice of topic and thus understand the meaning of behavior from the child's point of view, not just tally it. "Quantitative research implies that one knows what to count," as psychologist William Labov points out, "and this knowledge is reached only through a long period of trial and approximation, and upon the basis of a solid body of theoretical constructs. By the time the analyst knows what to count, the problem is practically solved" (1972, 305).

Because science has aimed at establishing general laws that hold true regardless of context, experimenters—whether chemists or psychologists—have sought to remove the objects they study from the influence of any specific environment and observe them in pure form in laboratories. But human beings live and learn in particular contexts, such as families, classrooms, and cultures. We can neither live nor learn anywhere else. These contexts shape our experiences and what those experiences mean to us. Thus laboratory experiments do not yield a truthful, complete picture of human behavior, as Elliot Mishler argues in his wonderfully entitled article "Meaning in Context: Is There Any Other Kind?" In fact, a chemical laboratory and a psychologist's office are in themselves contexts, but contexts whose influence is not taken into account. When we observe individuals in their own environments, such as students and teachers in classrooms, part of what is observed *is* the context. Context then becomes, as Mishler puts it, a resource for understanding rather than an enemy of understanding. While the findings of research in context may be less universal, they provide a more holistic view than the results of laboratory experiments.

If case studies can't prove theories, they have the power to disprove them, as language researcher Jerome Harste argues:

> It doesn't take much to disprove a theory—just a single exception. . . . In language research all phenomena are significant: for the theories we develop—if they are to have power—cannot wallow in frequency or convenience, but universality. It is for this reason that the case study is a powerful theoretical tool. Because all phenomena demand explanation, theories developed from this source have more generalizability rather than less. Now that's the opposite of what the profession as a whole seems to think. But experimental studies don't have generalizability. Experimental studies assume that exception is handled when it is termed "error" and statistically it can be shown that it is "insignificant." They think by labeling it "error" and "insignificant," it is *error* and *insignificant.* And so they trick themselves and confuse the profession with generalizations and models which end up explaining the behavior of no one. I'm not trying to be radical; I'm just trying to bring some standards back to the profession. A good model, now don't you agree, ought to at least be able to explain the behavior of one child before it gets implemented. (1981, 368–69)

Research methods are not neutral tools; they embody assumptions about causation and control, about how knowledge is acquired, and about the researcher's relationship to what is being studied. For example, the many studies of the effectiveness of different methods of teaching reading, using experimental designs with control groups, assume that the crucial variable in learning is the instructional method, rather than the backgrounds or characteristics of the learners, the quality of interpersonal relationships in the classroom, or any other factor. This is a top-down vision of control, with students viewed as receivers of instruction, and learning as a product of external conditions. This assumption of external and controllable causation would seems to underlie all studies based on experimental and control groups. Yet observational studies of children's language development and preschool literacy have revealed children to be creators rather than mere recipients of their learning. This research approach allows individuals to be seen as actors and as interactors with their normal environment; it lets us view learners as in control of their own learning—as self-directed or interactive. It is no accident, then, that experimental research in education has focused largely on issues of *teaching* (i.e. external control), while observational studies have directed more attention toward *learning* (i.e. internal processes reflecting various educative influences including, of course, teaching).

Research methods also carry assumptions about the proper distance to be maintained between researchers and the objects of their research—about objectivity. We may envision a scientific researcher wearing a white coat, suggestive of the antiseptic environment of his researching. He may observe his material not directly but through specialized instruments, further maintaining his distance and objectivity. Reports of his findings contain lots of numbers which, being impersonal like the instruments, are seen as objective and factual, even though decisions about what to measure and why a particular problem is worth investigating involve subjective choices. There is knowledge to be gained through this kind of detachment, especially knowledge about the nonliving world, but objectivity is not the sole route to knowledge. There is knowledge of a different sort to be gained through empathy and involvement, through sympathetic observation that seeks to understand the experience of other persons rather than their behavior as objects. "An observer who is not emotionally involved will be unable to empathize, to see things from the perspective of his subject, and therefore will miss much of the meaning of what he sees. Consequently he will not know how to ask the right questions . . . and look in the right places," claims Paul Diesing in his book on research in the social sciences (1971, 280).

The notion that we can come to know people and human situations by distancing ourselves from them must seem as strange to a case-study researcher as to a literary storyteller, though both need at times to see their work through the eyes of an outsider in order to gain perspective. Our research tools should not hamper a full view of what we are researching. No single research design, no single angle of vision or set of assumptions, will enable us to see the whole picture. We need methods that will allow us to use our empathy and intuition while giving us the distance to look critically, as a writer alternates between the roles of involved creator and critical reader of his own work. Scientist Evelyn Fox Keller proposes the concept of "dynamic objectivity" in place of an objectivity that is static, detached, and controlling. "Dynamic objectivity aims at a form of knowledge that grants to the world around us its independent integrity but does so in a way that remains cognizant of, indeed relies on, our connectivity with that world. In this, dynamic objectivity is not unlike empathy, a form of knowledge of other persons that draws explicitly on the commonality of feelings and experiences in order to enrich one's understanding of another in his or her own right" (1985, 117). This sounds like the description of an ideal relationship between teachers and students as well as between teachers and their research.

The image of the white-coated scientific researcher I evoked was clearly, in my mind, that of a man. The differences between the research approach he stands for and the more humanistic, naturalistic, and holistic case study approach I have been describing seem to parallel the gender differences in values described by psychologists such as Carol Gilligan, who argues, in *In a Different Voice,* that male morality is based on separation, on distancing oneself from concrete situations in order to determine general, objective rules or principles, while feminine morality is based in a sense of connectedness to others and on judgments related to specific contexts. Since our society's concept of knowledge, and thus of the methods through which we gain knowledge, has been dominated by a scientific view embodying values associated with men, it is not surprising to find that women have been influential in opening up alternative research methodologies. In education, I think especially of Patricia Carini's important theoretical work on observation and description and the research she has nurtured for many years at the Prospect School in North Bennington, Vermont. Carini was one of the first to support teacher-research in this country, guiding detailed classroom observations, long-term studies of individual children, and reflective conversations with teachers. The history of case-study research in psychology, including education—to which Freud, Piaget, and Erikson have contributed—as well as case-study research in the natural sciences, is replete with work by women. Janet Emig, a pioneer of case-study research in writing, concludes her essay on "Inquiry Paradigms and Writing" by stressing the importance of our choice of paradigms. What is involved, she holds, is "no less than how we choose to perceive the world and how we elect to define what is distinctly human about human life" (1983, 73).

In a speech entitled "Passionate Scholarship," psychologist Barbara DuBois extends this theme:

> Our models of inquiry, of science-making, are also models of reality: they reflect how we conceptualize what is, what is to be known, and how it is to be known. . . . And the science-making that is in fact based in *different* values than those prevailing in the culture at a given time, and that thus attempts to discover, explore and explain *different* realities, tends to be

ignored—or attacked as "unscientific." This judgment can frequently be understood for what it really is: not in fact a judgment about science, but a charge of heresy.

We need to discuss not only *what* we see but *how* we see, realizing that choices exist. Research methods provide selective lenses, sharpening our focus on some things while excluding others from view. Methodologies and their acceptability also raise the political issue of who is empowered to see— to research, to know, and to be known as an authority. Let us enlarge our gallery of images of researchers to include not only the white-coated scientist but also the naturalist in the salt marsh observing wild ducks, the parent carefully recording a child's monologues, the ethnographer in New Guinea observing and experiencing life in a different culture, and the teacher listening to tapes of his own writing conferences. If such research is a slice of life, it is a slice of carefully examined life.

Composition teacher Ferguson McKay transcribes his conference tapes noting where he has talked too much and his instruction has silenced rather than informed a student. He is observing himself. His next writing conference will be different. "The research makes you become aware of what you do as a teacher," says fellow teacher-researcher Jacqueline Capobianco, although her case study focuses not on herself but on two of her junior high students who were having trouble with school. A secondary teacher who set out to observe peer conferences told me, "I never knew I did all that stuff until I started recording it." As a researcher myself and in my work with teacher-researchers, I have come to value the research *process*. In traditional research the emphasis has been on results; in observational research the process *is* part of the result. "I learned. I became a listener. I saw the kids as individuals. The biggest thing I learned was to become a listener," reports Capobianco (1985).

The *process* of observing even a single individual sensitizes us that much more to other individuals. As one teacher commented at the conclusion of her case study, "I focused on two children but I learned about twenty-three." In other words, the process of seeing in a certain way is generalizable. One characteristic of school that has obstructed this kind of seeing is an evaluative mind set that readily leads teachers to respond to individuals and situations—and also to themselves—in terms of praise or criticism, approval or disapproval: grading rather than understanding. Case-study research is directed largely toward understanding; such descriptive research requires us to suspend judgment and just look. Researching in this way can be transforming because it changes the way we see others and ourselves. It can, in the very midst of being carried on, change the teaching of the researcher without years of waiting for reports of someone else's results or decades of waiting for the effects of university research to trickle down to classrooms.

First-grade teacher Carol Avery, who has done case-study observations in her classroom for several years, comments:

> There are no big conclusions coming out of the classroom researching process, but there sure are some very powerful learnings. The whole process is open-ended. Researching does not bring answers but rather raises questions. It keeps opening doors. When I was a child I had a book and on the cover of that book was a little girl reading a book and so on. I think teacher researching is like that book cover. It offers the potential to keep going on and on. That's exciting to me.

Thus classroom-based case-study research by teachers becomes a powerful instrument for self-directed inservice education and staff development. Teachers can test out and put to use immediately what they learn through their research. In the course of studying her sixth-grade students' commonplace books, Judith Boyce discovered that some students interpreted her questions, written in response to their entries, as criticisms. Since criticism was not her intention, she investigated responses to which students were more receptive and changed her teaching accordingly. And since she wasn't conducting an experiment in which conditions had to be held constant, she was free to make such changes and then take them into account in her later observations. "The kind of knowledge of a living system that case study methods provide is essentially suited to enabling a person to work within the system," claims social scientist Paul Diesing (1971, 264). Participant-observers, he continues, test the objectivity of their knowledge by seeing whether it is understandable to others in the system (the students in one's classroom or other teachers, for example) and by attempting to act on it.

Certain aspects of learning can be studied *only* by people engaged in teaching as they research, argues British teacher and researcher Michael Armstrong:

> It is characteristic of classroom research, indeed of most research into the processes of intellectual growth, that it excludes the act of teaching from its techniques of investigation. The research worker observes children and teachers, either in a natural setting or in a laboratory, and seeks to interpret, and sometimes to control, their behavior, but without attempting to participate directly in their activity. It is often assumed that the demands of scientific objectivity force this exclusion upon us a researchers. Yet its effect is to deprive us of vital sources of information and understanding:

those sources which depend upon asking children questions and answering their questions, exchanging ideas with them, discussing each other's opinions, chatting and joking, trying to probe their intentions and appreciate their problems, offering help and responding to appeals for help—those sources, that is to say, which depend upon teaching.

It was for this reason that I felt I had to continue teaching children in order to investigate their learning. It seemed to me that the act of teaching was indispensable to the study of intellectual growth; that to refuse the opportunity to teach was greatly to diminish the prospect of understanding the understanding of children. My own interest, in any case, lay in discovering what insights were to be obtained from a research strategy that was almost the reverse of the normal procedure: from continuing, that is, to participate as a teacher in the life of the classroom while seeking to develop a degree of objectivity and a concern for close observation, analysis, and description adequate to the task of examining, in a more or less systematic way, the character and course of children's learning. (1982, 53)

Although teachers may teach sizable groups of students, it is only individuals who learn; and it is the learning of each individual for which teachers are ultimately responsible. Thus an awareness of the individuals in their classrooms and of the shapes of their learning is of prime importance for teachers. And when they closely observe individual students in their classrooms, they come to appreciate the many resources students utilize in learning, including but not limited to instruction. Teachers, and perhaps especially teachers of writing, are daily confronted with individual differences. Commercial teaching materials cannot take these differences into account; teachers cannot ignore them. Traditional research blurs and ignores individual differences in its search for similarities and generalizations. While generalizations can guide teachers, they may become meaningless or useless in any particular educational encounter with an individual student. As Kathleen Hogan remarks, case study "highlights the enormous complexity of one single writer, telling us how oversimplified most traditional approaches to teaching writing are" (1985).

Because of the varied individuals and settings and interactions involved, several teachers might carry on similar investigations in their classrooms and yet come out with different findings. This need not lead to discrediting some findings, as would be expected in the realm of traditional research with its demand for replicability, though we would want to be able to explain the differences. The main concern should be whether each teacher had learned something that will illuminate his or her particular teaching situation.

On the other hand, if several teachers engaged in similar studies learn similar things, this should not be viewed as uselessly reinventing the wheel. The analogy does not fit. A mechanical invention that can be used by anyone is not like the understanding that we must each gain for ourselves through our own thinking. Understanding is not transferable, however much the thinking of others contributes to our own. This is why Piaget said that to understand is to reinvent.

At its worst, teacher-research might reduce itself to an uncritical documentation of a teacher's preferences—a selective gathering of evidence to support a preconceived conclusion. This hazard is not unique to participant-observer research. Teacher-researcher Ferguson McKay comments that "if you observe yourself as well as the students, you can prevent slanting the evidence—getting the results you predicted" (1985). Observing what they *do* may lead teacher-researchers to discover what they *know*—to make their knowledge-in-action visible to themselves and to others.

A new body of educational research is already building up, one that informs us about teaching and learning from the inside, as experienced and understood by teachers and their students. May the result of this research never be the generation of even more prescriptions to be laid on other teachers but rather a heightened awareness on the part of the teacher-observers themselves and their colleagues and thus an increase in their responsiveness and effectiveness as teachers and learners. All the teachers I've worked with were changed by their own research.

References

Armstrong, Michael. 1982. "A Seed's Growth." In *What's Going On? Language/ Learning Episodes in British and American Classrooms, Grades 4–13*, ed. Mary Barr, Pat D'Arcy & Mary K. Healy. Portsmouth, NH: Boynton/Cook.

Atwell, Nancie. 1984. "Writing and Reading Literature from the Inside Out." *Language Arts* 61 (March): 240–52.

Capobianco, Jacqueline, Personal Communication. July, 1985.

Carini, Patricia. 1975. *Observation and Description: An Alternative Methodology for the Investigation of Human Phenomena*. Grand Forks: University of North Dakota.

———. 1979. *The Art of Seeing and the Visibility of the Person*. Grand Forks: University of North Dakota.

Carrighar, Sally. 1965. *Wild Heritage.* New York: Ballantine.

Diesing, Paul. 1971. *Patterns of Discovery in the Social Sciences.* Chicago: Aldine Atherton.

DuBois, Barbara. 1979. "Passionate Scholarship." Paper presented to the First National Women's Studies Association, Lawrence, Kansas.

Emig, Janet. 1983. *The Web of Meaning: Essays on Writing, Teaching, Learning, and Thinking.* Portsmouth, NH: Boynton/Cook.

Gilligan, Carol. 1982. *In a Different Voice.* Cambridge, MA: Harvard University Press.

Harste, Jerome, Carolyn Burke, and Virginia Woodward. 1981. *Children, Their Language and World: Initial Encounters with Print.* Final NIE Report. Bloomington: Indiana University.

Hogan, Kathleen. Personal Communciation. June, 1985.

Keller, Evelyn Fox. 1985. *Reflections on Gender and Science.* New Haven, CT: Yale University Press.

Labov, William. 1972. "The Study of Language in Its Social Context." In *Language and Social Context,* ed. Pier Paolo Giglioli. Harmondsworth, England: Penguin.

McKay, Ferguson. Personal Communication. July, 1985.

Mishler, Elliot G. 1979. "Meaning in Context: Is There Any Other Kind?" *Harvard Educational Review* 49 (February): 1–19.

Rawlings, Marjorie Kinnan. 1942. *Cross Creek.* New York: Charles Scribner.

Rubin, Donald L. and Gene L. Piché. 1979. "Development in Syntactic and Strategic Aspects of Audience Adaptation Skills in Written Persuasive Communication." *Research in the Teaching of English* 13 (December): 293–316.

Weisskopf, Victor F. 1966. *Knowledge and Wonder.* Garden City, NY: Doubleday, Anchor Books.

Annotated Bibliography of Selected Case Studies

These studies suggest the range of designs possible within the case-study approach. They look at single individuals or a small number of individuals or interactions among individuals. They also extend the notion of a case to the unit of a particular classroom or community. They demonstrate various ways of organizing and focusing case studies. The subjects of these studies are persons of many backgrounds and ages, from young children through mature adults, including a researcher studying herself.

Armstrong, Michael. 1980. *Closely Observed Children*. London: Writers & Readers Publishing Cooperative Society. (Available in the United States through Heinemann–Boynton/Cook.) A teacher-researcher documents the learning of children in one primary-school classroom during one year, with particular attention to writing, art, pattern, and play.

Atwell, Nancie. 1984. "Writing and Reading Literature from the Inside Out." *Language Arts* 61 (March): 240–52. An eighth-grade teacher examines the growth of two students' personal responses to reading.

Bissex, Glenda L. 1980. *GNYS AT WRK: A Child Learns to Write and Read*. Cambridge, MA: Harvard University Press. A parent-researcher describes one child's development, from age five through ten, as seen through his activities at home and at school.

Calkins, Lucy M. 1983. *Lessons from a Child*. Portsmouth, NH: Heinemann. While this study focuses on the writing development of one third grader, it also discusses the teacher and the classroom.

Carini, Patricia F. 1982. *The School Lives of Seven Children: A Five Year Study*. Grand Forks: North Dakota Study Group on Evaluation, University of North Dakota. Carini documents seven modes of learning in seven children, prekindergarten through third grade, and includes useful suggestions for other researchers on ways of looking at learners.

Emig, Janet. 1971. *The Composing Processes of Twelfth Graders*. Urbana, IL: National Council of Teachers of English. This pioneering studying of composing examines one writer in depth and seven others more briefly.

Field, Joanna. 1958. *On Not Being Able to Paint*. Los Angeles: J. P. Tarcher. In looking at her own struggles and discoveries as a learner, this psychoanalyst and educational researcher raises some fundamental questions about the creative process and about education.

Heath, Shirley Brice. 1983. *Ways with Words: Language, Life, and Work in Communities and Classrooms*. Cambridge: Cambridge University Press. The cases in this ethnographic study are two communities—a black working-class and a white working-class community—contrasted as environments in which children learn oral and written language at home and in school.

Johnston, Peter H. 1985. "Understanding Reading Disability: A Case Study Approach." *Harvard Educational Review* 55 (May):153–77. This close look at three adult readers, through interviews and observations, reveals much about social and psychological contributions to reading failure.

Paley, Vivian G. 1981. *Wally's Stories.* Cambridge, MA: Harvard University Press. A fascinating exploration of children's thinking by a teacher-researcher who, through listening closely to her kindergartners' conversations, appreciates how they interpret their world.

Perl, Sondra and Nancy Wilson. 1986. *Through Teacher's Eyes: Portraits of Writing Teachers at Work.* Portsmouth, NH: Heinemann. The authors present in-depth studies of six very different teachers and their classrooms, both elementary and high school.

Schaefer-Simmern, Henry. 1948. *The Unfolding of Artistic Activity.* Berkeley: University of California Press. This work, with an introduction by John Dewey, offers intriguing studies of the artistic processes and development of mental defectives, delinquents, refugees, and business and professional people.

Selfe, Lorna. 1979. *Lorna: A Case of Extraordinary Drawing Ability in an Autistic Child.* New York: Harcourt Brace Jovanovich. This fascinating document raises the question, Why study a rare if not unique case? and suggests some reasons for doing so.

On Learning and Not Learning from Teaching

1988

AN EVENT FROM MY HIGH SCHOOL TEACHING YEARS returns in memory again and again to nudge me about what I didn't learn from it. When it visits me, I feel both a kind of warmth and enlightenment because of what *did* happen, and a sadness and puzzlement that this was an isolated incident, an anomaly. It was as though a door had opened and then just as quickly closed. Perhaps it is time now—some twenty-five years later—to try to hear what it has to teach me.

I had, back then, put together a dittoed booklet of Chinese and Japanese poems in translation for one of my English classes—I believe it was the Juniors. This was one of the poems:

JADE FLOWER PALACE

The stream swirls. The wind moans in
The pines. Grey rats scurry over
Broken tiles. What prince long ago,
Built this palace, standing in
Ruins beside the cliffs? There are
Green ghost fires in the black rooms.
The shattered pavements are all
Washed away. Ten thousand organ
Pipes whistle and roar. The storm
Scatters the red autumn leaves.
His dancing girls are yellow dust.
Their painted cheeks have crumbled
Away. His gold chariots

And courtiers are gone. Only
A stone horse is left of his
Glory. I sit on the grass and
Start a poem, but the pathos of
It overcomes me. The future
Slips imperceptibly away.
Who can say what the years will bring?

Tu Fu (A.D. 713–770)
translated from the Chinese by Kenneth Rexroth

And this was the homework assignment I gave:

Read the poem through slowly several times. Write a paper of 1–2 pages describing as precisely as possible what went on in your mind while reading the poem. What did you see in your imagination? Or hear? What associations or memories came to mind? What trains of thought or questions? If something that occurred to you seems foolish, don't just dismiss it but try to think *why* it came to mind (there may be good reason). State which lines or words in the poem led to your impressions. DO *NOT* EXPLAIN WHAT THE POEM "MEANS"!

The papers were astonishing. Every student in that class, including certain boys who generally had trouble saying much of anything about literature, wrote a paper which both interested me and conveyed a clear empathy with the mood of the poem. I loved those papers. If Xerox machines had existed then, I might have had the sense to copy them to keep. As it was, I joyfully read the papers aloud to the class and returned them. And returned to my usual English teaching.

I sensed that some revelation had occurred, but what exactly was it, and what was I to do with it? Perhaps it was the fact that I couldn't see what to do with it that prevented me from probing what it was. What did I teach next that year—was it *Macbeth* or *Lord Jim*? In any event, it was no doubt something from the canon, a piece of Western literature that already had a load of certified interpretations attached to it, unlike that ancient Chinese poem about which I knew nothing, which came to me free and clear of critical baggage—a poem out of a different culture and time that I could not hope to recreate as interpretive context. I see now that what was different in that teaching moment wasn't just the responses of my students, or the kind of assignment I gave, but my relationship to the literature we were reading.

As I read over the assignment now, I think of Peter Elbow's "movies of the mind," but Peter Elbow certainly wasn't writing any books back then to keep me company. Louise Rosenblatt was a voice crying in the wilderness, and I taught in the city. Twenty years or so later the notion and practice of reader-response approaches to teaching literature were widely published. I didn't, at the time, hear anyone who could help me make sense of what had happened in my classroom. This is something else reflection on this incident has taught me: You can't do it alone—or at least I couldn't. Learning from experience is not automatic; it requires certain conditions.

I've called this incident an anomaly. I didn't know then what one of the teacher-researchers I've worked with more recently has taught me: that an anomaly is the beginning of inquiry. An anomaly raises a question to be pursued, challenges us to account for it, and likely challenges the very assumptions in terms of which it appears as an anomaly—in this case, my assumptions about interpreting literature which, in a sense, I had set aside in making that assignment. I reaped the results and turned away from them as an oddity to be treasured but kept separate so as not to confuse the rest of my teaching. The seeing amazed but did not empower me as it might have if teacher-research had existed then, if I could have been a student in my own Case Study course, and if—even with support—I'd had the courage to ask the meaning of that incident.

Only now have I come to consider seriously what I might have done differently then, how I might have responded to what I saw. I think I would not only share with my students my response to those papers (as I did) but find out what happened to them when they were doing the assignment, find out what they thought they learned, find out from them how they saw this sort of associative, rather than analytical, understanding. I would consider with them how we might build on this experience in the class. If I had done this, I would not have been alone.

"And what does that prove?" one faculty member challenged me during an interview for my first full-time college teaching job. I had just finished telling him about my dissertation, a longitudinal study of my young son's writing and reading development. Nobody on my dissertation committee had asked me that question, nor had I asked it myself in all the years I collected and pored through data, searching for patterns. I was confronted with an alien view from which—I too keenly grasped—my research appeared worthless. I don't remember what I answered then, across the gulf between us, but I have not forgotten the question.

What had I proven? I hadn't set out with a hypothesis to test in order to prove something to somebody. I'd started out with a curiosity whetted by transcripts of children's talk I'd read and thought about in Courtney Cazden's

Child Language course when I was carrying the child I would later (unknown to me then) study. When that child started to write and a former high school English teacher of mine put me in touch with Charles Read's work on invented spelling, I was even more fascinated by what I was seeing. I guess I was so busy learning that I didn't worry about proving anything. Here was this wonderful growth unfolding in front of my eyes, and I wanted to truly see it. I wanted to probe it in places so I could know more than was on the surface. I was constantly looking for patterns as I reviewed piles of writings, tape recordings, and notes. Again and again, I asked "What does this mean?" What does it mean that Paul is reinventing writing conventions from other times and cultures? What do changes in the questions he asks about print mean in terms of his growing understanding? What do the similarities and differences I see between Paul's literacy efforts and those of my remedial reading students mean for my teaching or other people's teaching? As I look at it now, the question of what I proved appears thin and pale and irrelevant beside the richness of all the meanings I discovered, of all that I learned. I wouldn't have had any trouble answering the question, "And what did you learn?"

Like the incident with my high school English class, this interview question has returned in memory many times to nudge me. I'm hearing its lessons more clearly since I've become a teacher of teacher-researchers.

I remember getting together with my first group of Case Study students—teachers who were doing research in their own classrooms—at the end of winter, after they'd been gathering data for months. As we went around the table where we sat and each spoke, there was an accumulating disappointment that they had not arrived at any monumental conclusions and a relief to find that others had the same experience. I did not feel disappointed and realized clearly then that their expectations and mine, neither of which had probably been made explicit, were different. What *did* I expect? Why did *they* expect to come to earth-shaking conclusions? What *is* to be learned from this sort of research? Only after working with teacher-researchers for several years can I see how little I knew, and even now know, about it. I'm just beginning to learn from my students what teacher-research is for them—or, I should say, what together we make it.

What do insights about our own teaching, like the following ones, prove?

- A teacher-researcher who had been listening to tapes of some of her writing conferences this year told me she never realized how directive she sounded.
- Another teacher, who set out to study several of her advisees, wrote me that her case study was "still changing and growing. Now, instead of

seeing my story and the student stories as separate, I can see that the student stories help to tell a bigger story—the story of an advisor/instructor struggling to define her role in working with students in academic difficulty."

- I compiled a list of the central research questions each of my Case Study students had defined for himself at the beginning of this year only to realize that these "central" questions often didn't convey as much to me about their research as did their stories of what had led them to ask the questions.

It would be hard to say what any of these insights "prove," yet they have changed our teaching.

I don't know that any of the dozens of teacher-researchers I've worked with have felt they came up with earth-shaking conclusions. I also can't think of one who felt that she or he hadn't learned something from doing the study. If they learned less than they sought to learn, they also learned more; for they learned how to observe, they learned "why" they were teaching the way they were, they learned to reinterpret some events through seeing them from their students' points of view, and they learned, among other things, that they could trust their own powers of learning. Their excitement about these insights filled the void once left by the lack of earth-shaking conclusions.

How could I know what teacher-research was about until my students told me what they were learning and what effects that learning had? The word *research* suggests the researcher is "proving" something, frequently to someone else. (What do we call, then, the "research" which has "proved" something that was later disproved by other research?) While "research" has the right literal meaning—to look again—its connotations may be wrong for what teachers are doing. We are not researchers in other people's classrooms, looking for proofs or generalizable truths, but reflective practitioners in our own classrooms, searching for insights that will help us understand and improve our practice. That does not exclude us from finding generalizable truths, although we may not know when we have found them.

We don't yet know exactly what teacher-research is because we're just exploring it—what forms it can take, what purposes it can serve. What teacher-research means to me and to the teachers I work with may not be exactly what it means to other teachers. We can let these differences enrich our exploration of what teacher-research is, or we can try to narrow it at once by arguing what it isn't. Let's not bind its feet while it's still growing.

In writing this piece I re-searched moments in my life—looked at them again to reflect upon their meanings. What do they prove? What does any story, any biography or autobiography, or Frost's "Death of the Hired Man" or Shakespeare's *Macbeth* prove? We show our proofs to other people so that they may be convinced. We share our meanings with each other in the hope that the meanings of one person's story will help others seek and find the meanings of theirs.

Small Is Beautiful

CASE STUDY AS APPROPRIATE METHODOLOGY
FOR TEACHER-RESEARCH
1990

MY TITLE IS TAKEN FROM E. F. SCHUMACHER'S *Small Is Beautiful: Economics as if People Mattered.* "Small is beautiful": We live in a society where bigger is seen as better not only for business but often for research as well. (Is there a connection?) The larger the number of subjects, the more reliable the results. Numbers generate truth—or do they? "Economics as if people mattered": Why not research as if people mattered—as if students and teachers mattered more than externally imposed programs, as if classrooms were centers of humane activity rather than production lines?

"Appropriate methodology" echoes the concept of "appropriate technology"—tools compatible with their contexts. For a teacher to teach one class by an approach he believes in and another class by an approach he is at least less convinced about, in order to have a control and an experimental group, is inappropriate methodology. For a teacher to observe and inquire into and reflect on the events and persons in his classroom is to use methodology in keeping with his role as an educator—methodology that does not alienate him or intrude on his teaching.

I am not asserting that case studies are appropriate solely and exclusively for teacher-research as a sort of small-scale version of "real" research. Case study has a long tradition as a major way of knowing and of teaching in a number of disciplines and professions. Nor am I suggesting that case studies are the *only* route to knowledge, for teachers or for anyone else.

185

A *case* can be a single individual in her environment, or several such individuals, or an interactive group such as a writing conference group, or a special project as viewed through a close observation of responses from the individuals involved in it. A *case study* I see as a reflective story of the unfolding, over time, of a series of events involving particular individuals. The persons studied are regarded as full human beings, having intentions and making meanings, not merely "behaving." The researcher includes these intentions and meanings in the meaning that she makes of the story and, as interpreter if not also as actor, is herself a character in it.

What can we learn from a single case? What can we learn from Angelou's *I Know Why the Caged Bird Sings* or from Conrad's *Lord Jim*? Why is the study of individual cases an essential part of the training of lawyers, physicians, psychotherapists, social workers, and business managers? What do we learn from reading a biography or an autobiography—from one life? Or from studying an historical case like the French Revolution? Consider the expression "getting down to cases," meaning getting down to the specifics that really matter in a situation.

Donald Schön in *The Reflective Practitioner*, a set of case studies of professionals reflecting in action, speaks of cases as "exemplars" (a term he borrowed from Thomas Kuhn). An exemplar is a situation or experience seen as similar to a subsequent one and thereby instructive about it, or an example of a way of thinking about something that is applicable in another situation. Professionals learn to see new problems as similar to ones they've already encountered. As they build a repertoire of exemplars, they become more knowledgeable, resourceful, and successful. Schön's comments suggest the value of case studies as exemplars not only for the researcher herself but for others: teachers, teachers in training, and other researchers.

Science has accustomed us to looking for cause and effect relationships in order to predict and control behavior. As psychologist Robert White observed about the individual lives he studied, "Many forces operate at once on a given personality, producing an elaborate lattice of interconnected events rather than a simple model of cause and effect" (1952, 329). Looking closely at an individual, we see that lattice. The end of a case study should be insight, not control—an understanding of others and of ourselves that helps us to be educators, not manipulators.

As educators we teach individuals in the context of groups. In the statement preceding my case study *GNYS AT WRK: A Child Learns to Write and Read*, I stressed the importance to education of the individual and his context:

> Except in the form of an individual person's reading a particular text or writing a particular message in a specific situation, reading and writing do not exist. "Reading" and "writing" are abstractions, convenient abbrevia-

tions enabling us to *refer* to certain kinds of human activities. These terms can also lead us to believe that what they refer to has a concrete existence. For example, we are told the "reading" level of various groups of children, although *groups* do not read. We are not told what these individuals have been asked to read or under what conditions, nor are we reminded that "reading" tests can only indirectly measure "reading." Unless we keep reminding ourselves that "reading" and "writing" are abstractions and abbreviations, we may come to believe—or, just as dangerously, to act as though we believe—in their disembodied existence.

Furthermore, someone reads or writes something *for some purpose*. We do not read for the sake of reading, nor write for the sake of writing. Consider why you are reading this now. "Reading" and "writing" are meaningless as well as disembodied if they are regarded as ends in themselves, not as means of learning, imagining, communicating, thinking, remembering and understanding.

We cannot always specify who is reading or writing what under what conditions and for what purpose—but we sometimes must, to bring us back to the only concrete reality there is. Grade levels, test scores, and statistical analyses of "reading" and "writing" are very abstract—are abstractions about abstractions—although they may appear reassuringly tangible. Only individuals read and write particular messages, under particular conditions. (1980, xiv)

Traditional, empirical science has accustomed us to seeking meanings in similarities, in generalizations. It is of no relevance to the laws of gravity whether the falling apple happens to be a Red Delicious or a Granny Smith. But in the understanding of human beings, differences do make a difference. So Peter Johnston, leading us to understanding reading disability through three case studies, explains: "Case studies were used on the assumption that there can be substantial individual differences in experience and in important dimensions of behavior (both overt and covert) which are as critical as the commonalities between individuals" (1985, 155). Statistical studies cause differences to appear as one-dimensional, as differences in degree, blurring the qualitative differences among individuals which teachers confront daily in their classrooms. There is reason to believe diversity should not be viewed as an inconvenience or an anachronism but, as in biology, as conferring survival and evolutionary benefits, which we dismiss at our peril. If our students were all alike, wouldn't we be bored to death?

Harold Rosen has observed another value of case studies:

Intellectual life is more and more haunted by a dilemma. On the one hand, it produces powerful propositions, abstractions and principles which offer the seductive possibility of making sense of a chaos of evidence. On the other hand, such a formidable armoury often leaves a sense of dissatisfaction. The sense of the actual, the particular, the idiosyncratic, the taste of direct experience seems to get lost or buried or made to appear irrelevant. This is particularly true when we ourselves are the object of our study. The demand for "case studies" arises from that powerful feeling that there is more to life than generalizations can encompass. We are always greedy for accounts of "actual" experience which give off that special aroma of the authentic. Such accounts are neither atheoretical nor anti-theoretical, for always, however implicit, there are principles and assumptions at work. So it is with all narratives of personal experience, including narratives of teaching experience. (1988, 171–72)

Case studies can only disprove the universality of generalizations; they cannot generalize from one case to many. Conversely, we cannot presume to know an individual in terms of generalizations drawn from groups. Marjorie Kinnan Rawlings in *Cross Creek* put it this way: "Thoreau went off to live in the woods alone, to find out what the world was like. Now a man may learn a deal of the general from studying the specific, whereas it is impossible to know the specific by studying the general" (1942, 359).

Those of us who love and teach literature know that. We appreciate what can be learned from a single case—from *I Know Why the Caged Bird Sings* or from *Lord Jim*. "The more particular, the more specific you are, the more universal you are," writer Nancy Hale is quoted as saying (Murray 1990, 133). A similar sense of the illuminating quality of the particular led William James to claim that to study religion one should study the most religious man at his most religious moment.

Movement from the particular to the *general*—the way of science—is a different mode of thought than movement from the particular to the *universal*. "Instead of a movement of mental abstraction from the particular to the general, there is a perception of the universal reflected in the particular. . . . The universal is the unity of the intuitive mind. The general is the unity of the intellectual mind" (Bortoft 1986, 43). By disciplining and trusting the intuitive mind, as well as the logical and linear mind, we approach a more holistic research.

Jerome Bruner, in *Actual Minds, Possible Worlds*, speaks of two modes of thought:

I discovered that there were two styles of approaching narrative, a discovery pressed upon me while I was teaching concurrently two seminars on narrative. One of them, at the New School for Social Research, was dominated by psychologists. The other, at the New York Institute for the Humanities, was made up of playwrights, poets, novelists, critics, editors. Both seminars were interested in literary questions. Both were interested in readers and in writers. Both were interested in texts. But one group, the psychologists, was dedicated to working "top-down," the other to working "bottom-up". . . .

Top-down partisans take off from a theory about story, about mind, about writers, about readers. The theory may be anchored wherever: in psychoanalysis, in structural linguistics, in a theory of memory, in the philosophy of history. Armed with an hypothesis the top-down partisan swoops on this text and that, searching for instances (and less often counter-instances) of what he hopes will be a right "explanation." In skilled and dispassionate hands, it is a powerful way to work. It is the way of the linguist, the social scientist, and of science generally, but it instills habits of work that always risk producing results that are insensitive to the contexts in which they were dug up. . . .

Bottom-up partisans march to a very different tune. Their approach is focused on a particular piece of work: a story, a novel, a poem, even a line. They take it as their morsel of reality and explore it to reconstruct or deconstruct it. They are in search of the implicit theory in Conrad's construction of *Heart of Darkness* or in the worlds that Flaubert constructs. . . . The effort is to *read* a text for its meanings, and by doing so to elucidate the art of its author. They do not forswear the guidance of psychoanalytic theory or of Jakobsonian poetics or even of the philosophy of language in pursuing their quest. But their quest is not to prove or disprove a theory, but to explore the world of a particular literary work.

Partisans of the top-down approach bewail the particularity of those who proceed bottom-up. The latter deplore the abstract nonwriterliness of the former. The two do not, alas, talk much to teach other. (1986, 9–10)

Because there are different modes of thinking, of knowing, of understanding, there are different modes of researching. Since these different modes of thought coexist in the human mind, let us hope they can also coexist in the research community. Case study is a genre of research—most effective, I believe, for understanding (not controlling) human beings, most suitable for studying the human acts of composing and of interpreting literature, and most appropriate for teachers of English, whose commitment to and education in literature and writing, and whose personal engagement with students would seem to create an appreciation of case study. It seems altogether fitting, then, that teachers who know the ways of interpretation should interpret the texts of their own classrooms, and that teachers who understand the value of story should see and tell the stories of themselves and of their students. If any mode of inquiry speaks from and to the heart and soul and mind of our professions, it is surely case study.

References

Bissex, Glenda L. 1980. *GNYS AT WRK: A Child Learns to Write and Read.* Cambridge, MA: Harvard University Press.

Bortoft, Henri. 1986. *Goethe's Scientific Consciousness.* Tunbridge Wells, UK: The Institute for Cultural Research.

Bruner, Jerome. 1986. *Actual Minds, Possible Worlds.* Cambridge, MA: Harvard University Press.

Johnston, Peter H. 1985. "Understanding Reading Disability: A Case Study Approach." *Harvard Educational Review* 55:153–77.

Murray, Donald. 1990. *Shoptalk: Learning to Write with Writers.* Portsmouth, NH: Boynton/Cook.

Rawlings, Marjorie Kinnan. 1942. *Cross Creek.* New York: Charles Scribner.

Rosen, Harold. 1988. Postscript to *And None of It Was Nonsense* by Betty Rosen. Portsmouth, NH: Heinemann.

Schön, Donald. 1983. *The Reflective Practitioner: How Professionals Think in Action.* New York: Basic Books.

Schumacher, E. F. 1973. *Small Is Beautiful: Economics as if People Mattered.* New York: Harper & Row.

White, Robert W. 1952. *Lives in Progress.* New York: Dryden.

Teacher-Research

SEEING WHAT WE ARE DOING
1994

THIS YEAR LAURA PITTS, ONE OF THE TEACHER researchers I'm mentoring, is studying the effects on her students of a new global studies curriculum she's team-teaching. Recently she wrote me:

> You know, if it hadn't been for this case study project, I don't think I'd have appreciated the changes in Andrea nearly as much, nor would my other students have noticed the changes in themselves that my questioning has brought into focus. Would I have such a visible record that Andrea really has changed inside and out? Without my periodic questioning and faithful recording and analysis—which she's seen all along the way—would she write pages for me in response to the big inquiries, or forge a friendship with me and my team teacher beyond the classroom? She never did before, according to her previous teachers and the support staff of our school.

An inquiring frame of mind, relatively simple research tools—such as a double-entry notebook for recording events and reflecting on them—and audio or videotapes of classroom events and of interviews with students enable teacher-researchers to see things that otherwise might not be evident. Dora Glinn, a special educator, and John Goekler, a reading teacher, cotaught and co-researched a first grade. They reported that they wouldn't have listened to the children's conversations among themselves if they hadn't been doing research; instead, they probably would have been concerned with keeping the kids quiet. As researchers, however, they had videotaped a number of activities in their classroom, and the more they reviewed one particular tape, the more

191

they saw—for example, how the children were actually supporting one another's learning. Although these conversations were going on right under their noses, they could easily have heard them as only noise interfering with work. This kind of research requires a certain frame of mind—a readiness to hear and to see, a capacity for suspending, or being jolted out of, our usual interpretations of classroom events.

Looking and Seeing

When you start researching—looking again, which is often actually looking for the first time—there's no limit to the kinds of things you'll see. Some time ago, as I was responding to student papers, I caught myself doing what I'd doubtless done for many years without questioning it. I found I was responding differently to students whose papers were quite accomplished than I was to students whose language and thinking seemed unclear. To the more accomplished writers, I responded as a reader and as a colleague: I talked mostly about their ideas, sharing my own thoughts on issues that obviously interested me, too. To the writers of the more troublesome papers, I responded as an instructor, helpfully describing how they might improve their organization and explanations. I wish I knew what triggered my recognition of that difference. Possibly it was some combination of internal readiness and an external prod such as reading other research. Anyway, I stopped my pencil in its tracks as I thought of how I must sound to Alyssa, who was just orienting herself to American academia, juxtaposed with how I might be heard by Maureen, an already accomplished writer and historical researcher. I'd been responding to the Maureens as thinkers, as persons with something interesting to say. In contrast, I realized, I'd been indirectly telling the Alyssas that they had nothing to say that I took seriously enough to converse with them about, and I realized how lifeless and demeaning my "helpful" responses were. The snowball effect on the Alyssas of years of such responses, not only from me but surely from many other teachers—none of us taking their ideas and interests seriously—may have been devastating.

What if, instead of instructing them from behind my teacherly desk, I stepped out and sat with them, conversing? I decided to find out. One thing that happened was that responding to them became less tedious. Changing my role enabled me to see them differently, less negatively, as I looked for ideas, even incomplete ones, to discuss. What was in their papers, I discovered, was determined by the reader as well as by the text. As soon as I assumed an instructor's role in reading them, my vision and response narrowed. Unlearning this role has taken time, and still I catch myself in it. But having seen, I can never blind myself again. I can only keep catching myself and changing my responses into those that make me a better teacher and Alyssa a better learner.

Teacher-research means seeing what has been in front of us all the time. It means seeing something we didn't expect to see, a sure sign of learning since what we expect is what we already know. Teacher-research is not about what we can prove but about what we can learn—about what we can see in our classrooms that we have not seen before, that instructs and empowers us. Some people refer to this as "action research." Indeed, our wonderings and questions arise from the *actions* in our classrooms. Our investigations are carried out in the midst of those classroom *actions* and inter*actions*. And our *actions* as teachers are changed as researching allows us to see what had been unclear or invisible.

The most difficult things to see are often those closest to us—so familiar that we overlook them, or are hardly aware of them, or don't think to question them. Or things we don't see because we're blinded by what we "know," which means that our first step must be unlearning. "What happened in my classroom changed because suddenly I observed what was going on there," reports Nancie Atwell:

> At the end of each quarter I conferred with individuals about their uses and views of writing, documenting and analyzing what they said, set goals with them for the next nine weeks, and set a grade on their progress toward the goals of the previous quarter. One November, during our first round of evaluation conferences, I made an occasion for students to articulate the themes of the opening months of writing workshop by asking, among other things, "What's the most important or useful thing you've learned as a writer in the first quarter?". . . In the mini-lessons that autumn I had stressed leads and conclusions, self-editing and proofreading, and a writer's need to be his or her own first critic. I assumed that my students would give me back what I had given them, so that I could begin to formalize a sequence of mini-lessons for the eighth grade. Instead, the twenty-three students in just one of my classes named almost forty different kinds of knowledge, from new conventions to new techniques to new habits. . . . I had to rethink my teaching again. (1991, 4–8)

What enabled Atwell to see—to get beyond her initial assumptions? Her systematic research practice of asking students about their learning, of recording their responses, and of reflecting on them. What she could not see with her eyes, she could see through her students' eyes once she had taken that bold step of asking them what they saw and of accepting what they reported seeing. Teacher-researcher Susan Hohman pointed out to me another value of getting beyond our own perspective by seeing through our students' eyes: "By conversing with our students, we can figure out the important questions, the ones that might not even occur to us when we look from our single perspective. That may be even more important than finding the answers. We probably have a pretty good idea of the answers to our pre-conceived questions already."

New Questions

A student provided his teacher, Pat Fox, with a provocative question that changed the direction of her research. Fox was seeking to understand the variations in quality of writing she observed within individual seventh graders. "Some writing tasks you do better than others, " she told her class. "What kinds of writing do you do best and worst?"

> Etai's response to my question created our first striking moment, a moment of tension, a moment of discovery, and a major turning point in our study. "Best and worst according to whose standards, yours or ours?"
>
> At the moment I turned to him and said, "Now that's a good question—is there a difference?" our fruitful collaboration began. Etai had reserved the right to value a piece of writing in a way other than the way in which the teacher valued it, and he was not alone. This point was made over and over again in the discussion that followed. My student writers had a strong sense of their own strengths and weaknesses as writers which was based on their own criteria for good and bad writing. (1988)

Fox's research pursued this new question of students' criteria for evaluating their own writing, revealing significant differences from teacher evaluations.

Questions we had not envisioned can arise as we listen to replays of classroom events, when we are relieved of the pressures of being participants and can become spectators. One of Lolly Ockerstrom's responsibilities was training new teachers of writing. As a teacher-researcher she wanted to explore what happened when first-year teaching assistants began to teach for the first time. Ten new teaching assistants volunteered to be her informants, and she set up a series of meetings with them, which she taped:

There was no agenda for the meetings; I simply wanted to hear what first-year teaching assistants thought about as they began their teaching. . . . Through a free-form structure, I might learn about issues facing new teachers of writing that researchers in composition might have overlooked previously. As I reviewed the tapes of the meeting [I noticed that] the voices that dominated were male voices. I told myself that it didn't matter, that the women in the group were a little more shy than the men in speaking out, and that as we continued to meet and get to know each other better, the women would speak, too. But I realized that I was ignoring the voice within myself that screamed a protest: Why did I hear male voices and not female voices speaking? Why were women not speaking? When they did, why did they allow themselves to be interrupted by males voices, and displaced in the conversation? What was going on in those group meetings that I didn't understand?. . . I knew that what isn't spoken is as important as what is spoken; I found myself listening to gaps and silences and in particular to the absence of women's voices as much as I listened to what was said and who said it. . . .

I had no idea I would study gender differences when I began this case study. But the nature of the verbal interactions between the men and women in the group struck me immediately, and the more I noticed men speaking and women not speaking, the more I realized that this was important to look at. As I focused on gender and language, I realized that I was looking at issues in my own teaching and learning—why I felt blocked from speaking up in groups, why I doubted my own authority, and, most important, how I could change self-defeating behavior into action that allowed me to speak when I needed to speak.

Systematic records such as field notes, comments on student works, and tape recordings that we review and reflect on *with the intention of learning about our practice* can improve our vision. Ferguson McKay heard himself more clearly through tapes of his student conferences:

I've been using a tape recorder much more than I was before because I found that it makes me honest. You don't really understand what you've heard somebody say until you listen to it two or three times. What really helps is making a transcript. You've got to pay attention to what's on the tape. I listened to my tapes, copied them out, and wrote comments on them, either the day they were made or within a few days thereafter, but usually the day they were made. Then I went back and reexamined them and reinterpreted them later on while writing the paper. And the second interpretations were not the same as the first. The interpretations I made of the conference in the morning always caused me to see the conference totally differently from the way I'd seen it when I was meeting. . . . [I had] had a whole series of ideas about what the effect of this or that procedure was which half the time weren't right. Seeing that is threatening and exciting at the same time. (1987, 153)

And what enables teacher-researchers to see things that are threatening? McKay describes his experience: "This kind of research makes you aware of yourself—because it gives you some internal support, some increased self-respect; it makes it easier to look at yourself. You're not so afraid, or threatened, by the revelations that come" (1987, 155).

Understanding

Neither I nor the teacher-researchers I've worked with are doing what Stephen North in *The Making of Knowledge in Composition* calls "practitioner inquiry"—accumulating practices that "work" in their classrooms. All teachers do this, but not all teachers are, formally or informally, researchers in their own classrooms, looking again at what has happened there. In contrast to North's notion of practitioner "lore," the focus of teacher-research is not essentially on what "works," on collecting practical strategies, but on gaining understanding and awareness. Teacher-research is more interpretive than pragmatic. Carson's phrase "the hermeneutics of practice" (1990, 173) aptly describes it. Schön's "reflective practitioner" is a fitting description of teacher-researchers, whose understanding and awareness reshape, reform, their practice (1983).

Writing this paper was for me an act of teacher-research. I've examined again (re-searched) eight years of inquiries—conversations with my students, letters to and from them, drafts and final reports of their research. I've reviewed comments these teachers made, in writing and in taped discussions, about how their research affected their practice. I've looked again at my field notes and constantly revised teaching plans. Writing and rewriting this paper has taught me more about the kind of thinking and the kind of knowing that teacher-research is.

I understand better now how I have invented and evolved my way of teaching teacher-researchers—why, for instance, naturalist Samuel Scudder's little autobiographical reflection on learning from his teacher, Louis Aggasiz, to look and look and look again at the fish he was given to study is central to my case-study course and is often recalled as most helpful by participants. As a teacher-researcher, I'm seeing what I do. You could say I'm uncovering the theory underlying my own practice. As a teacher, this awareness of the ground of my practice is the most valuable fruit of my researching, more valuable than building an overarching theory or model of teacher-research— although I am, of course, tempted to lay my truths on other teacher-researchers.

After much researching to find what for me was the essence of teacher-research and thus the title for this paper, I reread a discussion among the first group of teacher-researchers I ever taught—a discussion about their experiences. There, right in front of me where it had been from the beginning, was what I had just discovered. Peggy Sheehan had said it: "We examine ourselves more; we look at ourselves more while we're in the classroom as teachers and *see what we're doing* [my italics] and how we're interacting. I think that's a value, if nothing else" (1987, 159).

The Process of Reflective Learning

For Anne Alpert, who teaches at a magnet school, teacher-research meant the shock of seeing for the first time the assumptions or theories on which she had been basing her practice as a writing teacher. As a final instance of teacher thinking and teacher knowing, I offer her complete essay on her inquiry, which allows us to follow the process of a teacher's reflective learning.

"JUST LIKE LIGHTNING!"

Anne Alpert

Someone once told me, and I'm sure it was a teacher, that often it's more important to figure out the right questions than to come up with answers. I have been struggling for a long time with the problem of motivating children in my fifth grade class who produce very little writing. What was I failing to do for them that I seemed to be doing for the others?

I decided to concentrate on finding out what I was doing wrong. I began taping my conferences with the children I had labeled "reluctant writers," hoping that, by listening to my part in the conferences, I would

---

Reprinted by permission of Anne Alpert and the Connecticut Writing Project

find some answers. After hours and hours of taping and transcribing, however, I was no closer to any real insights than when I had started.

Ironically, a conference with one of my [other] students, Tom, helped me to find some answers and pose some important questions. I had not taped my conferences with Tom because he was not one of those I had targeted as a reluctant writer. By March, when we had this conference, he had already published ten pieces. He is very cheerful about writing. He confers with friends often and loves to share his pieces with the class at whole-group share—not at all what you would call a "reluctant writer." Since I didn't tape the conference, this is approximately how it went.

Anne: What would you like me to help you with, Tom?

Tom: I'm publishing this piece.

Anne: How long have you been working on it?

Tom: Since Monday. [Two days.]

Anne: Are you sure it's ready to be published?

Tom: Sure . . . I'm done.

Anne: Okay, let's hear it. [He reads the piece to me.]

Tom: Can I publish now?

Anne: Is there anything you want to add?

Tom: Nope . . . That's it.

Anne: What will you do next?

Tom: I'm going to write about going bowling with Rohan yesterday.

Anne: Tom, would you consider trying a different form of writing, like those poems I've been reading to you, or a fairy tale?

Tom: I like this.

Anne: I know . . . and you worked hard at Writers' Workshop. You can mess around with different things, too.

Tom: Can I publish now?

Anne: It's your choice.

Tom: Okay . . . I'll publish.

I watched him saunter over to the computer to "publish" his piece and I realized that most of his conferences were like this. They were boring for both of us and I never felt satisfied that we had accomplished very much. After school, I decided to take out Tom's "Final Copy Folder" to see what he had published so far. All of his pieces were personal narratives, and all about his best friend, Rohan. They were all about the same length and pretty much the same level of complexity. Tom certainly wasn't a risk-taker, and he had been resisting my suggestions for a long time. He had been turning out pieces, though . . . so why was I feeling so uneasy about him? After conferring with him all year long, I realized I really didn't know him as a writer.

I began to think about the three students I had been taping all these months. What did I really know about them as writers? Maybe instead of asking questions about their writing, I needed to ask them questions about themselves as writers. I decided to have individual conferences with each of them . . . very different conferences than I had been having. These are the conferences verbatim: the first is with Jesus, the second with Samantha, and the third with Ronnie. Jesus and Ronnie have published one piece each this year, and Samantha has published none. (This is March.)

Jesus

Jesus never initiates a conference with me, and I have to force him to meet me about every other week. I poke and prod him when we confer and he reacts by agreeing with everything I say just to get away from me.

Anne: Read me what you have, Jesus, and then I want to ask you some questions.

Jesus: [He reads his piece to me. It's about a mouse named Itchy who has adventures traveling around the world. In each place, he makes a new friend and the friend joins him on his travels. He has been working on the same piece all term. He makes lots of starts, puts it away, starts again. It seems to me that he never commits himself to anything.]

Anne: What do you think of it, Jesus?

Jesus: It's good, I guess.

Anne: You don't sound too sure.

Jesus: What do you think?

Anne: I think I talk too much when we have a conference. I want to hear what you think about writing.

Jesus: I like it. [Long silence . . . He's waiting for me to say something.] I like this Itchy character. I have to use the globe to find the countries he'll go to next . . . and then I look up the country to find out about it and make up his friends' names and stuff like that. I keep getting new ideas for new places. It's fun.

Anne: That's what writers do all the time . . . They do research like you're doing.

Jesus: It takes time to do it . . . sometimes the whole writing period and I'm still not done. I read slow. Sometimes I have to ask Greg to help me with words.

Anne: I see. What do you plan to do with your Itchy stories?

Jesus: It's a chapter book. Every chapter is a different place. I have six places already. But it's taking me long to put it all together.

Anne: Read me the very first one you have.

Jesus: Why?

Anne: I don't remember hearing it. Don't you want to?

Jesus: OK. [He reads the first draft he started months ago. He stumbles where sentences end and begin and has to go back to correct himself.]

Anne: Why is that happening?

Jesus: I don't have any periods. I can't use them when I write.

Anne: How come?

Jesus: It stops me from thinking so I put them in after. I haven't done it yet.

Anne: Oh . . . I see . . . It's good you know that about yourself.

Jesus: Yeah.

He continues reading his piece. It really is very funny. I realize I never asked him before why he was stumbling over words. I though it was because he has difficulty reading and didn't want to embarrass him.

Anne: You're a great storyteller. Did you know that about yourself?

Jesus: Yeah. I was trying to write poems and mysteries and stuff like you wanted us to write, but it's too hard for me. I like to write funny stuff like this. It's easier to write about animals than about people too. You laughed at all the right places, Anne.

Anne: Was this a test?

Jesus: Yeah. [Laughs.]

Anne: What will you do now?

Jesus: I think I'll try to bring Itchy home again and go back and see what I can change from the beginning. It might take me a long time.

Anne: Should I wait for you to sign up for a conference when you're ready?

Jesus: Yeah. Sometimes I'm not ready when you call me.

Anne: Okay. Thanks, Jesus.

I felt bewildered after this conference. What made him think that I wouldn't value his piece because it wasn't as "hard" as a poem or a mystery? And why didn't he tell me before why he wasn't ready for a conference when I called him? And why didn't he object to being called in the first place? The usual procedure for a conference with me was to sign up when you needed one. The implication was that he couldn't be trusted to do that for himself. Why didn't I trust him?

Samantha

Samantha never wants to confer with me or with other children. I have to seek her out. She's very noncommittal at a conference. She always makes me feel as though I'm intruding on her privacy.

Anne: What are you working on, Sam?

Sam: The same thing.

Anne: Read me some.

Sam: [She proceeds to read a piece she has started months ago. It's a "chapter book" about a brother and sister who decide to run away because their mother is getting married again and they hate their prospective stepbrother. The first chapter is very well done. She has set up the characters very carefully. The second chapter, the one she is reading to me, is an elaborate explanation of how they plan to run away and where they're going to go, etc. She reads slowly and methodically, with very little expression or enthusiasm. She seems uncomfortable and angry at having to share it with me. She obviously wants to get it over with.]

Anne: I feel as if you don't want to share this, Sam.

Sam: Well, I wasn't ready.

Anne: Do you think I should wait until you sign up for a conference by yourself?

Sam: Yes. You don't call the other kids . . . just me. Why do you do that?

Anne: I guess because I'm afraid you're not writing anything and I need to find out what you're doing. You haven't published anything all year.

Sam: So what? You said authors take a year . . . sometimes two years to write a book. Nobody tells them they have to publish seven books a year. I don't think you're being fair.

Anne: How come you never told me that before?

Sam: Because nobody else seems to care about it.

Anne: Oh.

Sam: You let everybody else sign up for a conference when they need it. Why don't you wait for me to be ready?

Anne: Do you want to talk about your piece now?

Sam: Not really.

Anne: Okay.

Sam: I'll sign up when I'm ready.

Anne: Okay.

Sam: Maybe tomorrow or the next day.

Anne: It's okay, Sam . . . really. I'm glad you told me how you feel.

Sam: You see, when I write, it takes me a long time to figure out how something ends up. I try it different ways in my mind, but only one way fits right. I have to do it with every chapter because there's something that happens in each chapter that leads to something else in the next chapter. I have to think about things a long time without writing anything.

Anne: . . . and you don't need to talk to anyone to help you solve the problems.

Sam: No . . . it just interrupts me and I have to start thinking all over again.

Anne: Oh . . . so when I call you for a conference, it just interrupts you.

Sam: [Big sigh.] Yes!

Anne: Thanks, Sam . . . that's a big help to me.

Sam: Okay.

I've told my students so often that writers make many starts and sometimes take a long time to finally come up with a piece of writing that satisfies them. By saying that, wasn't I giving them permission to take as long as they needed? If I meant that, then why did I decide to require seven published pieces? Is that why Samantha has seemed angry at me all this time?

Ronnie

Ronnie does everything but write at Writers' Workshop. Mostly he draws or reads or talks to other people about their writing. He loves to have peer conferences and he'll confer with anyone who asks him. He has produced one piece of writing, a fairy tale of some length that he worked on for about six weeks. He made many revisions and was very proud of the result. Since then, he hasn't produced anything.

Anne: What's happening, Ron?

Ron: I can't think of anything to write about.

Anne: I know . . . that's what you tell me every time we have a conference. Don't any of my suggestions help you?

Ron: No.

Anne: Tell me how you get an idea for a piece.

Ron: Myself?

Anne: Yes.

Ron: Why do you want to know?

Anne: I don't know . . . It occurred to me after listening to all the tapes of our conferences that I never asked you that and I really want to know.

Ron: Well, it usually takes me a very long time. I never know when it hits . . . it just comes to me . . . like that. Then I write and write and . . . like my fairy tale. I got the idea from Andy when she was telling me about this movie she saw then it just hit me . . . just like lightning.

Anne: Okay . . . so you get your idea and then you write and write and then what happens?

Ron: After I publish, it's like I'm worn out . . . like when a balloon loses its air . . . just flat. I don't feel like writing again for a long time . . . so I do other stuff and just wait for another idea to hit me again.

Anne: Is there any way to make the ideas come faster?

Ron: I don't know. Do you know any?

Anne: I guess not . . . the ways I knew I shared with you and they didn't seem to work.

Ron: I know. I guess writers all have their own way and nobody can really help them.

Anne: I guess real writers know that about themselves.

Ron: What should I do now?

Anne: What do you want to do?

Ron: I think I'll read some more Shel Silverstein. I really like his poems.

Anne: Okay. Let me know when another idea hits you.

Ron: Okay. Thanks, Anne.

Ronnie was really happy with himself as a writer. So why was I feeling so frustrated all year? If he had been less independent and secure would I have felt more useful? What did all this have to do with Ronnie being labeled a reluctant writer?

Reflection

As I looked over my transcripts of past conferences with these three children, I realized that my focus was constantly on ways to move them along to publish. I heard myself remind them over and over that they needed to publish seven pieces and they were nowhere near that number. I accused them, also, of doing nothing constructive at writing time, which, as you can see from these conferences, was the furthest thing from the truth. And most important, they knew themselves as writers much more intimately and intelligently than I did.

So then what is a "reluctant" writer? Is writing a social act for everyone? What drove me to require a particular number of published pieces? Where was the ownership of the writer in that decision? Are we talking about "writing" or about "composing"? And if we're talking about "composing," isn't it much more than "writing"?

It seems clear to me now that "writing" is only one piece of the puzzle that is "composing." I should have known that from my own experiences struggling to compose. Composing is the getting reading to take the risk; it's the struggling to develop an idea; it's the self-doubt, the inner critic constantly challenging you; it's all the revision that happens before you ever get a word down on paper. Composing is the thinking, the problem solving, the choices. It's the totality of every act that finally produces "writing." And this whole process is different for each one of us.

If all this is so, then what is the purpose and value of Writers' Workshop? Is it to help children to know themselves as writers, or to publish? (That question is rhetorical since one of the revelations that came to me "like lightning" is that Writers' Workshop time is for helping my students see themselves as writers and be secure with what they know.) Publishing is important if the writer thinks it's important, but it's no more important than any other piece of the composing process. It took these three children all term to get up the courage to tell me who they are. I read in a "teacher book" that children decide what is important not by what you say, but by what you do. My message to these children had been that publishing is writing, but they had the courage to resist me so that they could be true to themselves. There is nothing "reluctant" about them. There are other times of the day to be concerned about product. Writers' Workshop will be a time to be concerned about the process of composing.

There's another issue that can't be avoided. If I really believe that the writer must have ownership of decisions about his or her writings, what drove me to establish a requirement for published pieces? Knowing what I know about my own writing process, I could never have met this requirement myself! I suppose it was my "easy way out." Evaluation of writing has always been impossible for me. Except for mechanics, everything else seems arbitrary. The final product is the end of a long road. I've never been able to simply look at the "finished" piece all by itself. Maybe setting a required number of pieces helped me to avoid the real issue: Why should writing be graded at all? How is this helpful to anyone?

As you can see, I have a few answers, but many more questions. Thinking about Tom, for example, I realize that he is much more afraid of writing than Jesus, Ronnie, or Samantha. He won't even talk about himself as a writer. It may be that he is whipping off all these pieces just to keep me happy and avoid having me ask him the questions I know now that I need to ask him. Would I call Tom a "reluctant" writer? He's reluctant to reveal himself, he's reluctant to share, he's reluctant to ask for help or admit he has needs. Maybe the real question is, why label him anything? It just gets in the way of knowing who he is. Schools shouldn't be for judging . . . they should be for listening, and respecting, and helping.

So . . . how do I help Tom? And how do I break it to the class that there is no required number of published pieces?

Reflections on a Teacher's Reflection

Alpert's research starts from a teaching problem: How can she motivate children in her fifth-grade class who produce very little writing? Embedded in that problem are theoretical issues that her research eventually leads her to unearth and examine.

Her first clue comes unexpectedly from a conference with a prolific writer, Tom, an event she has not seen as useful to her inquiry and, thus, has not recorded, except in her memory. Perhaps because she's in research mode, she pays more attention to the uneasiness she's felt for some time about Tom as a writer, which leads her to question what she knows about her "reluctant" students as writers. In her next conferences she asks them questions about themselves as writers and truly listens to them as informants, enabling them to "get up the courage to tell me who they are."

Her conference with Jesus leads her to a new set of questions about him and about herself:

> What made him think that I wouldn't value his piece because it wasn't as "hard" as a poem or a mystery? And why didn't he tell me before why he wasn't ready for a conference when I called him? And why didn't he object to being called in the first place? The usual procedure for a conference with me was to sign up when you needed one. The implication was that he couldn't be trusted to do that for himself. Why didn't I trust him?

Anne's conference with Samantha leads her to see a contradiction between the pedagogical beliefs she has asserted and her practice. Her awareness of this contradiction is a wedge that further opens up her inquiry. After completing her research, Anne reflects: "I've learned so much about myself from writing this paper . . . about how easy it is to be a hypocritical teacher and not know it unless someone or something forces you to look at yourself and your practice and measure these against what you say you believe." As often happens in teacher-research, the focus shifts from students to the teacher herself.

Her conference with Ronnie raises questions about her own expectations rather than, as originally, about her students' failure to live up to them. Recognizing that these students know themselves better as writers than she does forces her to redefine her research problem. Instead of asking how she can motivate these students to write more, she asks, "What is a 'reluctant' writer? Is writing a social act for everyone?" "Are we talking about 'writing' or about 'composing'?" "What is the purpose and value of Writers' Workshop?" Confronting the assumptions beneath her research problem as she originally framed it raises a host of theoretical questions.

Alpert's answers, explicit and implied, to these theoretical issues lead her back to her pedagogy—to her requirement that students publish a certain number of pieces—in the light of which she had viewed Jesus, Samantha, and Ronnie as unmotivated. "Maybe setting a required number of pieces helped me to avoid the real issues: Why should writing be graded at all?"

All of these questions have been raised in the service of her teaching, and it is to her teaching that she returns in the end: "So how do I help Tom? And how do I break it to the class that there is no required number of published pieces?" When she wrote to me the following school year, Anne described further changes in her teaching:

> Writers' Workshop has been a lot more fun for me this year. Since I'm not requiring a set number of published pieces, my fifth graders are using the time to experiment, read, learn from each other, and share their attempts. Some have even published. I think they have the idea now that publishing five pieces in ten days is missing the point. The main thing for me is that I'm enjoying what each person is doing and thinking and trying at the moment—not feeling uneasy because they're not where I want them to be three months from now. That's a great relief.
>
> Some wonderful writers are emerging and just about all of them have moved on in some way from where they were when they came to me. You know I teach in an inner-city school. My class is completely heterogeneous—racially, economically, in every way. I really feel my kids are so willing to accept each other's efforts because I am and they see that I am.

What seemed like a straightforward question about the external problem of motivating students turned into a critical analysis of Alpert's practice and her theory. She hears both her students and herself with new ears. "By using the child as our curricular informant, we have a self-correcting device built into our model of curriculum and curriculum development," as Harste and McInerney point out (1990, 304–5). Teacher-research enables Alpert, like other teacher-researchers, to listen to her informants, to tune in to these self-correcting devices. Her inquiries into the meanings of student behaviors have turned the categories of her initial research question upside down. She now sees important ways in which her "reluctant" writers were neither reluctant nor noncomposers, and she redefines a prolific writer as "reluctant." Furthermore, she has posed questions on several levels—about these four students, about the relationship between her own principles and her practice, about the purpose of Writers' Workshop in her curriculum, and about the nature of writing.

Doing this research didn't suddenly give Anne a new way of thinking— she's probably always been a questioner—but it supported and confirmed the value of such thinking, validated the time to pursue it further, provided conversation with other teacher-researchers about her issues, and yielded the clarification that came from writing and revising her research paper. Teacher-researchers are often amazed at how conscious and articulate even young students can be or become when their knowing is valued. The same is true for teachers.

What does Anne know as a result of her research? She knows her students more fully. And she knows herself, especially the principles on which her practice is based. Awareness rather than hypotheses may be the fruit of teacher-research. An awareness is something I carry with me that changes how I see and interpret and thus how I respond and act. In this sense it's a beginning rather than an end, which is why teacher-researchers can never go back to teaching as usual. As Cora Five, who has done research for years in her fifth-grade classroom, told me, "Once you do teacher-research, everything becomes something to investigate."

For experienced teachers, teacher-research provides an avenue for professional renewal and growth; for all teachers, including those just beginning, it offers a way of learning with dignity from our experiences, be they frustrations, failures, or successes. Professors teach most education courses and write the texts, managing the domain of knowledge, while cooperating teachers are valued for contributing to the domain of practice, of doing. Teachers' knowing and teachers' thinking are missing links. Prospective teachers, beginning teachers, and all of us, need models of courageous, inquiring teachers. We need to see teachers in the process of thinking and learning.

Researching as a teacher can bring about the critical consciousness of oneself as a meaning maker that Paolo Friere talks of, a consciousness that is liberating and empowering. We look at our knowledge, our assumptions, our interpretations as our practice renders them tangible, as re-searching makes them visible, and as critical consciousness opens them to questioning. What we see then are not merely faces or events, but meanings that re-form our practice.

References

Alpert, Anne. 1991. "Just Like Lightning!" In *Teacher Research: Guess Who's Learning*, ed. Glenda L. Bissex, 1–10. Storrs: Connecticut Writing Project, University of Connecticut.

Atwell, Nancie. 1991. *Side By Side*. Portsmouth, NH: Heinemann.

Carson, T. 1990. "What Kind of Knowing Is Critical Action Research?" *Theory into Practice* 29: 167–73.

Fox, Patricia. 1988. Unpublished case study. Northeastern University.

Harste, Jerome and J. McInerney. 1990. "Whole Language: Starting New Conversations." In *Portraits of Whole Language Classrooms*, ed. Heidi Mills and J. A. Clyde, 301–7. Portsmouth, NH: Heinemann.

McKay, Ferguson. 1987. "Roles and Strategies in College Writing Conferences." In *Seeing for Ourselves: Case-Study Research by Teachers of Writing*, ed. Glenda L. Bissex and Richard H. Bullock, 77–101. Portsmouth, NH: Heinemann.

North, Stephen. 1987. *The Making of Knowledge in Composition: Portrait of an Emerging Field*. Portsmouth, NH: Boynton/Cook.

Ockerstrom, Lolly. 1989. Unpublished case study. Northeastern University.

Schön, Donald A. 1983. *The Reflective Practitioner: How Professionals Think in Action*. New York: Basic Books.

Scudder, Samuel H. 1992. "Take This Fish and Look at It." In *Community of Voices: Reading and Writing in the Disciplines*, ed. Toby Fulwiler and Arthur W. Biddle, 641–46. New York: Macmillan.

Sheehan, Peggy. 1987. "On Becoming a Teacher Researcher." In *Seeing for Ourselves: Case-Study Research by Teachers of Writing*, ed. Glenda L. Bissex and Richard H. Bullock, 145–63, Portsmouth, NH: Heinemann.

The Romance of the Mallards

OBSERVING AND INTERPRETING
LIFE ON MY POND
1995

THIS ROMANCE OF THE DUCKS MAY BE AS WELL THE romance of their observer and the narrative bent of the human mind. Yes, I saw with my bare eyes and with binoculars all the events that I record—saw them in my backyard, which is partly a pond of perhaps a quarter of an acre. I thought I'd been following the triangular tale of two drakes and their lady love until I was shaken several days later by the appearance of four drakes together in my pond. I'd assumed continuities—that the three ducks I observed were always the same three. If I could not assume continuities, there would be no story and no meaning to events either on the pond or anywhere else.

What I saw raised more questions than I could answer from my own observations. In my search for information I read that "The very art of bird watching is to develop the ability to put a name to a bird that is seen less than perfectly." I wanted to do much more than name; I wanted to know their lives. Yet I, too, was seeing them imperfectly, "perhaps for a split second, or at a great distance and in poor light." The pond was nearby, but the distance between the ducks' lives and mine was greater. The daylight was usually adequate for seeing them, but was the light of my understanding?

As soon as the ice was off in early April, the mallard pair visited the pond. The third successive day, they were here at sunrise—sunrise being a red smudge on the clouds in the east. The drake was splendid in his breeding plumage—deep green head and neck separated by a white band from his plump cinnamon chest, and over his rump, elegant curls of black feathers scrolled above the white vee of his folded tail. He swam beside a mate painted by a different artist who dealt not in bold color contrasts but in varied small patterns of brown on tan, from the dark flecks on her head and neck to the tapestry of brown feather tips edged in tan on her wings and flanks. Only identical blue shoulder patches, edged in white but hidden now in their folded wings, marked them as the same breed.

They swam from the edge of the pond, where they'd been foraging, out to the safer middle as my golden retriever Teddy, a bird dog, sniffed around the shore, then turned away sniffing the field, its odors released by the snow melt, and headed down the hill for his morning jaunt. The mallards returned to the edge of the pond, where they nibbled early spring greens under the shallow water, but soon the drake pumped his head up and down and swam out to deeper water. His mate pumped her head and followed him out—a dialogue I was to see many times, a dialogue about leaving. One after the other, they jumped up and winged off into a blustery northwest wind.

Half an hour later I look up from my cereal to see outspread gray wings lowering from the east down onto the pond where the wings compose into a mallard drake. I look around for his mate. He doesn't. Beneath his quiet body, the paddling of his orange legs and webbed feet hold him in place against a wind that would blow me to shore at once were I out in my canoe. Through a break in the clouds the sun gleams; the drake's green head glistens, then blackens as clouds again cover the sun. After foraging, he sits on the shore and tucks his beautiful head under his wing to rest. His exposed shoulder patch glows violet where I'd seen blue before, transformed by a change in the light or in the angle of his wing. Seeing is not simple.

While I'm working at my desk, his mate returns. Did he know where she was? Did he need to know? Was she looking for a nest site already? Now she rests while he stands protectively alert nearby. When I next look, they're gone. The rhythm of my life is not to spend hours staring at the pond. The rhythm of their lives is not to stay here long. And so I collect scraps of scraps, not foreseeing how my rhythm will become disrupted when scraps of scraps are not enough for me.

My friend Toby looks gently amused when I talk about watching the ducks. Talk about sitting on Church Street in downtown Burlington watching people might sound more sensible. I do watch people, but watching ducks and other creatures opens up new worlds, gives me a glimpse of lives being lived all around me that I know hardly anything about. I know how people behave, but not ducks.

The next morning the pair is swimming along the edge of the pond, foraging. When they walk up out of the water, they look around cautiously.

Perhaps Teddy is sitting at his lookout post at the corner of the deck, easily visible from the pond. No, in his spot sits my small black cat, looking over the field and down the road just as Teddy does. Doubtless they don't see the same things. Kit must watch for the movement of birds or mice in the grass, Teddy for a deer crossing the field or someone walking on the road to bark at. Kit notices me behind the glass door and decides she wants to come in. The sound of the door opening sends the ducks off northeastward. Are they headed for Pigeon Pond?

The drake returns alone an hour later. Without his mate he swims faster in his foraging, then he rests on the muddy bank where they have rested together. I seem to see the eye turned toward me blink; now it's bright yellow, now black. Why do I say I "seem to see," as though my not expecting to see a duck blink makes me doubt what I observe? Through the binoculars I see very clearly that he blinks, but I still can't be sure if his eye lid is black and his eye yellow or the other way around. The picture in my duck book, doubtless drawn from a dead model, shows a black bead of an eye. Is his absent mate building a nest on one of the neighboring ponds that offers more cover than my little basin in an open field—Prescott's beaver pond, a twenty minute walk southwest through the woods, or the larger Bancroft Pond, as far to the southeast, or Pigeon Pond, the largest and farthest—even as a duck flies, more than two miles northeast? I'm typing at my desk when she flies in and so I don't see which direction she came from. This is a story of missed observations as well as observations not quite believed and beliefs shaping observations. It is a movie with many frames missing and continuity supplied by the narrator.

When my husband walks out toward the opposite end of the pond from the ducks, they walk with dignity—or perhaps indignation—heads held high, out of the shallow water, up the bank and into the field where they eventually take off when I'm not looking since I expect them always to take off from the water. After sunset I see them return to feed, and when the dusk is too deep for me to see through, I suppose they took off again, and before dawn, returned. Though they're here when I awake the next morning, I suppose this discontinuity because I doubt they'd spent the night in such an unprotected little pond.

They always forage together, as though yoked by a cord only a few yards long, tugging them back together when they separate at all. Like us, they seem to need sociability along with their food. Now the drake bobs his head and chest under water, tipping up his rear end and showing his pale gray underbelly. When he bobs up, his mate bobs under, the backward thrust of her feet, cupped like hands, keeping her upright in the water. Mostly they maintain this alternating rhythm of one up, one down. Perhaps their sociability protects them during this vulnerable time of eating when they cannot watch for dangers.

The pair stop feeding, swim across the pond trailing a long vee over the still water, climb up on the bank and stand together unmoving for a moment before she pumps her head, signalling departure. They run a few steps, expanding their wings, and lift off together, veering toward the most distant pond.

In less than five minutes I see a drake at the end of my pond, as though he'd simply made a large circle and returned. It hardly seems they'd been gone long enough to have flown to Pigeon Pond and for him to return. Did he bid her good-bye in the air? I don't suspect yet that there might be more than one drake and certainly not that the simple thread of this love story will become almost too tangled to unravel. All seems peacefully in order as, later that morning, I see two ducks swimming together, then none, then a splash down at dusk as they scoot across the surface like water skiers. Later, after my eyes adjust to the darkness and when the water, by contrast to its surrounding black rim grows faintly luminous, I see them no longer. These comings and goings have become a familiar pattern.

In the next morning's twilight, I hear a quack amid the shrill chatter of frogs but can see no ducks. Usually they are silent. In daylight, when I get up, a pair of mallards swims on the pond. Again, they fly away after foraging, and minutes later the drake returns. Soon I see a duck fly in and land beside him. Why has she changed the pattern? I look through my binoculars. It's not her—it's another him, and they look identical! How can I ever tell the drakes apart and keep their story straight? Not quite identical; one is lighter gray, but is that anything I could distinguish unless I saw them together? I look for another mark. The neck ring of the lighter drake looks brighter and wider. He holds his tail higher, like a jaunty sailor. I'm quite sure he's the new one.

Like the male and female pair, they stick close together but they forage with more gusto, even swimming across the pond to continue foraging rather than working their way slowly around the edges, movements that to a female like me might seem wasting energy. They have no eggs to lay, and it is spring and they are in love—it turns out, with the same woman. They swim together toward the middle of the pond, the lighter drake pumping his head up and down so vigorously I wonder if he's trying to dislodge something caught in his throat. The darker one opens his bill several times as if to speak but no sound comes out. Abruptly they swing 180 degrees around in the water and fly off in unison, curving together in the air so they're headed toward Prescott's beaver pond. The water, until now agitated with their activity, lies flat, still and gray under thickening folds of clouds. A few chickadees and juncos bop around the bushes and a sparrow sings.

Now that there are no ducks to disturb, I put on my jacket and boots to go out and rake last summer's dried grass and ferns away from the shore. But a duck I didn't see swims out into the water from the end of the pond—a drake holding his tail low. As he stretches his neck, his narrow white ring widens a little, making me wonder if perhaps the subtle differences between individuals arise more from how they hold their feathers than from the plumage itself. While he paddles to hold his place against the breeze that has come up, he calls in a soft bass voice. Three crows stand on the bank. One flies over the pond, cawing. The drake quacks and spins around. He hasn't foraged at all and swims quacking now against a background of more rapid and strident caws. Pursued by one crow, the elegant, lonely drake flies away. Less than a minute later a female mallard splashes down and revolves in place in the water, uttering a high pitched ticking sound. I want to tell her he was here and just left, chased by a crow. How far can either her ticking or his muted quacking carry? Or do ducks have sharper hearing than humans? Where, I wonder now, are their ears? The questions hook me and I sit down at the kitchen table by the glass door to watch the story unfold.

The four-caw call that preceded the pursuit of the drake sounds again like a warning but distant now. Is he still being harassed? The female lowers her head to scoop water onto her bill, then stretches her head back to swallow it. She swims to the edge of the pond where she starts foraging but soon stops, floats, watches, and listens while I sit at the kitchen table in my boots and jacket as though my life depended on what will happen next. Is this the ducks' story or mine?

It's the first time I've seen her alone on this pond though she must have been alone on another pond when her drake was here. Whether as mates or as buddies, these mallards have stuck so closely together that I feel lonely for her now. Or for something abandoned in myself? In her foraging she approaches a sparrow who's come down for a drink but quickly flies off while the duck continues around the pond, nibbling the water grasses. A large bird flies overhead. The mallard, too, looks up but it's only a crow. She moves out toward the middle of the pond, the usual take-off spot, looks around and leaps up from the water, leaving fast-spreading, deep ripples—the energy of her take-off so unlike the smaller, gentler movements of her foraging and expectant waiting. Is any creature's life simple and uniform? Why should it be, or why should we expect it, of others or ourselves?

Half an hour later another duck floats in the middle of the pond quacking, a drake with a thin white neck ring and dark gray and brown shadings on his back—the mate again. I think he must be anxious and that she, on whatever pond she's flown to, must be worrying where he is. I imagine them just missing one another not only at my pond but at other ponds where they have fed together. *I* would be worried. Is it just me? "Since birds often respond to situations at a highly instinctive level and their senses are so different from our own, it is essential that behavior watchers avoid assigning human motives and values to bird behavior," cautions the author of one bird book. I can see him frowning upon my story. These events would doubtless appear differently to him. His knowledge of birds and his assurance that their motives are unlike ours would distance him, while I sit on the edge of my chair with my binoculars, trying to figure out what's happening and taking sides.

An hour later, at noon, the drake is still here alone. Anxiously I phone my neighbor Bill Prescott to ask what ducks he's seen this morning from his house overlooking his beaver pond. He'd seen two when he was out earlier but he wouldn't swear they were a pair, so they could have been the two drakes who flew off in that direction. I want him to go out *now* and see whether a female is there, searching, but Bill's old and ailing; I can't ask him to.

The drake, who's been standing at the edge of my pond, swims out into the middle and flies up, leaving less of a wake than his mate did. I lose sight of him behind my barn. Running out into the road for a better view, I look up into a vacant sky. I'll never know if he flew toward Prescott's or toward Bancroft Pond. The chickadees call an alarm from the bare lilac bush beside the house. Since no cats are outside, they must be alerting me to their empty feeder. It's lunchtime for all of us.

In the wet, gray light of the afternoon, the crowns of the maples beyond the quiet pond glow red, the color of swelling buds. All color fades in the murky dusk, and I see only the swinging white tails of two deer grazing in the field. The frogs, silent all day, trill and peep from the pond where no ducks have landed.

Next morning a black cloud broods over the pond. At five-thirty, no ducks. At six o'clock, no ducks. At six-thirty, as I close the refrigerator and turn toward the glass door, two ducks are in the middle of the pond, the female vigorously bathing, dipping her outspread wings low to splash water on her back and then shaking it off as I've seen mallards do after mating. Now she composes herself and floats calmly. The dark sky is breaking up; a swath of blue between cloud banks flushed with morning pink is reflected in the water. The mirror quakes. A drake splashes down boldly beside the drake already here and both fly up together, leaving an empty pond. Could the female have gone without my noticing, or has she hidden herself? One drake, and another almost on top of him, splash down in the corner of the pond they've just taken off from. Then they're in the air again, skillfully following one another through every shift in direction, like a pair of dancers. But this is not a dance; it's a pursuit. Only one returns, splashing down in the corner of the pond. He holds his tail low and his neck ring looks thin. A wind gust stipples the pond as he swims to shore. In a moment his mate, no longer invisible against the dead brown reeds, stands beside him on the bank, facing into the wind. She preens while he stands guard, swiveling his green head. As they fly off toward Pigeon Pond, sunlight floods over them.

"Congaree" calls a redwing blackbird from the top of a bush beside the pond, claiming the water as his territory now. But a drake who looks like the one that just flew off with his mate lands in the middle of the pond. Will I ever get any breakfast? Though it's 7:30 already, I risk missing part of the story by turning away toward the fridge or stove. Most of the pond is still shadowed by the house; on the far edge sunlight gleams on the irridescent green head and thin white neck ring of the drake. More wind gusts blow dark splotches of roughened water across the surface of the pond, and he swims out into them. Then another drake lands beside the swimmer and pursues him across the water and into the sky. Robins and grackles forage the banks for their own kinds of food, as I finally prepare mine while waiting for the next scene.

When I can wait no longer, I strike out the mile through the woods to Bill Prescott's pond where a light gray drake, holding his tail high and quacking softly, swims down the pond into the reedy islands and dead trees at its end. He swims not feeding but searching. I head back home and, coming out of the woods into the field overlooking my pond, I see the darker drake, tail low, swimming and quacking. One drake in each pond, calling for a female who is somewhere else.

The drake in my pond bobs up, chomping some morsel he's found, then dips down again and again, searching for more. Back in the house now, I make myself a pot of tea. When I check the pond again, I see a pair of mallards and, as if my coming to the glass door flushes them, they fly up and off over the valley to the northwest—to yet another pond where the light drake may not find them? He isn't far behind. Several minutes later he swoops in and swims around the perimeter of the pond as though patrolling. Abruptly, before he's even completed his circuit, he flies back toward Prescott's pond. I, too, leave for the afternoon. One stop will be the library for books about ducks.

Since I see no ducks when I return, it looks like a good time to rake the herb garden behind the house. As I rake, my back is to the pond; when I'm finished and turn around, I see a drake swimming. Slowly I walk around the house to go in the front door, away from the pond, pick up my binoculars from the kitchen table and observe the beautiful ripple rings his departure has left on the glassy pond. Which one was he? I don't know whether to trust my fleeting impression that he was the light drake, come to fight again for the already mated female.

No ducks to watch on the pond the next morning, so my eyes are free to read about them. "Wild ducks are basically monogamous for the nesting season." According to this book, the pair may have chosen each other only a few months or even weeks ago. I'm caught up in the intensity of their brief encounter and the passion of the drake who would seize the female for his own. "There are many unmated males in mallard populations and it is these birds that create so much havoc at mating time." Yes, havoc in their lives and in mine. The magnetic energy they bring to the pond draws me in. "Rape is common." This scientific observer of animal behavior uses the word "rape." "Such brutality may lead to disasters and there have been many cases of females being drowned by overzealous males."

I look up from reading. Ripples are radiating toward shore, so the drake I see must just have landed—the dark drake. He seems to have come here merely to feed, and goes about his business along the pond's edge. Rain pocks the water. He swings his head from side to side and flicks his tail, then glides swanlike across the water. In an hour the shower is over and the sun shines thinly. The floating drake turns round and round, quacking. Where is she? Alternately he forages and calls. I can read his actions in the glassy water: a trailing vee when he swims, radiating ripples when he dabbles or tips, and only his reflection when he floats. On the deck just outside the glass doors a junco is pecking seeds dropped from the bird feeder above. My cat watches, crouched to spring, inside the glass. The drake swims the length of the pond again. Clouds cover the sky once more. The drake calls.

Another duck lands and the two swim toward each other until they meet and then swim side by side to shore, the dark drake and the light one. They walk out of the water but immediately return, dabbling and swimming, always together, one shadowing the other. Fifteen minutes later, flying in from the direction of Pigeon Pond, a female lands in the middle of the pond. Both drakes speed toward her and both leap on her. Amid the thrashing bodies and churning water I see two heads only—green heads. When the female's brown head emerges from under the bodies of her suitors, they cease battling one another with their outspread wings and jump on her once more. Finally, out from the turmoil, the desired female surfaces again and swims calmly, demurely toward the north end of the pond. Following her, the dark drake stands watch while she forages, then preens his feathers and forages himself in the shallow water. The light drake retreats to the opposite shore and stands rearranging his ruffled feathers until the darker drake, running across the water straight for him, drives him up into the air and chases him over the woods toward Prescott's, then circles back to land beside the woman I assume he's won at last.

The floating female preens her feathers vigorously—to straighten them after the attack or to prepare for whatever will come next? The pair swims to the water's edge. He stands on the shore, neck stretched up, surveying. A crow flies over their heads, caws, and they scoot back into the water. When the crow disappears behind the barn, they move again toward shore and scurry up into the field, the drake leading, his bill opening as though he's saying something. Then they're off in the direction of Pigeon Pond—white forms, seen from below, soaring against a hillside of dark cedars. The pond is empty of their energy. Only rain flecks its surface. The edge of my awareness of these ducks relaxes. Like a mother attuned to her young children, I've lived the past three days mostly with the ducks; even when they weren't here, I've thought of them and watched for them, needing to know their story.

Whoosh! Splashing down, sweeping back and forth across the water, his neck stretched up to its full height, the light gray drake fills the pond. Then the whole surface reverberates from the thrust of his skyward leap. I run out the door to follow his flight, but I've lost him. Is he pursuing the lovers to Pigeon Pond? Even if I drove the five miles to the gate and and hiked in to the pond, what chance would I have of finding out? I'm doomed to partial knowing—to piecing together what I see with what I can imagine and what I learn about ducks through reading others' observations.

The pair is together the following morning on my pond. At rest on the bank, she's almost invisible against the unruly dead grasses I'd wanted to burn. With their heads tucked under their wings, both show their blue shoulder stripes. Kit creeps silently along the bank toward them. The drake rouses and swims out into the water while Kit walks away from the pond as though she never was interested in ducks anyway. The drake returns to the side of his mate, who scratches her head with one orange foot. Later, after they fly off, the drake returns to forage. Feeling comfortable now with this familiar pattern, I turn to housecleaning. When I take a break and check the pond, a dark and a lighter gray drake are swimming side by side, only one long vee trailing behind the two of them. They tip up, preen, do everything ensemble. Have they resolved their rivalry and become buddies or is there a sinister edge to their togetherness? After I've mopped the spring mud off my entranceway floor, the drakes are gone.

An hour later, as I'm thinking about lunch, I hear the muted quacks of a drake. The dark one floats in the middle of the pond. After lunch, he swims over to meet a duck who's just splashed down—not his mate but the light drake. This is not the familiar pattern and I have trouble concentrating on reading the manuscripts that are my afternoon's work. Once again I hear a quacking and, looking out, realize I've missed another scene, for the mates are together in the middle of the pond while the light drake rearranges his feathers on the grass at the same corner of the pond where he's retreated after earlier contests. The pair swims toward shore as far as possible away from the light drake, but while the female forages, her mate flies just above the water straight for his rival. Together they rise up, the mate chasing away his rival and returning with a great slide across the water. But the light drake is only circling over the pond and drops down again. Again the mate flies at him, this time pursuing him far into the western sky. When he returns, the darker drake, as though to seal his triumph, grasps his mate by the back of her neck with his bill and holds her, thrashing under water, while he mounts her. After he releases her, she shakes herself, stretches her wings out and stands up on the water. He stands up, too, spreading his wings. Then both contract into swimming ducks, shake their tails vigorously and resume foraging—their casual coda to a Hollywood ending.

This was the final battle scene I witnessed, but was it the final battle? What is the ending of the mallards' story? In all romances, the story ends when the obstacles have been overcome and the lovers reunited, before the intensity of courtship subsides into the daily rounds of domesticity. "The pair bond in mallards begins to weaken with the beginning of incubation," I read. I can expect the dark drake's devotion to wane as the eggs hatch and he retreats with other males to a safer place than my pond to molt his fine plumage and even his flight feathers. At that time what he needs most is quiet and camouflage, not passion and glory. The female will raise her brood until they can fly and then she'll molt her own feathers in preparation for the next adventure, the great fall migration south, when the flock instead of the pair bond is needed for survival.

And what of the third character in this drama, the routed light drake? More than three weeks later, he appeared in my pond with a female. I assume it was not the female he'd fought over but one who perhaps had lost her mate or her eggs. Out in the middle of the water, she starts to pump her head up and down as though talking about taking off, but instead she's apparently talking about love. The drake responds by opening and closing his bill silently, then both disappear underwater. I want to say what I saw: that they dived, however shallowly, though mallards are not diving ducks. Up again, they're soon thrashing and splashing as he mounts her, holding the back of her neck in his bill even as he submerges her. It was the only time I saw them here, as though he was showing off the female he had won, which is blatantly "assigning human motives and values to bird behavior." But birds or animals or humans, don't we share passions like devotion, desire, and jealousy? What would draw me to observe an utterly alien species to whom I felt no connection?

Yet something in the ducks' difference draws me, too—the focused quality of lives lived more fully in the present than mine. My human mind shuttles restlessly between past and future, remembrance and expectation, cause and effect. Observing—the discipline of seeing what is "seen less than perfectly"—fixes me in the present, here and now, and I begin to see how much I do not see. When, after these events, four drakes appear together on my pond, the motion picture I painstakingly spliced together breaks up into a disarray of single frames. I never considered there might be more than two drakes; above all, I never questioned my sense of continuity. Now that four drakes force me to, the question threatens to fragment every movie, every story, of my life. I walk on a quaking bog and must reinvent ground that may give way again. Observing is creating as well as re-creating. It is the art of brightening the "poor light," of closing the "great distance," and of extending the "split second." It is an art practiced by ducks and dogs and cats as well as by humans, but only they know what stories their observations weave.